Stillwater Flies
How and When to Fish Them

First published in 1982 by
Ernest Benn Limited
Now published in 1985 by
A & C Black (Publishers) Limited,
35 Bedford Row, London, WC1R 4JH

First edition 1982, reprinted 1985

ISBN 0 7136 5535 6

Filmset in 10/12pt Baskerville by
Reproduction Drawings Ltd, Sutton, Surrey
Printed and bound in Great Britain

Other books by John Goddard

The Super Flies of Still Water
Trout Flies of Stillwater
Trout Fly Recognition
Big Fish from Salt Water
The Trout and the Fly (with Brian Clarke)

Stillwater Flies
How and When to Fish
Them

John Goddard

with contributions by
Syd Brock
Bob Carnill
Bob Church
John Ketley
Dick Walker

and illustrated by
Ted Andrews

A & C BLACK · LONDON

Dedication

I dedicate this book to my good
friend of many years, Leslie Cardew
Wood. Now a veteran angler, he has
been addicted to our wonderful sport
all his life. Past President of my old
society 'The Piscatorial', and an
angler of great skill and experience,
he was responsible for the original
concept of this volume.

Contents

Colour Plates

The colour plates appear between pages 96 and 105

Traditional patterns
Alexandra
Allrounder
Blae and Black
Black Zulu
Bloody Butcher
Coachman
Coch-y-Bonddu
Dunkeld
Gold Ribbed Hare's Ear
Greenwell's Glory
Grey Duster
Invicta
Mallard & Claret
Orange John
Peter Ross
Red Palmer
Short Orange Partridge
Teal Blue & Silver
Teal & Green
Wickham's Fancy

Imitative Patterns
Adult Buzzers
Black Duck Fly
Alder Larva
Amber Nymph
Black & Peacock Spider
Bloodworm
Caenis Nymph
Cased Caddis
Collyer's Nymphs
Corixa
Daddy Longlegs
Footballer
Fiery Brown Sedge
Damosel Nymph
Floating Snail
Grenadier
G & H Sedge
Hatching Sedge
Hatching Midge Pupa
Hawthorn
Last Hope
Longhorns
Pheasant Tail Nymph
PVC Nymph
Mating Shrimp
Mayfly Nymph
Poly Rib C Pupa
Pond Olive Spinner

Persuader
Red and Green Larva
Small Hatching Midge
Walker's Sedge
Sedge Pupa
Stick Fly
Suspender Midge
Super Grizzly
Williams
Tadpolly

Lures and Attractors
Ace of Spades
Baby Doll
Appetiser
Badger Matuka
Black Bear's Hair
Black Chenille
Black Ghost
Black & Orange Marabou
Christmas Tree
Concorde
Church Fry
Dambuster
Dunkeld Lure
Jack Frost
Goldie
Jersey Herd
Leprechaun
Mickey Finn
Missionary
Nailer Fly
Muddler Minnow
Mylar Minnow
Popping Bug
Orange Marabou Muddler
Pearly
Pearly Nobblers
Polystickle
Ruby
Special Baby Doll
Viva
Sweeny Todd
Squirrel & Silver
Whisky Fly
Yellow Hammer
White Marabou Tandem Muddler
Worm Fly
Streaker
White Muddler

6

Illustrations

Introduction

Fly fishing on stillwaters, particularly the larger lakes and reservoirs, can often be extremely difficult and frustrating since, unlike fishing on trout rivers, you can seldom see your quarry or the food upon which they may be feeding. It is therefore very often a question of knowing from past experience which artificials are most likely to be most successful and how best to fish them. Now when this book was first conceived it was quickly realised that no one person was sufficiently qualified to write in depth on all the different styles of fishing involved. Even the most experienced allrounder tends to specialise at least to some extent, and it was for this reason it was decided to seek a different contributor to cover each method or style of fishing.

First and foremost, this is a reference book, and should be used as such. Basically, it should be referred to when planning a day's fishing, or perhaps even taken with you on the day. The season is covered month by month, starting in April and finishing in October. March is not covered, because few of the larger waters open until April. By referring to the chapter of the month you are fishing, and then to the heading of the style of fishing you wish to employ, all will be revealed, as they say. You will be advised of the best artificials to use during that month and also how to fish them, under varying weather conditions. It must be appreciated, however, that the patterns and techniques recommended are for average waters, so the angler himself will have to take into account local variations. It will also be noted that there is considerable duplication on patterns and even, in some cases, techniques by the various contributors; this is, of course, inevitable, for even with the different styles and methods covered, similar basic techniques and patterns are often employed. In addition, where a contributor describes a particular technique in one month which applies again in another, the information is often repeated again in full. To repeat, this is a reference book, and in such there is nothing more annoying than being referred to a previous chapter. Most of the artificials mentioned in the text are included in the colour plates, to assist the less experienced quickly and positively identify the appropriate pattern in his fly box, assuming that it is present. Also, to assist those fly fishers who dress their own flies, a large percentage of the lesser known patterns, as well as some of the more popular ones, are included in the back of this volume. These have been set out in simple, step-by-step tying sequences by that gifted illustrator, Ted Andrews.

After much consideration, it was decided not to deal with fly fishing on small waters in the month-by-month chapters. Unlike the big lakes and reservoirs, small waters are, first and foremost, less affected by weather conditions, require fewer patterns to fish them successfully and, furthermore, rely far more on the approach and presentation of the fly than on specified techniques. For this reason, a completely separate chapter has been designated to cover this very different style of fly fishing.

The contributors have been chosen with extreme care, so it is hardly surprising that the final list includes anglers that are household names in fly fishing circles, each being considered the top expert in the country today in his own particular field.

Our first contributor covers the art of lure fishing from a boat, and let us say here and now that, contrary to the belief of many fly fishers, lures, in the hands of an expert, under the right weather conditions, can be a very killing method. This fact has been proved on countless occasions by Bob Church, who is undoubtedly one of our greatest all round trout anglers.

Our second contributor, Syd Brock, covers lure fishing from the bank, and there is really no fly fisher better qualified to cover this technique, in which he has specialised for many years. In this period he has proved his exceptional ability with some staggering catches of massive brown trout.

Up to now, all international fly fishing matches have been restricted to traditional boat fishing methods, so there can be no-one better qualified to write on this aspect than John Ketley, captain of the England international team for many years.

Our next contributor, Bob Carnill, is looked upon with great respect by the skillful anglers of the Midlands, where he fishes, and has developed a reputation second to none as an exceptional fly dresser and fly fisher, specialising in fishing imitative patterns from the bank, the technique which he will cover for us.

Our last contributor, Dick Walker, really needs no introduction; a fine all round angler, he must surely be the most knowledgeable and respected authority this country has yet produced. In recent years he has taken a keen interest in stillwater trout fishing, and latterly has tended to specialise in fishing the smaller waters, the topic which he will be covering for us in this volume.

Finally, I shall deal with fishing imitative patterns from a boat, as this is the area on which I have concentrated in recent years. At one time I much preferred bank fishing but, with advancing age, I am afraid that the comforts of a boat became more and more appealing.

In conclusion, I am sure that most anglers will appreciate that fishing, and in particular fly fishing, is a very individual sport, so for those anglers that have enquiring minds and are not afraid to experiment, wonderful opportunities still exist in both techniques and development of new patterns to improve our sport. The knowledge imparted by the experts who have contributed to this volume is provided for the benefit of all. The extent to which it leads to further development is a matter of personal choice and inclination. But never forget that progress will only come from original thinking, experimentation and, above all, close observation of both the trout and the natural creatures upon which it feeds.

John Goddard, 1981

1 The Weather — wind and currents

Since the last war, stillwater trout fishing in this country has progressed at a tremendous rate. Prior to this, few advances had been made, as most fly fishers were quite content to fish mainly on the Irish and Scottish lochs in the traditional drift fishing style. On the comparatively few English lakes and reservoirs, drift fishing also predominated, although a small minority were beginning to take an increasing interest in bank fishing.

Today, the picture is very different; most reservoirs are stocked with trout, and there has been a literal explosion in the numbers of small private waters that have now become available. As the availability of water has increased, so have the numbers of fly fishers, and it was inevitable that this vast influx of new anglers would bring with it new ideas. This has resulted in many new styles and techniques being adopted, with the accompanying need for new tackle and equipment, as well as a proliferation in fly patterns. The situation is now very different from when two or three dozen patterns in one's fly box would suffice. It is hoped, therefore, that this volume will at least provide most of the answers under average conditions and assist not only beginners, but many of the more experienced fly fishers as well, in their choice of pattern and the most rewarding technique.

The main purpose of this opening chapter is to give the beginner or less experienced angler as much information as possible on the various styles of fishing, as well as basic details on standard techniques and guidance on how and where to find trout.

Weather — General

Let us first look at the weather, for this can affect fishing tremendously, particularly when there are extreme conditions, or any sudden climatic changes. Now it is obviously not possible to lay down hard and fast rules for any set of weather conditions. Trout, like any wild creatures, are at times as completely unpredictable as the weather itself. Thus, the following information should only be taken as a basic guide.

In the early spring, when the water temperature is still low, the trout are usually to be found in deeper water, feeding close to the bottom. However, should there be a prolonged spell of warm weather, which does happen on odd occasions, the trout, although still keeping to the deeper sections of the lake or reservoir, may well feed much closer to the surface. The same situation applies again in the late autumn, except that at that time only a prolonged spell of exceptionally cold weather will drive them back into the deeper water. As the season progresses, and the water temperature increases, the trout will move into the very shallow margins to feed, particularly in the early morning or late evening; this usually applies from early June through to the end of September. The sun and the wind, as well as the water temperature, also play important parts. The ideal conditions for fishing occur after a spell of settled weather with, for example, a light and steady south-westerly breeze, with a good cloud cover. Later in the season, good fishing can also be experienced on wet and windy days after a prolonged hot spell. On the other hand, days to be avoided if at all possible are those that occur only too frequently, when the heavens open, and we are treated to heavy or torrential rain, particularly when these conditions are accompanied by gusty winds. Wind in itself is often conducive to good fishing, even when the wind is strong, as long as it is steady. But beware of very strong and gusty winds, where the frequent squalls seem almost to flatten the wave tops. These are possibly the worst conditions of all, and unless one can find a sheltered bay, it is probably better to have a rest until conditions improve. The other condition that all stillwater fishers dread occurs during a heat wave, when the sun shines down out of a brassy sky, and the water surface is like a sheet of glass.

Usually under these conditions it is all but impossible to catch fish, but if one perseveres, it is sometimes possible to take the odd trout on a deep fished nymph. One other point to be borne in mind in connection with the weather is the effect that the sun can have on our fishing. Most fly fishers appreciate that, during bright sunny conditions, trout will rarely venture into shallow water, particularly when it is very clear. Neither are they likely to be found near the surface, unless there is a good breeze. The problem then to be solved is to find out at what level the trout may be lying or feeding. This can only be achieved by trial and error, by fishing at different levels until the fish are found. It is also worth noting that on many stillwaters, daphnia form a staple diet for trout, at certain times of the year. These minute creatures form vast clouds in the water, but as they dislike bright light, the sunnier the day, the deeper they descend, and, of course, the trout go with them.

The wind and current

One of the most important aspects the fly fisher must take into account when fishing on windy days is the direction of the wind, particularly in the early part of the season. Always fish on or adjacent to a lee shore (the shore onto which the wind is blowing), as this is where most of the trout will be concentrated due to the higher water temperature. If you are bank fishing, this means you will be casting into the wind, which can be unpleasant as well as difficult; you will not be able to cast far, but then it will not be necessary, for the trout will be much closer to this bank. (*Illustration No. 1.*) You will also, on most waters, catch far more trout than those anglers fishing in comparative comfort with the wind behind them. This also applies throughout the season, but to a lesser degree and for a different reason. From June onwards, it is not the temperature (which will now be fairly constant) that will attract the trout to the lee shores, but the effect the wind and current has of concentrating most of the available surface food towards one end or side of the lake. A good compromise is to fish with the wind running along the bank, preferably from the left to the right. In fact, later in the season this is to be

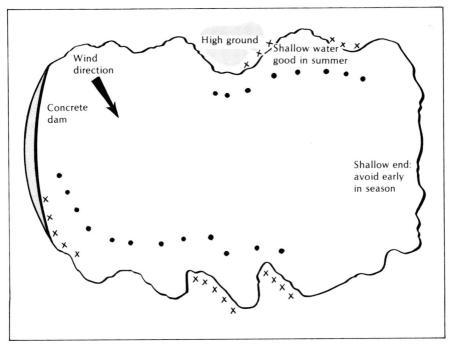

Illustration No.1: The best areas to fish on a typical reservoir
× Bank anglers
● Boat anglers — drift or anchor within 100 yards of the bank

favoured as you are then moving your flies across the front of trout that usually travel in an upwind direction. If you feel happier casting with the wind behind you, seek a section of bank with fairly shallow water in front of you. From mid-May onwards, when the shallows warm up, trout will often gather to feed where the water increases in depth. The current driven by an offshore wind will carry any hatching nymphs, larvae and terrestrial flies from the shallow water out to the waiting trout. (*Illustration No. 2.*) You should present your artificials just where the water begins to shelve off. Also in very windy conditions you will often find an area of calm water extending some considerable distance out from a high bank with an offshore wind. The effect of surface tension seems to be more adhesive in this calm water, hatching insects will take much longer to break through, and so the trout are likely to gather where the ripple begins, to take advantage of easier pickings.

When the wind exceeds a velocity of about ten miles per hour, a curious phenomenon often occurs; this is the formation of wind lanes. These are narrow channels of relatively smooth water which, in rough weather, are often lined with streaks of foam. These lanes, according to at least one authority, are formed by two circulating currents of water which meet in the centre of the lane, and these concentrate any food in the area. (*Illustration No. 3.*) The trout are obviously well aware of this, and often shoals of rainbows can be seen feeding actively upwind along them. Also, in strongish winds which blow along the bank, lakes or

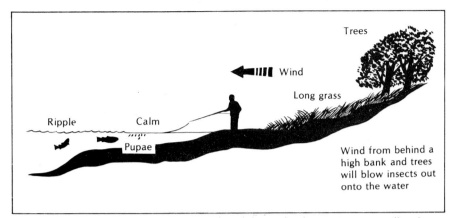

Illustration No.2: Trout will feed along the edge of the ripple where most pupae will gather to hatch, or will cruise along the edge of a shelf looking up to the surface for any insects blown offshore.

Illustration No.3: This diagram shows how two opposing circulating currents may cause the formation of a wind lane.

reservoirs with predominantly muddy bottoms will be clearly marked downwind by bands of discoloured water. The offshore edge of it forms an all but invisible wall, along which feeding trout will travel. If you can reach this clearer water from the bank or, better still, drift along it in a boat, a few nice trout may be forthcoming. (*Illustration No. 4.*) When in a boat, however, you must ensure that you do not come too close to any bank anglers.

In very light breezes during the day, or when the wind drops in the evening, areas of flat, calm water will be bordered by areas with a nice ripple. Under these conditions, trout may be located moving and feeding along the edges of this ripple. (*Illustration No. 5.*) It should also be pointed out that when these conditions occur, fishing in the ripple is far more productive than fishing in the areas of flat calm.

13

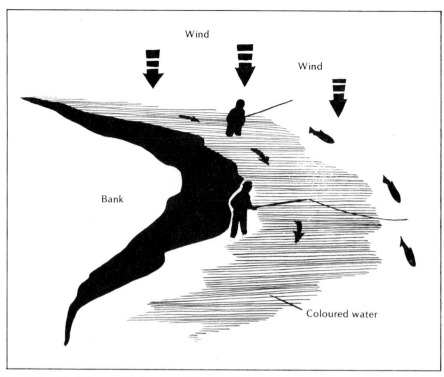

Illustration No.4: Trout will often patrol the outside edge of coloured water. The diagram shows the perfect positions for intercepting them.

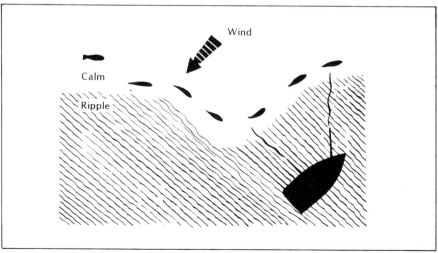

Illustration No.5: Always fish the edge of the ripple from the rippled side, since your fly line and leader are less visible to the trout on the broken surface.

It may surprise many stillwater anglers, but even on the calmest of days a reservoir or lake is never still. Currents and cross currents are always present, and the direction of these will be dependent upon both the contours of the banks and the direction of winds both past and present. The stronger currents carrying food to the trout are always found around the shores or any banks, shoals, etc. that may be present. For this reason, unless one is surface fishing and drifting, there is little point when boat fishing in anchoring too far off shore. (*Illustration No. 6.*) Current can be very important when fishing deep either from the bank or an anchored boat; just as in a river the trout will either be lying facing the current, or moving up it, so if you are fishing nymphs, ideally your artificial should be moving across or with the current towards them. The current on the surface seldom, if ever, travels in the same direction as the current below the surface, and unfortunately (unless we are surface fishing) it is this unseen current that we are more interested in. It is therefore important to ascertain in which direction this unseen current is moving. This will usually be (allowing of course for unusual bank contours) against the wind (*Illustration No. 7*), but here it is important to take into account the predominant direction of the wind over the last few days. If the wind has changed on the day you are fishing, this rule of thumb will not work, as it can take many hours for the direction of the currents to change under the influence of wind from a different quarter.

One other, very important effect that the wind or current can have on your fishing, is the direction your lure or wet fly is retrieved. This applies whether you

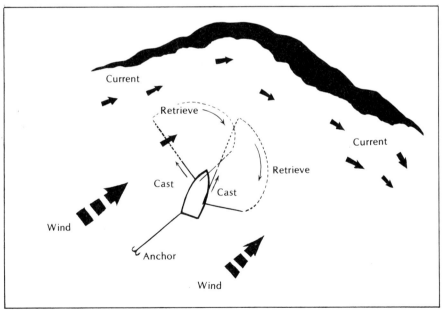

Illustration No.6: With their boat anchored by the stern about 100 yards offshore these anglers are in the perfect position to make full use of both wind and current, which will work their lines around in an arc and cause their flies to cover a large area.

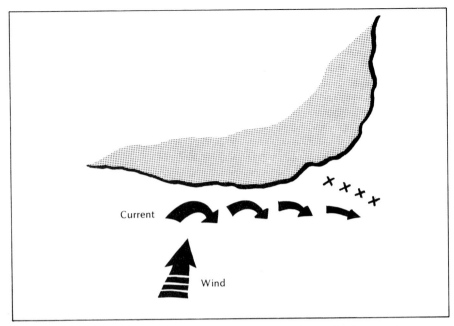

Illustration No.7: A wind blowing into this bank has set up a current flowing past the headland. The crosses indicate the best place to intercept trout moving along its edge.

are fishing on or below the surface. As a direct result of considerable experimentation recently carried out by myself, I have proved, at least to my own satisfaction, that trout following a fly from directly behind are far less likely to be securely hooked than those trout that take a fly from the side when it is being retrieved across their path. In the former case, if the trout is hooked at all, it is invariably in the front of the mouth, and the percentage of trout that one fails to hook is quite high.

Most fly fishers that have practised the art of traditional loch style fishing from a drifting boat downwind will be only too well aware of the number of trout that come short or are pricked, in many cases after following the fly for a considerable distance. In the other case, where a trout takes the fly from the side, or even at an angle, a successful hook-up usually results, and practically always the hook will engage firmly in the scissors. Now, dear reader, what can we do to ensure that the fly is presented to the trout across his line of vision? Well, the answer by now should be fairly obvious, but unfortunately, in practice it is not always so simple to achieve. The fly should be retrieved across the wind or current, as the trout nearly always swim upwind or upcurrent. So far as the current is concerned, the problem here is to ascertain in which direction it is travelling, which is not always easy, particularly for a sub-surface current. The bank angler can always find a section of bank that allows him to fish across the wind, but for the boat angler this can present a problem, particularly when drifting, unless, of course, he is alone in a boat, which is seldom the norm.

16

2 Bank and boat fishing — rise forms and buzzers

Bank fishing

The newcomer to stillwater trout fishing is usually introduced to this branch of our sport from the bank, and surely there can be no more daunting a prospect in any type of fishing than to arrive on the bank of a typical large reservoir, to look out over an apparently featureless expanse of water, and wonder where to start fishing. First of all one must take into account the wind, as already discussed, and then decide upon which stretch of shoreline to fish. Having made this decision, it is then a good plan to study the shoreline carefully, and if necessary walk along it. While most stillwaters may appear featureless, this is in fact far from the truth, as there are many fish-holding areas if you know what to look for. Most reservoirs are formed by erecting a dam at one end of a valley and then flooding it; when this has happened many clues are left for the observant fly fisher. First of all, the contours of the land will tell you where you may expect to find either shallow or deep water off the bank and, as already explained, the depth of water can often be important, depending upon the time of year and also the time of day. Promontories sticking out into the water are always hot spots which enable you to cover trout moving up or down the water. (*Illustration No. 8.*) The inside shorelines of bays are often good fish-holding areas. (*Illustration No. 9.*) Copses of trees close to the shore seem to encourage more insect life, and provide food to attract the trout. Always be on the lookout for old hedgerows, ditches and old roads which disappear into the water; these provide motorways up which the trout will travel and are always productive. Objects visible in the water such as old posts or treestumps usually attract a few fish, as do streams entering the water, and these are always worth trying. If you can find a weedy area of bank, or stretch that is littered with debris or old bushes sticking up out of the water, you can be sure they will hold some good trout. Most fly fishers avoid these spots for fear of losing their flies or a trout if it is hooked. The answer here is to use a much stronger leader, and to stop and hold the trout as soon as he is hooked. Even trout of five or six pounds can be stopped immediately with an eight or ten pound test leader, providing you hold the rod high and get the head of the trout above the surface.

Under windy conditions, always be on the lookout for the wind or scum lanes discussed in the previous section. These will sometimes run into the bank or parallel to it, and where you can reach them you will be assured of fish. All bodies of stillwater hide channels and deep holes, which always hold fish, and although you cannot see these, they will, over a season, become apparent. These will be the first places to be taken by arriving fishermen, and should be noted for future reference. Another clue to these spots is that the shoreline will always be well worn and trampled in their vicinity.

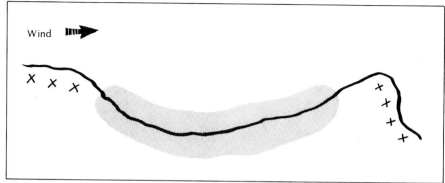

Illustration No.8: With the wind blowing across a long bay, as shown, only the marked locations at the points of the bay are likely to produce fish. The dead ground in between, marked by shading, should be avoided unless it is shallow enough to permit one to wade out a fair distance.

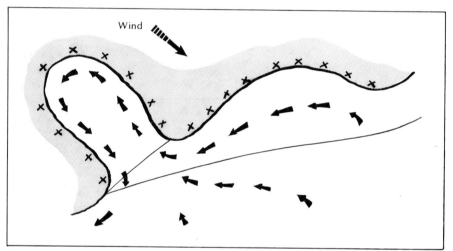

Illustration No.9: As long as it is not too shallow, a narrow bay can act as a two way funnel for trout nearing the shore after travelling against the wind.

The majority of bank anglers wear thigh waders and, in most cases, as soon as they arrive at the waterside and assemble their tackle, they immediately wade out as far and as fast as they possibly can, pushing a bow wave in front of them that will thoroughly scare off almost every trout in the area. Not content with this, they will then cast their flies out as far as they can in front, immediately lining any less wary trout that may be left and scaring them as well. They then wonder why they do not start catching trout right away. Eventually, if they are in the right spot, they will commence to catch fish as these gradually come back into the area, providing of course they are not constantly moving as, unfortunately, many have a wont to do. Personally, I can see no point at all in wading, except possibly along shores where the water is shallow a long way out, and I, along with many others, would be very happy to see it banned. Much of the trout's natural food is concentrated along the shoreline, and if they are not disturbed or frightened the trout will come tight into the very shallow water along the banks to feed, so that all that wading does is to drive the trout offshore and at the same time trample, disturb and destroy much of the natural fauna which grow fat and healthy trout.

Under the present system, where most anglers wade, we are all forced to do it in order to reach the trout, unless one is fortunate perhaps to arrive early and find a stretch of shoreline unoccupied. If this happens, stand well back from the water's edge and, aerialising quite a short length of line, cast your flies out about ten or fifteen yards at an angle along the bank and then retrieve. After each cast, take two or three paces along the bank. In this manner you can cover quite a long stretch of bank in an hour's fishing, and the beauty of this method is that you are constantly covering fresh water. I well remember the first year that Rutland water opened. I was invited to attend for a day's fishing on press day before it officially opened. Strange to relate, the fishing was not particularly good, and by lunchtime, many attending had drawn a blank. In the morning I fished a small bay in the company of seven or eight other journalists, who were all wading, and I struggled to get a couple of fish. As I liked the look of this bay, I returned in the afternoon only to find I had it virtually to myself. I therefore decided not to wade, and commenced casting, standing at least ten yards back from the bank. Unfortunately a lot of the rainbows I caught were black and had to be returned. Nevertheless, within two hours I had caught my limit of clean fish and had to pack up. There are of course exceptions when wading can pay off, if for example you wish to reach a scum line, or a shoal of rainbows moving in deeper water, or sometimes of an evening when the trout commence feeding on the surface on midges in the deeper water. But, personally, in the interests of conservation of aquatic life in the water I would be prepared to forego this pleasure. In any case if you are patient you will find eventually the fish will come in to where you can cover them.

Most bank anglers when wading return to the shore every time they catch a trout. Now, in the evenings when the trout come inshore to feed, providing one wades in and out again silently, this will not make a lot of difference to the amount of fish you catch. During the day it can often be a very different story, because then small or large shoals of trout, particularly rainbows, will be feeding along the shoreline. If you are quick you can sometimes take two or three trout from one of these shoals before they pass, but only if you are prepared to carry a bag or creel over your shoulder to hold your fish. Better still is one of those American type fish stringers hung from your belt. Usually, the time taken to wade carefully ashore and out again with a trout is quite long enough for the shoal to pass by. Finally, as a bank angler, always observe the codes of good behaviour and be courteous to your fellow fishermen. Never fish or enter the water closer than about 20 yards to a fellow angler. Never cast across or near his line of retrieve, and never rush over and try to help him land his trout, even if it is a monster, unless he asks for your assistance. Even then I advise you to avoid this if at all possible; there is nothing worse than losing a trout for another angler, even if it is an unfortunate accident.

Both in boat and bank fishing, the ability to detect a take is of paramount importance, and there is no doubt that the more experienced fisher will catch many more trout, as he has developed this ability to a very fine degree. To generalise, the faster you retrieve, the more positive the takes, and the more likely the trout are to hook themselves. The slower you retrieve, the less likely the fish are to hook themselves. The most difficult takes to detect are when you are barely moving the fly, as in nymph fishing, and in fact I am quite sure that most experienced nymph fishermen will readily admit that far more takes go undetected than those that are detected. I know from personal observations on clearwater streams, that a trout can take an artificial nymph into his mouth, chew on it and reject it, and then take it again, all without moving your leader a fraction of an inch.

However, many takes can be detected if you know where to look. If the light is good and it is not too rough, your attention at all times should be riveted to the end of your fly line where it joins the leader and any movement, even slight, should be rewarded with a tightening of the line — better to strike and miss than not to strike at all. At the same time, you should also try to keep at least half an eye, as they say, on the estimated position of your flies in the water. You will often see perhaps a slight boil of water on the surface, or a momentary flash of silver as a trout turns to take your fly; in fact, if you are aware of any unnatural sign or movement you lose nothing by tightening the line, and very often a fish will be your reward. In rough weather or poor light, watch the loop of fly line from your rod tip to where it enters the water surface. Takes will be indicated by a slight lifting of this loop or sometimes even by the failure of the loop to sink back down between retrieves. Even a slight quiver in this loop will indicate a take, so if you wish to be successful you must be prepared to concentrate on the end of the fly line or the loop at all times. Great nymph fishermen like Arthur Cove have developed this ability to an incredible degree and this is why they are so successful. A little tip to remember whether you are retrieving fast or slow — never point your rod straight along the direction of your fly line. Always hold your rod at a slight angle to the line as this will cushion the effect of the odd savage take which may occur.

There is an exception to this rule. The veteran angler, Leslie Cardew Wood, who always catches more than his share of large trout, recommends a special and most effective method of fishing lures or attractor patterns which he has been using for more than 25 years. With this method it is essential to hold the rod low with the top close to the surface, pointing directly along the path of your line. With the finger and thumb of one hand, lightly hold the line while you retrieve with the finger and thumb of the other hand. The retrieve must be continuous, fast and sharp, no more than one inch at a time. With practice you will quickly achieve a constant rhythm which, in time, will become almost automatic. The fly when retrieved in this manner, will swim slowly but steadily, which trout seem to find most attractive, and the sharp, short retrieve ensures positive hooking, while the line held in the other finger and thumb very lightly, guards against a break when the fly is taken. The technique is best performed from a kneeling or sitting position.

Boat fishing

While bank fishing allows you to present your flies far more delicately and is therefore preferable for most forms of nymph fishing, it also allowed you, at least in the past, far greater scope for differing techniques. This is no longer the case; in the last decade or so, thanks mainly to that master stillwater angler Dick Shrive and the Northampton School of Specimen Hunters, vast progress has been achieved, particularly in regard to boat fishing. Prior to the last war, boat fishing for trout was restricted mainly to the traditional Scottish drift fishing method, which entailed drifting broadside to the wind with or without a drogue trailing behind, fastened to the middle of the boat. A team of three or more flies are utilized and these are cast downwind on a short line and rapidly retrieved by raising the rod tip. This is still a very effective method of fishing, and with experience it is possible to bounce the top dropper or bob fly along the surface in a manner that many trout find irresistible. To watch a proficient loch fisher casting and retrieving in this manner is indeed a most pleasurable experience. The late Cyril Inwood was a great exponent of this style of fishing, and on the right day would produce trout after trout as if by magic. Many anglers fishing this style cast straight downwind and retrieve, but it often pays dividends to cast and retrieve at varying angles across the wind, as you will then be covering more fish and, furthermore, hooking will usually be more positive.

Knowing where to look for trout is just as important to the boat angler as it is to the bank angler. Should you decide to fish from an anchored boat, much of what has already been described for the bank angler will also apply, but please do remember to give bank anglers plenty of room. One of the great advantages of boat fishing when the weather conditions are favourable is that you can drift and thereby cover far more water, but you should always work to a pattern. If it is windy you can fish down the wind or scum lanes, or if it is calm you can drift along between the areas of calm and ripple. Alternatively, you can always try drifting along a stretch of bank or dam wall if there are no bank anglers present, providing the wind is favourable and allows you to do so. If you wish to do this and the wind is unfavourable, providing you have a companion in the boat, one of you can take the oars and row quietly along the bank while the other fishes. It is also possible to do this even with slightly adverse winds if you have a drift control rudder with you — but more of that later.

One of the best methods of locating fish in a boat is in a series of short drifts across areas and depths of water that you feel should hold fish for the time of year you are fishing. Always, before starting, look for recognisable landmarks on at least two cross-sections of bank, so that if you do locate fish on a drift, you can return to the same spot to ensure you will drift back over the same stretch again. Also, please be aware of the courtesies that you should extend to other drift fishing boats. Never go close across the front of another angler's drift, and never cut in or follow another fisherman's drift, particularly if you see him catching fish. This is rank bad manners, which I am afraid to say is only too common on many waters.

The most important factor with any style of stillwater fishing is to try to be in the right place at the right time with the right fly, so if one end or side of the water proves unproductive, do not be afraid to move; indeed, this is much easier for the boat angler than it is for the bank angler. On many waters different areas will produce better than others at varying times during the day. In many cases, this will be determined by purely local hatches of certain insects, and it is not at all uncommon to find that, if you stick to one area and possibly in consequence have a blank day, at least some other anglers, somewhere on the water, will end up with bag limits. Needless to say, this can be most annoying, and you will only have yourself to blame.

Now let us look a little more closely at drift fishing itself. First of all you will quickly realise that all boats have minds of their own when it comes to drifting; few of them will drift straight downwind. This can be due to several factors: the distribution of weight in the boat; the relative position of the fisherman or fishermen; and also the anchoring position of the rope trailing the drogue, if one is being used. It will also be found that some boats, irrespective of the above factors, will always drift at an angle across the wind. With this type of boat you will usually find that if you turn the boat around completely, then it will travel at an angle across the wind in the other direction. It is important to understand all these

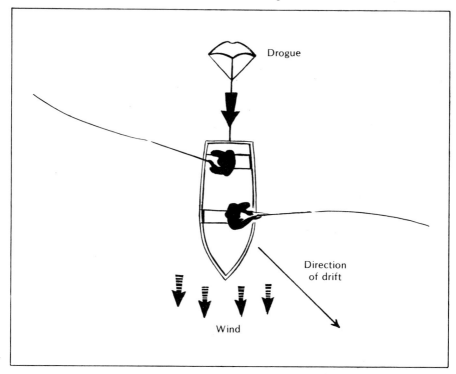

Illustration No.10: When surface fishing with floating lines, cast across the wind and immediately commence the retrieve.

various factors that influence the direction of drift, because if you know what to do, this can be turned to your advantage. You can then influence to some extent your direction of drift, which under some conditions is vital to success.

As already briefly mentioned, we now have many other methods of drift fishing available to us, in addition to the traditional drift broadside to the wind with the drogue over the side. The first of these is simple to perform; instead of securing the rope holding the drogue to the centre of the boat, you secure it in the centre of the stern. This means that the boat will now drift downwind, bow first. It also means there is less resistance to the wind from the stern of the boat so it will drift slower. In this position, it is naturally impossible for two anglers in a boat to fish downwind over the bow, so the angler sitting in the stern will now cast across the wind on one side of the boat, while his companion will cast across the wind on the opposite side of the boat. The angler upwind in the stern may find it a little difficult if he is right handed as he will have to cast over his right shoulder with what is in effect a right to left wind blowing. This is an excellent way to drift as it presents the fly across the front of trout which are generally feeding upwind into the wave or ripple. (*Illustration No. 10.*) It is also very effective using a sinking or sink tip line, pausing briefly to allow the line to sink a little. With the right amount of pause a bow will develop in the line, so that the fly or lure travels a short distance in the opposite direction to the boat, it will then begin to straighten out and lift, and it is at this point that most takes will come, mainly from rainbows, who seem to find this movement irresistible (*Illustration No. 11.*) Dick Shrive, the well-known Northampton angler, strongly recommends a 30 ft length of one inch link chain

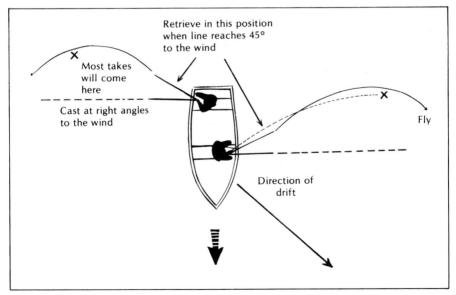

Illustration No.11: When using a sink tip or sinking line — and depending on how deep you wish to fish your fly — cast out at right angles to the wind, wait until the line is about 45° to the wind, and then retrieve.

hung over the stern of the boat in place of a drogue for this style of fishing, as he suggests this is far more effective. I have never tried this myself as the thought of humping a 30 lb weight of chain down to a boat every time I go fishing has up to now rather put me off. However, I can see the sense in this, as the amount of chain hanging over the stern can be adjusted according to the depth of water, and it will also provide you with a good idea of the contours of the lake bed as well. (*Illustration No. 12.*) When you come to a shallow bank, you will feel the boat momentarily slow as the chain hits the bottom. The chain should have a spring clip at one end for attaching an anchor when required, and the other end should have a link to which is attached a 30 ft double length of rope knotted together every yard. In deep water, this will allow you to trail all the chain and if you want to pay out more chain, you just pay out the rope yard by yard, and then hook one of the knots over a cleat on the boat. When at anchor, utilising this chain, it will hold the boat without dragging, even in strong winds, and by using the bow rope of the boat and securing the knotted end of the rope to the stern (*Illustration No. 13*) it will also hold the boat very steady. In very rough conditions it is safer to anchor bow into wind (*Illustration No. 14.*) It can also be used hung over the side and secured to the bow and stern for traditional drifting in place of the usual drogue (*Illustration No. 16*).

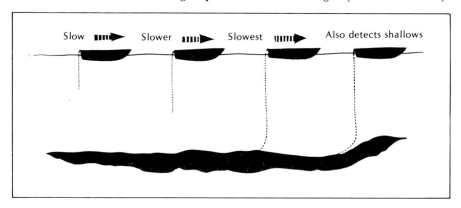

Slow   Slower   Slowest   Also detects shallows

Illustration No.12: As an alternative to a drogue try using a 30 ft length of 1 inch link chain. The more chain hung over the stern, the slower the drift. With this method an added advantage is that shallows can be detected by the boat slowing or stopping as more chain is grounded.

Another relatively new method of drifting uses a little device called a drift control rudder. Unfortunately this is now banned on many reservoirs, which is a great pity because it is an excellent device which allows you, up to a point, to control the direction of your drift, and also to change the direction of the drift merely by altering the position of this rudder. This is a tremendous help in following the contours of the bank, but it can only be used in light winds. (*Illustration No. 15.*) If you wish to use one of these rudders, it will have to be specially made and fitted to the stern of the boat with clamps (*Illustration No. 17*) when you wish to use it. Another refinement which allows you to drift across the face of the wind is the leeboard which, like the drift control rudder, was developed

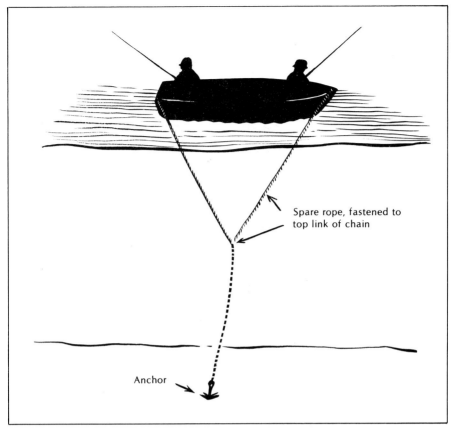

Illustration No.13: Anchoring broadside on to the wind. Fasten the spare rope to the chain, using the shackle, to hold one end of the boat. The other is secured by the double rope. This will hold the boat firm and steady, even in the strongest winds, but it is not recommended for very rough conditions, when it is safer to anchor bow into the wind.

by those maestros of stillwater fishing, Bob Church and Dick Shrive. This is now also banned on many waters, but in this case it is probably just, because this can be a very dangerous gadget in inexperienced hands.

Should you decide to anchor and fish, ensure that you take your own anchor, since the majority of those supplied are pretty useless. Better still, take two anchors if possible, these will then provide you with a stable platform from which to fish nymphs. If you have only one anchor in the boat, the best place to secure the anchor rope is to one corner of the stern of the boat. (*Illustration No. 18.*) In this position you will experience less yawing, which can make fishing very difficult. While fishing at anchor can be very effective and, under some conditions, necessary, I prefer to fish on the drift where possible. Today you are in fact more likely to see the majority of boat fishers casting from anchored boats, and I think the reason for this is that they just do not know how to drift fish correctly. You are also likely to see a large percentage of fly fishers standing up in a boat to fish, and I

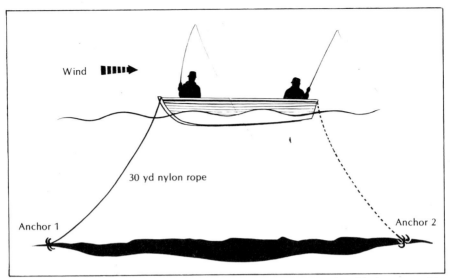

Illustration No.14: The 'Anchor 1' position is the safest in a strong wind and high wave, and is ideal for fishing lures and for sinking line techniques in any depth. 'Anchor 2' may be put out over the stern to eliminate swing and provide a more stable platform. That can be important for slow nymph fishing when sensitive control of fly line is necessary.

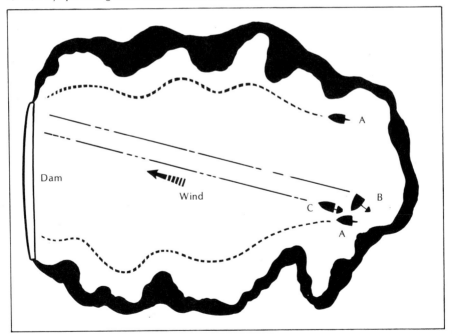

Illustration No.15: A clear demonstration of the advantages of using the drift control rudder. The rudder-controlled boat A follows the feeding contours. The other boats B and C are at the mercy of the wind direction, although boat C with the drogue trailing from the stern may permit more efficient fishing; the drogue is in fact essential if sinking lines are being used.

assure you that this is quite unnecessary; with a little practice you can cast just as far sitting down, where you present a far smaller silhouette, and scare far fewer trout. Apart from this, when you stand and cast you will inevitably rock the boat, and do so very violently if you are an indifferent caster. This rocking will send out waves all round the boat which are very fish scaring, particularly in calm conditions.

One last point. Choose your boat partner with care, as you will be in close confinement all day, and if you are incompatible, this can result in a very miserable day's fishing indeed. Also bear in mind that a bad caster in a boat can be very dangerous both to himself and also to his companion.

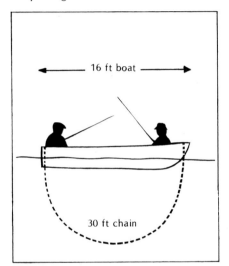

Illustration No.16: For a steady broadside drift, suspend the whole chain under the boat, from bow to stern.

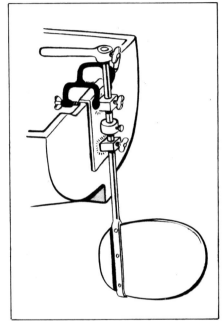

Illustration No.17: A drift control rudder.

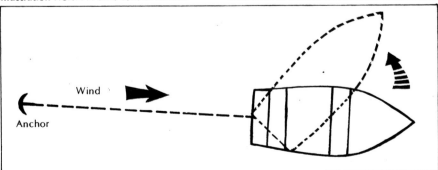

Illustration No.18: To prevent or minimise a boat's yawing from side to side when it is anchored, particularly under windy conditions, first secure the rope to the centre of the stern. Then wait till the boat stops swinging and transfer it to the corner of the stern.

Rise forms

No book on trout fishing would be complete without at least a mention of rise forms, as they can be of considerable assistance in identifying the type of food on which the trout may be feeding. Rise forms can be very complex and there are many variations, so let us pick out a few of the more common types which are fairly easy to identify, and look at these. The slow head and tail rise is one of these, and is usually confined to calm conditions. If you observe this rise closely, you will see first, the head of the trout, followed by the dorsal fin, and then finally the tip of the tail, before he sinks below the surface. There action is slow and deliberate, and is indicative of a trout taking food just below or in the surface film. If the rises are fairly frequent and erratic in direction, it is safe to assume he is feeding on hatching midge pupae hanging in the surface film, or, less commonly, taking floating snail. If he is rising rapidly and moving in a straight line, he is probably taking caenis nymphs hatching in the surface film. Another common rise later in the season is a rise where you will see the head of the trout appear above the surface, and if you are watching carefully, you will see his mouth open. This is caused by a trout cruising a foot or so below the surface and rising at frequent intervals, usually upwind in a ripple, and picking hatching sedges off the surface. Should you observe swirls just below the surface, these are made by trout chasing nymphs or pupae towards the surface. The sip is also another common rise, a very leisurely rise where you will see only the nose of the fish break the surface, sometimes followed by an audible sip or kiss. These are trout feeding on spinners or newly hatched duns trapped in the surface, and if it happens to be caenis spinners they are feeding on, you will note they always travel in a straight line, rising rapidly and repeatedly. Should you observe very violent splashing rises with the trout sometimes arching out of the water, you will know they are feeding on large mayflies where they occur; later in the season, they will either be feeding on adult sedges, struggling to become airborne, or on damsel nymphs wiggling along just under the surface. In July or August, if you see trout rising at regular intervals up wind lanes during the day, they will in all probability be feeding on tiny hatching midges. Should you be fishing to rising trout, if you are very quick and put your fly in the centre of the rise, he will often turn back and take it. But it is usually better to cast your fly a yard or two away in your estimated position of his next rise. With practice, it is possible to ascertain in which direction a trout is moving, but if you are unsure, it is good practice to cast upwind of his last rise as 90 per cent of trout feeding on the surface move in an upwind direction. In addition to this a useful rule of thumb is to cast your fly about a yard for very second of time away from his last rise.

The midges or buzzers

While it is not intended to cover the subject of stillwater angling entomology in any depth in this volume, I do feel it is necessary to mention the classification of the various species of chironomids (buzzers or midges, as they are commonly referred to by fly fishers). Without doubt, the larvae, pupae and adults of this family form the major diet of trout on most stillwaters, yet in the past they have been largely ignored by most angling authors. Those that have covered them have done so only briefly, and therefore but few common names have come into general use. I carried out what was probably the first in-depth study of these important insects in my book *Trout Flies of Still Water*, first published by A. & C. Black in 1969. There I have attempted to classify the more common species and give them common names which would be acceptable to most anglers, based mainly on the appearance of the adults. Since then, while some angling authors have adhered to my suggested nomenclature, others have coined new common names for the same species. Now this can only be confusing to the average fly fisher, so I feel the time is now ripe to look carefully again at this list in an effort to ratify it where necessary in a form that may be more acceptable to the majority in future.

Let us start with the very small midges. In my original list I refer to three of these, the small black, the small red and the small brown midge. Previous to my original research, as far as I know, none of these had been covered in the literature, and as they now seem to be generally accepted, I propose to leave these as they are in the new list. The next one in the list, the Blagdon green midge, I feel should also remain unaltered, as this medium sized, bright green bodied midge was first named by Sheringham, and has since been accepted by most leading authors. Next we come to the black midge, a medium sized species with a grey-black ribbed body. This is an early season species, referred to in Scotland as the Blae and Black, and as both J. R. Harris and Bob Carnill also refer to it by this name, I have decided to alter the name in the list accordingly. A similar species but with a black body is also common early in the season, particularly in Ireland, where it is referred to as the duck-fly. Bob Carnill also refers to it by this name, but I have not included it in the list as up to now I have been unable positively to identify the species. The next poses something of a problem. In my original list I referred to it as the ribbed midge; it is a medium to large species appearing in mid summer, and while the body is predominantly olive, the edge of each segment is an ivory or beige colour. This species is referred to by Bob Carnill as the ginger and beige, but since at least three earlier authors, namely Sheringham, Harris and Courtney Williams, all refer to it as the olive midge, I have decided to follow the majority and reclassify it under this name. We now come to a medium to large species also common in mid summer, which I referred to as the Golden Dun midge. This has a golden olive body with a brilliant yellow thorax, with two distinct black stripes or dots; so apart from the fact that this name seems most applicable, it must obviously be adopted, as all the leading authorities right back to Ronalds in the last century refer to it by this name. We now come to the three largest species. The first of these, an early season species, I referred to as the orange and silver midge; it had not been previously identified. It has a distinctly grey body with orange-red joinings of the segments, but as these joinings can only be seen against transmitted light, I feel that Bob Carnill's suggested name, Grey

Boy, is probably more appropriate. The large red midge in my list had never been previously mentioned in angling literature, unless of course this is the ruby gnat referred to by Leonard West. This late season species is referred to by Bob Carnill as the large ginger, so I think in the new list we should perhaps refer to it in future as the large red or ginger midge. The last in the list, and without doubt the largest of all the midges, is a late season variety to which I gave the name the large green midge. I feel that this should remain as it is; the only other author to come up with an alternative has been Bob Carnill, and his suggested name, the Large Dark Olive midge could be a little confusing since there are both natural upwinged flies and artificials of the same name.

This is the new, modified list:

Angler's name	Entomological name
The Large Green Midge	*Chironomus plumosus* — Group
The Large Red or Ginger Midge	*Chironomus plumosus*
The Grey Boy	*Chironomus plumosus*
The Golden Dun Midge	*Chironomus plumosus*
The Olive Midge	*Chironomus plumosus*
The Blae and Black	*Chironomus anthracinus*
The Blagdon Green Midge	*Endochironomus albipennis*
The Small Brown Midge	*Glypotei dipes paripes*
The Small Red Midge	*Microtendipes pedellus*
The Small Black Midge	*Polypedilum nubeculosus*

3 Tackle and tips

Rods

I do not intend to devote a great deal of space to this subject as it has been well covered in other volumes. In any case, a rod is a very personal item, and the action and feel of a rod that suits one fly fisher will not necessarily suit another. Having said that, I will offer a little advice to the less experienced. Always ensure, when purchasing a rod, that you use the correct weight of line with it; there is nothing more inhibiting to casting than trying to work a rod with a line that is either too light or too heavy. I would also advise any fly fisher purchasing a new rod to make sure he obtains the correct length and weight of rod for the style of fishing he intends to use it for. Without becoming too technical, a good rod for fishing from the bank should be 9 ft or 9½ ft long and take lines between No. 7 to 9. It should be as light as possible, yet powerful enough to push a line out when necessary, directly into a strong wind. For nymph fishing, you will require a lighter rod to take lines between No. 6 and 8, ideally it should be a little longer, about 10 ft. This will also make a good rod for general boat fishing on the drift. It will also be necessary to have at least one other rod and this should be about 9 ft long to take lines No. 8 to 10, which will be for fishing sinking lines from a boat. These three rods will suffice for most stillwater work, although you will probably require further, more specialised rods as you become more involved.

The relatively new carbon rods, although expensive, are ideal for stillwater fly fishing as they incorporate both lightness with power and a small diameter, which makes them less tiring to use over long periods. Also, they are much more tolerant of line weight, and many of them, at a pinch, will cope with lines between No. 6 and 10. One word of warning, however. Their power is such that, until one learns to strike more gently than with a glass or cane rod, you will be leaving flies in many fish. Although, in fairness, with recent improvements in design they are now less prone to do this than they used to be. If the price of carbon rods is a little beyond your pocket, do not be afraid to purchase a glass rod; providing you choose carefully, there are many excellent glass rods still available, and in many cases these have a better 'feel' than carbon, which is primarily a casting tool. One such rod is the 'Stillwater' which is marketed under my name. This is a 9½ ft general purpose glass rod which takes a No. 7 or 8 line, very pleasant to use. It is a versatile rod, meant for either bank or boat fishing, and is primarily a fishing tool, although it will cast a long line if required.

Reels

So far as I am concerned, I look upon reels as merely a container to hold my line. Rightly or wrongly, I seldom, if ever actually play a trout off the reel. I prefer to play a fish by holding the fly line with finger and thumb, as this gives me far greater control, and also more feel for what the fish is doing. I realise that many fly fishers will point out that to have coils of loose line in the boat or on the ground around your feet is asking for trouble, for if it becomes snagged, or if you stand on it, a break is inevitable. In practice, with a little care, this rarely happens, and in over 25 years of stillwater fishing, the number of trout I have lost due to this could be counted on the fingers of two hands. On the other hand, I have observed countless anglers lose trout while trying to take up slack onto the reel, as it is all but impossible to concentrate fully on the fish while trying to do this. I have also seen many fly fishers broken when the trout has made a sudden lunge and the check or brake on the reel has been set a little too firmly. In my opinion, the main points to consider when purchasing a reel are lightness and capacity. A reel for stillwater should be large enough to take a full fly line, and also a minimum of 100 yards of backing. I also like a reel that has an exposed rim, so that if I happen to hook a big trout that takes a lot of line on his initial run, I can control him with the palm of my hand on the spool of the reel. One little item that I do abhor in a reel is a loud, two way ratchet which operates every time you wind your line back onto the spool, and echoes all round the lake.

Lines

This is one item of tackle on which you can now spend a small fortune if you are so inclined. The variety of fly lines now available are legion. Double taper — Forward taper — Sink tip — Long belly — Floaters — Slow sink — Fast sink — Hi.D — Lead core. You can then add to this list a variety of shooting heads, and then multiply all the above by the different weights available, and it all becomes very confusing indeed. For this reason it is quite impossible to suggest what lines you start with, since this will depend entirely on what style of fishing you decide to concentrate on, as each of them is made for a different purpose. Whether you use a full length line or a shooting head is also a matter of personal choice. A shooting head is, in effect made by cutting the first 10 yards off any of the above lines, and then joining it to a special backing line. This can be anything from ordinary 25 lb test monofilament, to the new hollow core nylon backing that is now available. The main consideration here is to have a backing which will shoot freely through the rings of the rod, and above all not tangle when you retrieve into your line tray. In the last ten years we have seen many different types of backing produced specially for this purpose, including pre-stretched oval, and even flattened monofilament, but in my opinion the new hollow core braided nylon backing is by far the best. It is very soft and limp and therefore rarely tangles, and it also shoots beautifully. In addition, with its hollow core it makes the chore of joining a shooting head or even a full line to the backing delightfully simple. Take a thick needle such as an old darning needle, and push it up the centre of the hollow backing for about an inch. Then with a lighter or a match, heat the protruding end of the needle. If you apply the right amount of heat (too much and the backing will melt), the backing will not close down over the needle as you withdraw it. The end of the fly line can then be easily pushed into the hollow core, and with a little instant glue spread thinly over the outside of the backing which it will penetrate you will have a super smooth join which will last for at least a season. A short length, about twelve inches, can also be used to join the butt end of your leader to the fly line. What are the advantages of using a shooting head? First of all, once you have mastered the art of shooting line, or better still, double hauling, a shooting head will allow you to achieve far greater distance. I have been using shooting heads now for stillwater fly fishing from the bank since 1957, and the main reason I favour them is that they are far less fatiguing to use. To cast 20 or 25 yards of a full length fly line requires four or five false casts to aerialise the line, whereas with a shooting head two false casts will give you 30 yards at least. In the past, a lot of rubbish has been talked about shooting heads hitting the surface so hard that they scare every trout for miles. Of course they will in the hands of an inexperienced person, and so will an ordinary fly line. Any reasonably competent caster can put a shooting head down on the surface as quietly as a double taper line.

Whether you use a full line or a shooting head, the colour you choose may well affect your fishing success, particularly with floating lines. Brian Clarke and I, in our book *The Trout and the Fly*, clearly demonstrated the fish-scaring effects of bright coloured fly lines in the air, and even more so on the surface in the mirror. This raised great controversy at the time, as the pro-white brigade were not prepared to accept this. They quoted many instances, such as Mr. So and So who took over 300 trout in a season using a white line. My answer is that he would probably have taken over 400 if he had been using a dark coloured line. This apart, few anglers seem to appreciate that using the right colour is much more important for some types of fishing than others. On a clear river or lake it makes only a minimal difference, as you can see whether there are any trout between you and the one to which you are fishing, but how different on a big stillwater where you are casting a long line on water into which it is difficult, if not impossible, to see. There could be any number of trout between you and the point in the water where your fly lands, and even after it lands, cruising trout may pass under the line. There may be a point for a white line for nymph fishing, as a white line on the surface can also be seen more clearly by the fisherman, and it is of vital importance when nymph fishing to see as clearly as possible the end of your fly line. However, I would suggest a better alternative is to paint the last yard or so of your dark fly line.

In 1981 I wrote an article for *Trout Fisherman* magazine entitled 'The Herringbone Effect', which pointed out the fish-scaring effects of retrieving a floating line even very slowly on still water. To overcome this problem I suggested that maybe one of the fly line manufacturers could produce a special fly line with a negative buoyancy which could be retrieved just below the surface film to eliminate the fish-scaring ripple. I am now happy to report that Garcia, one of the largest fly line manufacturers in the world, have now produced such a line, called 'The Intermediate', which should be available by the time this book is published.

Leaders

I shall dwell on these but briefly. In the past, a lot of nonsense has been suggested in respect of leaders, such as the necessity to make up leaders tapered down in steps by joining monofilament of different breaking strains, and even in some cases, with reverse tapers being employed towards the end. In the first place, they are difficult and time consuming to make, and secondly, they naturally include a series of ugly knots. They were designed to give your fly a better turn over and presentation, and it is doubtful whether they do so. I am a firm believer in having as few knots in a leader or line as possible. For general fishing, a 9 ft tapered leader which can be purchased in any tackle shop is quite satisfactory. Onto the end of this you can knot a length of ordinary monofilament of a breaking strain of your choice for tying on your droppers or point fly. For river fishing or for fishing on small, clear stillwaters, I normally mount a short leader with a maximum length of 12 ft; where you can see your trout there is really no point in having a longer leader, which is more difficult to control. It is also sensible to use a short leader for punching a fly out onto a wind. Having said that, I would strongly recommend for general stillwater fishing that you employ as long a leader as you can possibly handle. Back in the 1960s, I was largely responsible for publicising the use of these long leaders. As the result of experiments with the amount of noise and disturbance fly lines make when they land in the water, I quickly realised that the further a fly lands away from your fly line, the less trout you will scare.

The accessories

The amount or quality of the accessories you carry with you is largely a matter of commonsense. Good, sound clothing which is really waterproof is, of course, a must for use in foul weather; and for fishing in pleasant conditions, dark, drab clothing is to be preferred. Bright colours should be avoided, as trout have very sharp eyesight. A fishing vest or waistcoat, one of those with a multitude of pockets, is very useful, and one of those large capacity, waterproof reservoir haversacks which are now being specially made is a good investment. You should always carry a priest for despatching your trout humanely, and a specially made spoon for examining the stomach contents of the trout you catch is also a must. You can now purchase a combined marrow scoop (spoon) and priest. A large rush bag or bass (as they are called), which will hold all the trout you catch throughout the day, and also keep them fresh, is also a good idea. The old type of rush bag is now somewhat difficult to obtain, but a recent innovation is a specially made trout bass. This is an outer bag of hessian or flax which absorbs water, and which can be well soaked before you use it. Inside is a lining of open weave nylon to hold your fish, which breathes, keeps your trout beautifully fresh and can also be removed for cleaning. A good fly box and landing net are also necessities, but the range of these is so wide you must make your own personal choice. Floatant, line grease and a degreasant should always be carried as they are vital to successful fishing.

The boat angler will be well advised to take with him a comfortable cushion, and one of the inflatable varieties is to be preferred, since there is nothing better designed to ensure a miserable day's fishing than a hard seat in a boat. Some reservoir authorities do in fact supply foam pads to sit on, but they are not particularly comfortable. As previously mentioned, a good anchor or anchors in a boat are of great importance, so I strongly advise you to make your own and carry them with you. Even where they are supplied with the boat, they are invariably all but useless. The same applies to drogues; although these are sometimes supplied and satisfactory, it is better to be on the safe side and take your own. You can now purchase these in some tackle shops, but it is a fairly simple matter to make your own (*Illustration No. 19.*) Always carry a good quality stone with which to keep your hooks sharp, as this is of vital importance and something most fly fishers neglect completely.

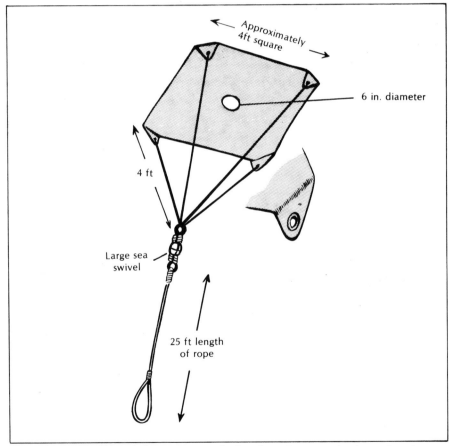

Illustration No.19: Although drogues are standard equipment on many boats, most are too small, and ineffective. An efficient drogue is easily constructed from heavy nylon, a few brass eyelets, a heavy swivel and a length of nylon cord. (The drawing — particularly the swivel — is not to scale.)

While on the subject of hooks, there is one golden rule that you should always observe when fishing, and I really cannot overemphasise its importance. The first thing you should always do after pricking, losing or landing a trout is to check your hook and make sure it is perfectly sound. I myself, even with all my experience, occasionally forget to do this, and it can often be a very costly oversight indeed. Only last season on Grafham one evening, I was guilty of failing to realise that the reason I lost six trout in succession was the fact that the first one pricked took the point of the hook with him.

Finally, may I make a plea in the interest of conservation? May I suggest that you give very serious consideration to using barbless hooks? This is really very simple to achieve, and does not necessitate the purchase of hooks without barbs. You can do it yourself in the manner described on page 41. All you have to do is purchase a pair of sharp-nosed modelmaker's pliers and carry them in your pocket. Then, after you have tied your fly onto your leaders, flatten the barb with the pliers; sometimes the barb will break off as you flatten it, which is all to the good, and rarely, very rarely indeed, unless you are clumsy, will the point break off. This is a plus really. Although it results in a wasted fly, it means that the hook was overtempered, and it is far better to break the point off in the hand, instead of in a trout. During the course of a season, we all return a percentage of unwanted trout, and a hook with a barb, even when removed carefully, can cause lacerations in the mouth of a trout, which may eventually result in his death. Apart from this, with a barbless hook there is no need to take the trout out of the water and handle it; slide your finger and thumb down the leader to the fly, a quick shake, and the trout is free. Contrary to popular belief, I can assure you that you will lose less trout if you use barbless hooks. Without a barb, the hook invariably penetrates right up to the bend. This means the trout is *less* likely to come off, even on a slack line, and furthermore, the point is less likely to break off or the hook open as there is less leverage. I have been using barbless hooks now for many years, and I do assure you I now lose far less trout than I used to.

I conclude this chapter with a selection of useful tips that I have picked up over the years.

Some useful tips

1. Have you ever found yourself in that most frustrating of all positions, late in the evening with the light almost gone, with big trout humping and swirling all around you, and your leader and flies in an impossible tangle? More often than not by the time you have unravelled them or tied on a new leader and flies the rise is over. If you have not yet experienced this situation you surely will eventually. It only requires one bad cast, or a small rainbow to take your top dropper. (Of course the danger of a snarl-up can be minimised if you come down to two or even better one fly, but as is often the case, particularly from a boat, your best chance of taking trout may be with three flies.) Now, is there a solution to this problem? Well, yes, there are several alternatives and probably the best is as follows.

First of all, in place of whipping or nail knotting your leader to the end of your fly line, form a small whipped loop. This is quite a simple operation. With a sharp razor blade or a knife remove a small amount of the plastic covering (about one quarter of an inch) on one side of the fly line as close to the end as possible and then form a small tight loop whip and varnish. (*Illustration No. 20.*) You will now have a permanent loop on the end of your fly line and your leader may be attached or detached at will. If you use custom-made tapered leaders that have a loop formed at the butt end, this will have to be cut off. To attach your leader to the loop on the end of your fly line you will have to use a blood knot or similar knot. Next you will have to purchase a set of Hills cast carriers or if you have handy fingers make a set yourself out of a sheet of plastic.

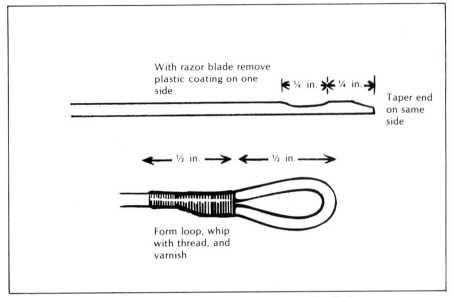

With razor blade remove plastic coating on one side

◄ ¼ in. ✱ ¼ in. ►

Taper end on same side

◄— ½ in. —► ◄— ½ in. —►

Form loop, whip with thread, and varnish

Illustration No.20: How to form a small whipped loop at the end of a fly line.

You are now all set for the next evening's fishing. As the magic hour approaches and you have decided which flies you are going to mount on your cast, make up a duplicate set and wind on to one of your cast carriers. Should a tangle then occur during the failing light, it will only take a matter of seconds to cut off the old leader at the fly line loop and tie on your duplicate leader.

It is also a good idea to utilise some of the other cast carriers in the set, to make up and wind on several other leaders, with alternative patterns for the time of the year. From June onwards trout have a perverse habit of changing their diet three or even four times during some evening rises. The switch from one species to another can often be rapid and sometimes shortlived, and unless you use this or a similar method you will have little success.

2. Now we are all aware, I am sure, that during an average day's fishing it is often necessary to change the fly lines several times in order to present your flies at the depth at which the fish may be feeding, this could necessitate using fast sinking lines, floating lines or any type in between. If one is using the leaders that are permanently fixed to the fly line it will mean that each time you wish to change to a different type of line, your outfit will have to be completely stripped down and remade. Those anglers that can afford two or three complete outfits can of course overcome the problem by making up all these outfits with different lines before they start fishing, but even so this is not always a good idea, as made up rods are often a nuisance, particularly in a boat where they can also be damaged.

A far better solution, providing that you can handle a fairly long leader, is to purchase several spare spools for your reel. It will then only be necessary to wind the butt of the leader down close to the reel on your rod, cut the leader off tight up to the loop on the fly line, then remove the spool from the reel, clip in a new spool containing a different line and re-tie the leader to the loop. This can be achieved in seconds rather than minutes, but it is necessary if one is using three flies to have a leader at least 16 ft in length, which will give you 10 ft from the butt of the leader to the first dropper. With a 9 ft or 9½ ft rod this will provide sufficient slack to re-tie the leader to the new line with the top dropper pulled up to the top of the rod.

3. During the past 25 years of fly fishing I have picked up or discovered many little tips that can make you a more efficient angler. Here are two of them.

3a When making up the rod many fly fishers thread the point of the leader through the rod rings. This is a fiddly job at the best of times, and with a very fine point on the leader it is only too easy to miss a ring and not to discover your error until after you have tied your fly on and you start fishing. If you double back the leader half way along its length you will find it much easier and quicker to feed the resulting loop through the rings. Furthermore, you would then have to be very careless indeed to miss a ring.

3b Most of us, I am sure, appreciate that modern fly lines have a plastic coating that tends to crack after a year or two of wear. One of the major contributory factors is the common practice of doubling the leader around the reel and securing the fly in one of the rod rings, thereby causing the fly line to be doubled back sharply around the tip ring. Most rods are fitted with a small keeper ring for holding the fly — use it! If your leader is longer than the rod you are using, as it should be, it will then result in the leader and not the expensive fly line being doubled over the tip ring.

4. What can be more annoying or frustrating than arriving at the waterside and finding you have misplaced or lost your scissors or clippers? In the past this has happened to me on many occasions. Nowadays I use a small pair of nail clippers, with a small eyeletted hole at the tapered end to which one can tie a length of cord. The other end of the cord can be tied to the flap of a pocket on your fishing vest, or better still, to one of those marvellous little spring loaded extension reels that you can buy to clip or pin onto your vest. I find that the small nail clippers I use are more convenient and less dangerous to carry than scissors, but they do have one drawback, they can very easily slip out of your fingers when the opening lever is depressed to cut, particularly when your fingers are a little stiff with the cold weather. To overcome this I glue onto the surface of the lever and also to the back surface of the clippers, two small strips of sandpaper or emery paper. This gives you a wonderful non-slip grip. (*Illustration No. 21*).

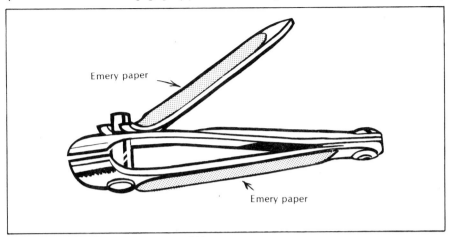

Illustration No.21: Nail clippers with a difference.

5. I am sure everyone has experienced the annoyance of finding the eye of the fly one is about to tie on is filled with varnish or dirt, and you waste valuable time trying to pierce it with your relatively limp nylon. You can of course re-open your fly-box, extract another fly and utilise the point of this to clear the eye, or seek the needle you carry specifically for this purpose if you can locate it. All this takes precious time, so I now carry a little tool which is very simple to make and solves the problem admirably. (*Illustration No. 22*.) Obtain an old exhausted *Bic* pen and remove the little plastic plug at the blunt end. In place of this insert a tapered wood plug which can be whittled to shape with a knife. Then, with an ultra fine drill make a hole slightly smaller than the diameter of a thick needle; this hole should not completely pierce through the plug. Next take a fairly stout needle and snap or

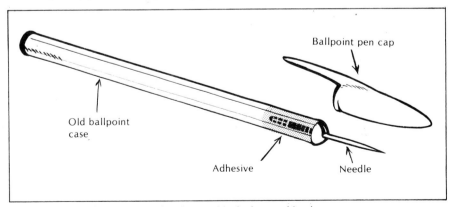

Illustration No.22: A simple tool for clearing blocked eyes of hooks.

cut this in half. The broken end of the upper portion is pushed into the hole, leaving about half an inch of the point extruding. This is then covered by the plastic pocket clip when not in use, which in turn allows you to carry it clipped in your pocket where it is instantly available. Alternatively, a quicker and possibly simpler method is to remove the empty ink tube from the pen, remove and pierce the plastic plug with a needle or even a pin, fill the end of the empty pen tube with an adhesive and replace the plug with the base of the pin or needle (which can be covered with a short length of the empty ink tube) extending half its length into the glue, which will seal it permanently in position when dry.

6. Most of us carry a selection of dry flies in our fly box, for those magic days that occur occasionally on still water when the trout are feeding avidly on surface fly. Dry flies fished on stillwater are often notoriously difficult to keep afloat, due to the length of time it may be necessary to keep them on the surface, so anything we can do to increase their floatability must be highly desirable. The vast majority of fly fishers annoint their flies with a floatant as they mount them on the leader, and then immediately commence fishing. This in effect results in a large percentage of the floatant being washed off as soon as it comes into contact with the water. Ideally your flies should be thoroughly dried after treatment before you commence fishing, but most of us are naturally not prepared to waste valuable fishing time on such niceties. The answer to this little problem is very simple. As soon as you purchase your flies, or if you dress your own, treat them thoroughly with floatant before you put them into your fly box. Personally I find it is best to treat them in batches and then lay out on clean newspaper in a warm room to dry thoroughly before mounting them in my fly box.

7. Here is a little but very important tip concerning your personal safety. Whether you are fishing rivers, stillwaters or even engaged in some casting practice, always wear a pair of glasses to protect your eyes. A badly cast fly, a sudden gust of wind, or a mistake by a companion angler, particularly in the close confines of a boat, can only too easily result in the loss of sight in an eye. This unfortunate occurrence has befallen too many anglers in the past, and will doubtless continue unless everyone takes this very simple precaution. Ordinary sunglasses may be used, although it should be pointed out that these may impair your eyesight if worn repeatedly over long periods. Far better to invest in a pair of good quality polarized spectacles which have the added advantage of allowing you to spot fish in the water if it is clear enough, particularly when worn in conjunction with a long peaked cap which cuts down overhead glare dramatically.

8. I am sure that many of you who have been fly fishing for some time have experienced the embarrassment and inconvenience of having the point and barb of a fly buried deep in some part of your anatomy. This usually necessitates a visit to the nearest doctor or hospital with consequent loss of valuable fishing time. Now, providing the hook is not buried in any particularly tender part of the body such as the lip or nose, or of course anywhere near the eye, it is comparatively easy and, if carried out correctly, relatively painless to remove it yourself with the assistance of a companion. The only instrument required to achieve this is a short length of thin but strong nylon line, which should present no problem to a fisherman. Tie an eighteen inch length of nylon monofilament securely to the bend of the hook, grip the other end firmly with one hand, and with the forefinger of the other hand press down fairly hard on top of the shank of the hook. A hard sharp jerk on the line should then remove the hook from the flesh cleanly, with the barb doing the minimum of damage. This only applies though to small hooks, if the offending hook is larger than size 12 it is better to seek professional help.

9. Since I first advocated the use of barbless hooks for fly fishing several years ago, more and more fly fishers are becoming converted. If you wish to return trout on those waters where it is allowed, or where the rules of the fishery state undersized trout should be returned, the use of barbless hooks means that they can be returned with the minimum of damage to their relatively tender mouths, and even more important, they can be released in the water without actually touching them. In addition, contrary to popular belief, it is very rare to lose a fish on a barbless hook; without a barb it is much easier to set a hook, and furthermore you will seldom if ever have a hook open up or the point break off. Over the years many anglers that have observed me fishing with barbless hooks have stated they have been tempted to try it but have been put off as they have either been unable to buy flies on barbless hooks or have been unable to obtain barbless hooks on which to tie their own flies. This is really no problem at all; I dress all my own flies on ordinary, barbed hooks (due to the difficulty in obtaining the right type of barbless hooks — although I understand that even this difficulty may shortly be resolved). I remove or flatten the barb at the waterside after I have mounted the fly on the leader. All that is required is a small pair of sharp-nosed, modelmaker's pliers which I carry permanently in my pocket. With these it takes but a second to flatten the barb, and more often than not the barb will break off as you flatten it. Very, very rarely, and then only if you are careless, the point also breaks off. Then you have wasted a fly, but in practice this happens so rarely that you can more or less discount it. Give it a try and I promise you, never again will you use barbed hooks.

10. While it is possible to purchase several different brands and types of degreasant, did you know that for a few coppers you can make one of the most effective compounds? All you require is a bottle of glycerine and a bag of Fuller's earth. This will last you several years and you can either make it all at once and store it in a large tin, or you can mix it in small amounts as and when required. Add the glycerine to the Fuller's earth (which you can purchase at most chemists) until it reaches a consistency of a thin paste. To use take a pinch between finger and thumb, and rub along your leader to remove all trace of grease. To degrease a fly immerse it in the paste; it will come out looking like nothing on earth, but do not worry, it will all wash off as soon as it is immersed in the water. I carry my paste in an empty plastic film spool container, as I find this is a convenient size and is also reasonably airtight. After a time the mixture tends to thicken, but to thin it down you can either add further glycerine or, if at the waterside, add a little water to do the job just as well.

11. If you are a newcomer to stillwater trouting, you will doubtless wonder why some fly fishers catch many more fish than others. Now there can be many reasons for this, including an essential ingredient — experience. However, in my opinion one of the most common causes of failure, particularly with the less experienced, is due to their inability to understand the importance of both grease and degreasant for different fishing techniques. During the summer in the very early mornings or late evenings when the trout are feeding on or close to the surface, most fly fishers quite rightly use a floating line. Now to generalise, unless you are fishing dry flies your artificials should be retrieved either below the surface of just beneath the film, yet on countless occasions I observe anglers, I am sure unwittingly, retrieving these flies along the surface, where they will scare fish rather than attract. Many fly fishers mistakenly think that flies and leader will only float if you deliberately grease them — not so. Both will pick up a certain amount of grease from your skin as a result of handling, so it is essential to treat both thoroughly with degreasant before starting to fish. Conversely, greasing your leader or flies for certain styles of fishing can be equally important. As an example, when you are drift fishing from a boat it is often expedient to bounce your top dropper along the surface to attract trout; now unless you well grease the butt section of the leader above the fly and also treat the fly with floatant, it will keep sinking and not do its job properly. There are of course many other instances where the correct use of grease or degreasant can make all the difference between success and failure.

12. Most fly fishers possess several fly reels and also spare spools containing different types of fly lines. Now there is little problem with those reels and lines you are regularly using. However, put aside any of these reels and lines for any length of time, and you will inevitably be scratching your head trying to identify them, for apart from the fact that light coloured lines are usually floaters there is little to distinguish one from another, particularly when it comes to different weights of line. You can write the details on each spool, but in time the writing fades or rubs off, or you can scratch the details on, but this is not really recommended as it can damage the spool. A far better solution is to cut off the part of the label supplied with the line that gives the type and size and secure this on the inside back of the spool with a waterproof glue. This can easily be removed if and when you change the line.

4 April

The weather

The difference in the weather between the South and the North, particularly with regard to temperature, may be considerable during this month, so the fly fisher must naturally take this into account when planning tactics. Showers, sometimes of sleet and snow, are not uncommon when the wind is in the north or north west, which will provide a bleak prospect for the angler. Also, high winds may be expected on many days, which will naturally make fishing difficult. The best April days are those bringing warm rains from the west, with intermittent sunshine, or the occasional southerly wind with the propsect of summer to come. Fishing during the month of April can vary tremendously from one season to another, depending upon the weather. In a normal year with average spring temperatures the trout are likely to feed closer and closer to the surface as the month progresses, so that towards the end of the month, boat fishing may begin to pay greater dividends than bank fishing. In the early part of the month, should it be cold, lure fishing will usually provide more fish, although it may be necessary to use sinking lines in deeper waters. From the above, it should be apparent that the level at which many patterns should be fished will depend very much on the temperature of the water. Large reservoirs and lakes can be very bleak places if the weather is unkind, so the fly fisher may be well advised at this time of the season to plan a few trips to the smaller waters, as these, apart from being less affected by the weather, are often more sheltered.

Boat fishing – imitative patterns
JOHN GODDARD

Boat fishing can often be less productive than bank fishing during April, so if your preference is for boat fishing, you must be prepared to work hard for your trout and take advantage of any opportunities that may occur. During the early part of the month, unless it is exceptionally warm, one's best chance is to fish from an anchored boat, using either a floating line with a long leader, or a sink tip or slow sink line. At this time of the year, the trout are most likely to be concentrated in small shoals in relatively restricted areas, particularly the recently introduced stockies. For this reason it is a good plan to keep on the move until the trout are located. Never spend more than 20 minutes anchored in one spot if no takes are forthcoming. Avoid the areas adjacent to feeder streams, channels or ditches early in the season, as they are more likely to hold the overwintered rainbows which will now be black and in poor condition, not worth catching. Also avoid the shore off which the wind is blowing, always fish adjacent to the lee shore, particularly early in the year, as this is where the trout are most likely to be, as the water temperature will be higher. Water between eight and twelve feet in depth should be favoured, and particularly good areas to concentrate on at this time of the year are drop-offs over the edge of banks or promontories, or towards the gradually sloping walls of dams on some reservoirs. Natural food at this time of year is at a premium, but on most waters freshwater shrimps are likely to be present in fair quantities, so a leaded shrimp pattern fished slowly, close to the bottom is often a good bet. In conjunction with a leaded shrimp on the point, I often mount a Mallard and Claret on a dropper. Early in the season this is an excellent general pattern. On many waters during March, April and May, where they occur, the larvae of alder flies are very active, as at this period prior to pupation, they regularly leave their burrows in the mud or silt of the lake bed, and roam along the bottom, where they provide easy pickings for the trout. Therefore throughout this month, a leaded Alder Larva pattern mounted on the point, and retrieved slowly, close to the bed of the lake on a slow sink line from an anchored boat, can often prove very productive. A useful alternative would be a red or green larva, as the larvae of the chironomids are also very active on the bottom at this time of the year. Whichever of these slow-moving bottom dwellers you are trying to imitate, I cannot overemphasise the importance of retrieving your artificials in a similar manner; if you retrieve too fast they will plane up from the bed of the lake and they will be less acceptable to the trout.

Towards the middle of the month, particularly if the water is starting to warm up, good hatches of chironomids (midges) are likely to occur, mainly in the early evenings. The predominant species are most likely to be either the small or medium sized black midge (Blae and Black or the Duck Fly) or the large orange and silver (Grey Boy), and there are appropriate hatching midge patterns to represent all of these. On calm evenings, some surface activity is likely to occur with the trout humping and swirling as they chase the pupae to the surface. When this occurs, I have had most success fishing from a slowly drifting boat, retrieving a couple of hatching midge pupae patterns, one of each colour, at a medium pace just below the surface.

The end of April is usually more productive, and providing it is not too cold, some surface activity may be observed during the day. The odd trout may be seen to swirl at the surface, and a few may also seem to be leaping out of the water. Under these conditions, standard drift fishing may pay off, but I usually confine my drifts to the slightly deeper water. Utilising a 10 ft boat rod with a No. 6 or 7 floating line, I have found a killing combination of patterns is a Small Black Midge mounted on the top dropper, with an Orange and Silver on the middle dropper, and a Persuader or Black Bear's Hair Lure on the point. I have also had a lot of success with a well-greased Black Palmer or Zulu mounted on the top dropper in place of the Black Midge, as this can be bounced along the surface and will often attract trout up to your flies from a considerable depth. If you can handle it use a long leader, around 20 ft with the flies spaced 3 to 4 ft apart.

Finally, if you encounter a nice breezy day near the end of the month, be on the lookout for hawthorn flies. These large black terrestrial flies, which can quickly be identified in flight by their long trailing rear legs, often get blown onto the water surface under windy conditions at this time of year, when they hatch, often in considerable numbers. If you are fortunate to encounter a good fall of these naturals on the surface, sport is usually assured, as the trout seem inordinately fond of these relatively large, juicy morsels, and a good surface rise is to be anticipated. There are several artificial hawthorn patterns available, and these seem to be equally effective either fished dry on the surface and given an occasional tweak to animate, or retrieved slowly just beneath the surface.

Boat fishing – traditional JOHN KETLEY

At the start of the season many fly fishers believe they must anchor to get their flies down to the fish and it is often true that the trout really do hug the bottom when the water is cold. But, even if there are no fish showing on the surface, and on bitterly cold days, traditional loch style fishing can produce a bag of the best condition fish in the water.

One of the positive aspects of fishing loch style early on is that one seldom catches the dark coloured rainbows and out of condition brownies, as such fish tend to congregate on the bottom in certain areas and are seldom cruising mid-water in search of food.

Many anglers associate traditional loch style fishing with floating lines, but it must be remembered the originators of the technique used ungreased silk lines and flies up to size six, so without bending tradition, sinking lines have a big part to play in this style of fishing.

At the beginning of the month, even if there is a cold wind there will be one or two periods when those hardy little devils, the buzzers, do leave the bottom and reach at least the top three feet of water, some of them may even continue up to hatch into flies. While the numbers will not equal those of later months, there will be enough to interest those hungry April trout and during these periods the trout are very catchable by traditional loch methods.

One thing that makes loch style fishing more interesting to many is the fact that the boat is always drifting sideways to the wind, so every cast made is covering, at least partly, a fresh area of water.

If the wind is strong, as is too often the case in April, a drogue can be a real asset, as it gives the flies a chance to get down that important foot or two. In fact, some of the very experienced fly fishers now use two drogues, one at each end of the boat, and it's amazing just how much they can slow down a boat in a good blow. With the modern fibreglass boats' tendency to skid across the water, some sort of drogue can make all the difference. The boats on which this technique was originated were made of wood and built really heavy, so they drifted slowly and deliberately in anything less than a force 8. On Loch Leven they still have the original boats, now nearly a hundred years old, believe it or not, in daily service. Fishing from these heavy monsters is a revelation to any modern angler on just how sweet a boat can drift.

The next problem is where to start and finish the drift and, as always, it depends on the weather, but as a basic guide consider the fundamentals affecting one's quarry rather than how it appears on the surface. The trout most catchable by loch style fishing will be feeding in the warmer layers of water during April and these layers will occur either where it is fairly sheltered, or where the wind has tucked the warm layer underneath on the windy shore. From the angler's point of view the sheltered shore is often too short of ripple for successful loch style fishing, so a logical place to start will be drifting onto the windy shore.

The greatest aid to the drifting boat fisherman is the sight of a rising fish or two, but this, sadly, is not a common occurrence in April. Nevertheless, if the day has some warmth, a cruise around likely parts of the lake between 1 pm and 3 pm may well show you a few fish on the top and then you will at least know you're over moving fish.

If you cannot find any moving fish, have a look round for swallows, swifts and even seagulls that appear to be feeding above, or, in the case of gulls, on the water. These birds may well be finding airborne midges and the occasional larger fly in confined areas of the lake. Even if there are no trout on the surface under these birds, it indicates an area where the insect life is active and in all probability you will find some trout feeding on the ascending nymphs a few inches, or sometimes feet, below the surface.

The next thing on any angler's list must be having a team of flies in which he has confidence, especially if there are no fish moving and not sufficient number of hatching flies to identify a likely candidate artificial. The fact is every angler has certain favourite flies and I, for one, would suggest you have at least one such fly on your cast, because this early in the season almost any of the famous loch flies can do the trick. But allow me to explain my own rationalisation for a choice of patterns for April.

The winged insects most likely to be trout fodder at this time of year are usually from the famous buzzer family. They will hatch out in surprisingly cold conditions. Even when they're not actually breaking through the surface film, there will often be considerable numbers of the pupae active below the cooler top layer of water.

The traditional patterns that best emulate the early buzzers are, in my opinion, the Blae and Black, the Mallard and Claret, the Black Pennel, the Williams or the Black Palmer. Slightly more recent is the wingless pattern originated by Dr Bell of Blagdon and now just called a Black Buzzer. There are many other colourways based on this basic pattern, all of which catch fish.

In certain light conditions, usually brightish days, I feel infinitely more confident when I also have a bright flashy fly on my cast and for this reason I would include one of the following in my candidate list for April. Wickham's Fancy (and Wickham's nymph pattern), Teal Blue and Silver, Teal and Green, Butcher or Dunkeld.

In early April the depth and area in which you fish is rather more critical than the choice of pattern, as the fish that are on the move are hungry and usually less selective than they become in later months.

For this reason the way in which you search through the water is of great importance, which leads me to the angle of the casts you make from a drifting boat. Many anglers cast straight ahead in front of the boat rather than fan out their subsequent casts to cover an angle of 45° during three casts. Employ the second method and your flies will not only cover and search a much greater area of water, they will be presented at varying angles to any fish that are there. Remember the fish are relatively torpid at this time of year and while they may take a fly that comes within a foot or so of their nose, they will not move to a fly yards away as they often do during warmer months.

Now to the speed of retrieve, which seems to be one of the most misunderstood parts of fly fishing, as so few people actually experiment to discover how much their flies move when they retrieve — especially from a drifting boat. The objective in the early season is to move your flies relatively slowly for two reasons.

Firstly, the fish are usually a little slow and ponderous as the water is still cold after the winter. Secondly, the flies will fish deeper if retrieved slowly. But it is no good pulling in line, assuming the flies are moving, because they may be virtually stationary in the water and all you are doing is catching up with them as the boat drifts forward. The most effective anglers I know have all developed a 'feel' that enables them to tell from the subtle difference in the resistance, or apparent weight of the line as it is retrieved through the water, just how fast their flies are moving.

The best experiment I know is to cast alongside another boat, or along a jetty or dam wall where a friend can watch your flies as you retrieve them and report on their action through the water. With a little trial and error you can quickly develop the magic 'feel' that catches fish so consistently.

Boat fishing – lures BOB CHURCH

Lure fishing from a boat can take on many forms, and as I describe a season's general approach we will cover all of them. Lure fishing is not just 'lure stripping', and in fact to be continuously successful a subtle approach is a must. There are, as you will see, many lessons to be learned.

Lures may be tied to be deceivers, that is, to resemble small coarse fish like roach, rudd, perch or bream fry. Or they may imitate minnows, bullheads or sticklebacks. Trout will regularly feed on these larger food items if they are present in fair numbers. Then there are the attractor lures; these are sometimes the quite gaudy creations which the Americans call streamer flies. When fished fast at the correct time of year and depth, they can be deadly trout catchers.

The weather is liable to be cold, wet and windy this month, so it is important to dress warmly and to be in possession of a good set of waterproofs, but above all a successful boat angler must have all the necessary gadgets to ensure he is master of his craft even under the worst conditions. Of these one of the most important is a good anchor, so purchase or make one yourself and take it with you on every boat trip. Nine times out of ten those provided by the authorities are quite useless in a strong wind and merely drag the bottom. Attach to your anchor ten yards of light chain, using a shackle, and then 30 yards of thick nylon rope. This should be wound onto a wooden holder for easy transportation and to eliminate tangles.

Because the water is so cold the trout are inclined to be lethargic at this time of year and are most likely to be found in small localized shoals on the side of the reservoir onto which the wind is blowing. So, it's no good putting the anchor down just anywhere and hoping for the best, especially on a big water.

Throughout April it is best to anchor about 60 yards from this lee shore. Not only will the water temperature be a little higher here, but the backwash of waves will also help create a good feeding area. The bottom-dwelling aquatic life gets disturbed in a good blow, making easy pickings for foraging trout. On all but the rarest occasions there will be many more trout along this shoreline than elsewhere.

Naturally I advise a sinking line, a fast sinker too, as there will be no weed to worry about. During this early period of the season I strongly advocate small lures and also a slow retrieve. A No. 10 long shank Black Chenille lure is my favourite and rarely fails, although a good alternative is a Baby Doll in a similar size. Two other lures which have also served me well in April are Ace of Spades and Worm Fly. The latter is a good old favourite and dates back a long time; both patterns produce well to slow and deep tactics.

Going back in time to the opening years at Chew Valley in the late 1950s, Worm Flies were traditionally tied on tandem mounts. This consisted of one hook facing upwards and one down, a good-hooking rig, no doubt, but personally I prefer the single hook version with exactly the same dressing.

Look out for some kind of feature as an alternative anchoring spot. By this I mean old submerged hedgerows and ditches, valve or aerator towers, or shallow reefs positioned well out in the reservoir such as at Draycote and elsewhere. If you ever drop anchor in a big wind and high wave, make sure the rope is attached to the bows only. This way the boat will comfortably ride the largest of waves. Once anchored safely, remember that such large waves often stimulate the trout into a concentrated feeding spree, so fishing can be excellent.

Towards the end of April the early season enthusiasm of many fly fishers has meant regular full house attendances at the leading reservoirs. Because of this the initial stocking of trout gets quite a hammering and the numbers are thinned out. To catch the remaining trout, which by now are pretty well educated, the boat angler has considerable advantage over the bank fisher. Start to experiment more with presentation — a sink-tip line can now be a very good approach. Cast across the wind and do nothing except keep in contact as the line and lures are swept round. I say lures because I often tie on a dropper when fishing this method. Basically the same patterns should be used, but remember it may now be necessary to vary the size as this can often be the key to success or failure.

If lots of black buzzer are coming off, the Black Chenille lure will still work well, but in the last week in April you will generally catch more fish with some kind of buzzer nymph — as detailed in the section on imitative fishing.

Most of the lure patterns I mention also fish well in tandem at the appropriate time of season, so it is very useful to know how to tie a tandem mount. It is time consuming, but nevertheless it pays to make a good strong job of the mount so that no breakages occur if and when you hook your big trout deep down.

I always make up several tandem rigs prior to an evening's lure tying. Materials used are No. 6 or No. 4 long shank and extra long shank hooks; 30 lb monofilament for joining them; some fairly sturdy nylon whipping thread on a bobbin holder; and varnish to finish off.

Place your hook in a vice, and thread the end of the 30 lb nylon through the eye and along the shank, then tie in half-hitch knot close up to the eye and trim the loose end level with the bend. Then whip it tightly to the shank and varnish. This is the rear end hook of your tandem rig. With the 6 inches or so of nylon that is left, I tie another half-hitch. When tightened this lies about 1 ½ inches in front of the rear hook. After trimming off the surplus I whip this nylon to the second hook, with the anchor knot positioned about half way along the shank. The gap between the two hooks is about ½ to ¾ inch. Make up a number of these rigs and varnish them one evening, then work on the lure dressings themselves another night.

Bank fishing – imitative patterns

BOB CARNILL

April is such an unpredictable month for the fly fisherman — both from the point of view of the weather and from the obvious effects it has upon the fishing. But no matter what the weather, it is the season of re-birth and a time of re-awakening. Both above and below the waterline overwintered creatures are becoming increasingly more active. Below the waterline this renewed activity will take place, for the most part, on or around the lake bed — the very place where the majority of the early season trout will be found.

The aquatic insects of greatest interest to the trout — and therefore to the trout fisherman during April, are as follows. Alder larvae are particularly active during this month, as they leave their burrows and migrate *towards* the bank, prior to pupation. So too are the caddis larvae, roaming the lake bed in their continual search for food and dragging their protective case along with them. Corixa (lesser water boatman) also take on a new lease of life, and can be seen in the margins of most still waters. Water beetles too are becoming more active, as are the freshwater shrimp (*Gammarus*). And if chironomids (buzzers or midge) are seen on, or around the water, then it is a positive indication that the buzzer pupa will be on the trout's menu also. So, while the trout's food is not yet 'thick on the ground', at least it is quite varied and does give the angler a fair choice of artificials.

At the beginning of the month I almost invariably tackle up and fish with these deep living, slow moving invertebrates in mind. For this kind of fishing I favour a 10 ft carbon fibre rod, taking a No. 8 weight forward floating line. My leaders are, by necessity, quite lengthy, 18 to 25 feet being common. I prefer to fish three flies given the right conditions, and they are spaced a little over three feet apart — making it possible to net a fish comparatively easily whatever fly it takes.

My first choice of flies would be as follows: point — my own Cased Caddis (leaded); first dropper — a Williams (leaded); top dropper — Buzzer Pupa (black or bottle green). However, the combination and choice of flies available for this style of fishing are legion — so here are just a few more which I would strongly recommend. For the point: Alder Larva, Stick Fly, Worm Fly and Shrimp. For the first dropper: Black & Peacock Spider, Zulu and Corixa. And for the top dropper: Buzzer Pupa (various patterns and colours), Mallard & Claret, Black Pennel and, if there's a bit of sun about, a small silver Butcher.

Long leaders and leaded flies are not the easiest of combinations to use, especially when casting into a headwind. The kind of spot I would choose, given the opportunity, would be a bank with a left to right wind, or as a second choice a right to left wind. Should that bank have points and bays — then so much the better. Fishing down wind from a point or promontory is always tactically sound. So too is covering a bay with the wind coming over ones back. Using the wind in this manner not only assists casting, it also holds the fly line out straight on the water without forming a 'windy-belly', thus avoiding drag. This in turn gives the angler as much time as is required for his flies to reach the desired depth. While on the subject of depth it should be mentioned that when choosing a spot for this style of fishing, both extremes of depth should be avoided. Clean trout are unlikely to be in very shallow water during April — although it will hold plenty of unwanted coloured cock rainbows. On the other hand, if the chosen spot has exceptionally deep water close to the bank, then the angler will have great difficulty in making his flies fish along the bottom. Such spots necessitate the use of sinking lines.

When retrieving the flies it should be kept in mind what we are trying to imitate — that being, a slow moving, bottom dwelling creature. A mistake all too often made by beginners and some ex-lure fishermen, is to fish their flies back much too quickly, this only serves to make the team of flies plane up and away from the bottom of the lake — completely defeating their objective.

The takes, when they occur, can be detected in a variety of ways, but I must admit that with the majority of the trout that I take, the offers are felt rather than seen. I attribute this to the strict discipline of keeping the rod tip low to the water with an angle between the rod and the line, and the line and the flies in direct conact with the rod tip. It is amazing just how sensitive this technique can be, even the smallest strand of weed picked up on the hook can be felt. However, on a very slow retrieve, the takes, under favourable conditions, can quite often be seen and should always be watched for. Should the tip of the fly line pull under, or should there be a straightening of the line between draws, then it must be tightened into, nothing should be ignored. It is better to strike falsely than not to react at all.

On some waters it can be distinctly advantageous to fish the 'lee shore', casting square into, or across the wind. If the wind strength, in this position, is anything other than light, I would forsake the floating line and the long leader, and in its place would go for a sinking line and a much shorter leader. The type of sinking line chosen would be dependent on wind strength and depth of water at that time. However, not all waters share this distinction of the lee-shore fishing well during a 'blow'. Rutland Water, for example, is becoming increasingly notorious for the 'reverse' being the better proposition.

It is quite unlikely that there will be any real changes by the middle of the month, and the aforementioned techniques should still be providing good results. However, I always take the added precaution of having another rod set up at all times, just in case a sudden 'rise' might occur. Chironomids and small shell-back beetles are usually the only insects responsible for instigating surface activity during the middle of April, consequently making the choice of artificials for the spare rod an easy task. My second rod is matched with the other rod in use, the only difference being that this time I would choose a No. 7 or 8 double taper floating line, and a 12 ft leader. On the point and the first dropper I would mount two buzzer pupa of different colours, a black one and a bottle green one for starters, and on the top dropper one of my Adult Buzzers — either a Blae & Black or a Duck Fly. During a rise this cast of flies is best fished just sub-surface, and fairly slowly. Every effort should be made to cover moving fish — and bearing in mind that springtime 'rises' can be short lived affairs, speed is of the essence and time must not be wasted should one occur within your reach.

By the end of April there is usually a marked increase in surface activity. This is due to the combination of a gradual increase in the water temperature, and a marked increase in buzzer hatches. It will be noticed that there are several species of buzzer on and about the water now, the largest being a fly that is known on my local waters as the Grey Boy. This, and the black Duck Fly, would be my first choice of Adult Buzzers to fish at this time — sometimes as a cast of three, or as top dropper flies with buzzer pupa on the point and first dropper. However, in order to make the right choice of flies, and to match the size and colour of the buzzer pupa, the importance of examing the stomach contents of a recently caught trout, in order to get a clear and a positive picture of what they are in fact selecting, cannot be over-stressed.

In between the periods of surface activity the trout may be cruising, and indeed feeding, at any depth from the bottom to just sub-surface. It is, therefore, necessary to fish one's flies at varying depths until the right level is found. The techniques previously discussed are ideal for this purpose, but when fishing away from the bottom and exploring the upper layers of water, the caddis imitations and the alder larva should be exchanged for more suitable patterns. For example, a Black & Peacock Spider, a Zulu, a Corixa or a large Pheasant Tail Nymph. Each of these point flies should be either weighted or dressed on heavy 'irons'.

Bank fishing – lures SYD BROCK

Fly fishing has changed so much in the last 15 years, and because of this I feel the modern day angler has so much more to take into account when he sets off fly fishing. Before he actually goes fishing the angler must know just what a particular line will do when it is cast upon the water. All too often the categories of lines are rolled into either sinking or floating items which are used to get the flies near, or as close as possible, to the feeding fish and after that the angler has no control over what happens to the 30 yards of line. This line of thought seems to be one of the lure fisherman's problems; whether consciously or unconsciously it rears its ugly head every time I go fishing, for it is the actions of the anglers themselves that brings this problem to light. So if you are using a form of sinking line you should know just how fast each individual line you possess sinks. For myself a slow sinker, a medium sinker and also a very fast sinking line are my main items. I know for instance that my slow sink line will descend at approximately one foot in 8 seconds, my medium sinker will take 4 seconds to sink a foot, and my fast sink line takes just over 1 second to sink the same distance. I memorise these statistics.

Now if we imagine a nice natural bank sloping away to say a depth of 8 feet at 30 yards, it is a great mistake to use the fast sink line, for the angler has to either strip in the lure very fast and risk not presenting the lure in the correct manner, or fish the lure properly for the first couple of yards and then be fouled in the lake bed's vegetation, when just a little thought can make all the difference. I would use a slow sink line, maybe wait a little longer for the line to reach the desired depth and then present the lure in the correct manner.

It goes without saying that if the lake bed were different, say a gradual slope out to 20 yards with a high ridge of vegetation and then a deep hole, I would in fact use a line to get me down in that hole, knowing that most fish would take the lure as it rose up from the hole heading for safety of the weed beds. You may be fouled in the weeds just the same, so it is a matter of thinking tactics all the time. Once you know what sort of water you are fishing over, and you can usually tell after a few casts, alter your tackle to suit the conditions, don't be afraid to sit on the bank for a while and consider just what your tactics will be. A few minutes well spent like this can make all the difference. Decisions made in a hurry can cause all sorts of problems and disappointments.

A lure is not just a lure — so many anglers make this mistake. There are several categories so let us take just a few that I use. The Black Ghost if fished correctly should cut through the water like a cheese knife cutting cheese, for it is a streamer lure and should be fished fairly fast for the best results. But the special Baby Doll (or Jersey Herd) is not affected by its shape altering when it is fished slowly, so it can be fished very slow if required, although I would recommend that as a general rule the slower you fish these flies the smaller size lure you use. Then there are what I call water movers, the Muddler or Pearly lures — these are very versatile, for the buoyancy of these lures enables the angler to fish them in so many ways. Their bulk creates quite a bit of water movement, so medium to slow retrieves are required to fish these lures correctly. However, there are times when this general rule does not apply but I will cover these as we pass from month to month.

I have touched very lightly on just a few points to remember, but these are very important to a lure man's tactics. There are so many other things that can affect your approach to a day's sport, such as weather, water conditions, the lack of fish showing, the abundance of fish showing, etc., that you must keep an alert mind to the ever-changing situations. Try to imagine just what each individual lure would look like when in its wet form and place it into its correct category, so you can fish each lure at its right speed of retrieve.

April is at first a test bed of what is to come. Depending on what sort of weather has preceded in February and March one can usually define what sort of sport to expect. Early April is when most waters open up for the start of the season, so a lot of fish will be fairly easy to catch. It is also a time to avoid fishing where feeder streams or any trickles of water enter lakes or reservoirs, for in these areas congregate dark, out of condition fish.

My local water, Farmoor 2, has taught me, over the years, to fish very deep at this time of year with either a Black Lure or Black Pearly, using a fast sink line (shooting head) and moderately slow retrieves to tempt the fish, but stay alert, for if your tactics are producing no takes, or even black fish, a change is necessary. I would change first to a streaker and try to avoid these fish, for I feel that out of condition fish do not swim as fast as good clean fish. If these tactics do not work I would then change my line to a medium slow sink and repeat the process again.

It may be that you find yourself fishing water other than your local water, so remember these rules if you can. Do not wade into the water; so many fish are disturbed by people wading that it can take hours before the fish return. Sometimes they never return, for rainbows shoal and tend to move around quite frequently. If they continuously get disturbed by shock waves of anglers entering the water, your best bet could be to move to a quieter area.

Keep your eyes open all the time for these tell-tale commotions at the bankside of stickling fish chasing the fry. If this is observed a slow sink line with a Baby Doll or Jersey Herd (size 8) retrieved slowly over the shallows can be a deadly method.

By mid April the fish have learnt a thing or two, and a change in tactics will be needed, except for early morning and late evening when fish seem to feed fairly close in to the bank. Long casting starts to pay dividends — this is where my tactics tend to split into two parts, one rod is kept tackled up for deep feeding browns with the fast sink line and a Black Lure, the other rod will have a slow sink line and a Whisky or Dunkeld lure for rainbows feeding between the surface and mid water — very rarely do I use a dropper. For a while I will fish for browns in the depths — my tactics are fairly long, fast retrieves using the count down method, that is to determine at just what depth I am fishing, so some casts I retrieve after counting to 20, and some after counting to 25, all depending on how deep the water is, so if you catch fish after counting to say 25, you know that you can constantly fish at that depth by just counting down to 25 before you start your retrieve. This can be a dull way of fishing but on occasions it does work well, especially for big browns, but the takes are usually far less in numbers to fishing a little higher in the water.

If these tactics fail I then pick up my other rod and fish between the surface and mid water, searching out those rainbows, and over the years the best lures seem to be with orange in them. Rainbows just can't resist lures such as Whisky Fly, Dunkeld, or Church Fry.

As April draws to an end there also becomes a definite split between the two species. In the early part of the month both rainbows and browns can be caught hard down on the bottom; now as the water temperature starts its long climb upwards so the rainbows start to move more generally into the mid and high water.

5 May

The weather

Unless we are unfortunate, the weather has now begun to settle down, and extremes between the north and south are less likely. May is often dry, and on average the second week is one of the five driest weeks of the year, and also one of the sunniest. Which means that the water temperature will now start rising quite rapidly, so surface activity with good rises of trout should be anticipated. Unfortunately, north-easterly winds are common during this month, and these are not generally welcomed by the fly fisher. Towards the end of the month, strong winds are often the order of the day, and while these can make casting a little difficult, they are usually warm and will often excite the trout which will then feed freely throughout the day. By the end of the month, the trout will have begun to populate the shallower water, and in the evenings may be found in very shallow water indeed. Some of the heaviest evening rises of the year may now be anticipated, and in addition, towards the end of the month, bank fishers may look forward to splendid sport with good rises very early in the mornings. In average years, May is undoubtedly the most productive and exciting month of the year for the stillwater fly fisher. Plenty of trout are only too eager to take your fly, and whatever style or method of fishing you may adopt, some success is likely to come your way.

Boat fishing – imitative patterns
JOHN GODDARD

The month of May brings a population explosion of aquatic creatures, so the choice of patterns and fishing techniques is increased accordingly. This can naturally pose problems for the fly fisher in his choice of pattern as well as to the techniques to be employed. It is therefore a good plan at this time of the year to commence the regular practice of spooning out the stomachs of all trout caught, as correct identification of these contents can often provide vital clues to the species on which the trout are feeding. In addition, close observation of the water surface for any species which may be hatching is also of vital importance and, finally, with experience it is often possible to ascertain on what the trout are feeding by the rise form. In early May on some waters, especially under windy conditions, falls of terrestrial hawthorn flies are still likely, and when large swarms of these are blown out over the water by the wind and eventually fall on the surface, a good rise is usually assured. They can be quickly recognised in flight by their long, trailing back legs, and the many artificial patterns available to represent them may be fished as a dry fly on the surface, or as an alternative, which is often even more effective, as a wet fly fished slowly just under the surface. If surface fishing proves to be unproductive at this time, I suggest you mount either a large Pheasant Tail nymph, an ombudsman, or a weighted alder larva on the point on a long leader. Depending on the depth of water to be fished, either a floating or slow sink line should be used, and the artificial retrieved slowly, as close to the bottom as possible. Under windy conditions it is best to fish from an anchored boat, but under calm conditions I favour fishing from a drifting boat as then more water can be covered. When fishing in this manner it often pays dividends to mount a Mallard & Claret or a small Bloody Butcher on a dropper, four or five feet above the point fly.

Throughout May, if the weather conditions are right, increasing surface activity during the day may be anticipated with trout swirling or even rising in the surface to the various species of chironomids (midges or buzzers), which are a staple diet of the trout at this time of year. The best technique to employ is drift fishing utilising a drogue, and for this style I prefer a light 10 ft carbon boat rod, mounted with a No. 6 or 7 floating line with a long leader. The predominant species of midge are still most likely to be the orange and silver or the black midge, although on some waters the olive midge (ribbed midge), which is olive brown with ivory bands, may now be encountered.

It is therefore good practice initially to mount three Hatching Midge Pupae patterns, one in each colour, until the favoured colour for the day has been established. On those days when the surface activity is spasmodic, I often mount a well greased Red Palmer on the top dropper and bounce this along the surface on the retrieve. This will often entice trout up to this bob fly where they inevitably turn and take one of the two pupae patterns following. When drift fishing in this manner you will sometimes find trout rising to your pupa patterns but failing to take them. If this occurs, try mounting a small unweighted or (as an alternative) weighted Gold Ribbed Hare's Ear on the point . For some unaccountable reason, this old but excellent pattern will often succeed when all else fails.

From the middle of May until early June, some of the most prolific surface rises of the year to midges are likely to occur in calm conditions, either in the very early mornings or late evenings. The slow, sipping head and tail rise to the pupae hanging in the film is unmistakable, and although fishing during these rises can often be very frustrating, it can also be most rewarding once the right formula has been found. Again, it may be necessary to ascertain on which colour, and even possibly size of midge, the trout are feeding, which can only be achieved by trial and error, unless a trout is caught and the stomach content analysed. In addition, it will be necessary to establish according to the rise form whether the trout are chasing the emerging pupae to the surface, or whether they are feeding predominantly on the pupae hanging vertically in the film. In the former case, two or three Hatching Midge Pupae should be mounted on a long leader, and retrieved at a slow or in some cases a medium pace just under the surface on a thoroughly degreased leader. In the latter case, it is better to fish from an anchored boat utilising two or three Suspender Midge Pupae. They hang vertically in the surface film and should be cast in the likely path of rising fish. If they are given an occasional tweak this will often tempt a trout, as this slight tightening of the fly line will tilt the pupa up into a horizontal plane, which is the position natural pupae adopt prior to emerging on the surface.

Towards the end of the month on some lowland and many upland waters, lake olives, a common upwinged fly, may be observed hatching and drifting on the surface with the wind. Hatches tend to be localised, often adjacent to weed beds, and if the trout are observed rising a Super Grizzly or similar dry fly pattern cast selectively will often take the odd trout. In the evenings, similar rises may occur when the spent female spinner falls exhausted on the surface. An appropriate spinner pattern such as the Apricot Spinner beloved of the late Oliver Kite, or my own Pond Olive Spinner, cast to individual rising trout will usually entice a brace of fish providing one has sufficient patience. At this time of the year on the shallower areas and margins in some waters, increasing numbers of tadpoles may be observed and as the trout are very fond of these, a pattern such as my own Tadpolly kills very well. This pattern should be fished on its own on the point, either on a floating line with a long leader, or on a slow sink line, depending on the depth of water you are fishing. Retrieve at a medium pace with frequent pauses. An interesting and very effective alternative is to dress this pattern with an oval piece of *Ethafoam* coloured black with a felt tip pen in place of the peacock herls which form the body on the standard pattern. You will now have a very buoyant pattern which can be mounted on a fast sink line, and when cast out into slightly deeper water from an anchored boat, the line will sink to the bottom while the tadpolly will remain near the surface. As soon as the retrieve is commenced, the artificial will dive towards the bottom, and this often proves irresistible to any cruising trout.

Boat fishing — traditional JOHN KETLEY

May is the first month when traditional Loch style fishing can really be considered a prime method of fly fishing. As always a lot depends on the weather. especially on the larger deeper stillwaters. Trout will respond to relatively minor changes in water temperature, but remember it takes many really warm days for the general lake temperature to rise those few critical degrees on the big stillwaters.

This is also the first month when you really must start to consider whether you wish to catch fish stocked a few weeks before or brownies and rainbows that have overwintered successfully. The reason I raise this fundamental question now, although it is relevant all season through, is that the fish are less mixed up in May and you can, to an extent, choose to fish for stockies, or avoid them. The recently introduced fish will still be in shoals, although the size of the shoals will be steadily decreasing, from both stockie-bashing angling, and a natural dispersal as they become more confident in their new environment. Therefore these fish should be the easier to locate, and take, than either the overwintered rainbows or brownies, which are more used to lack of a daily ration of pellets and prepared to await a proper hatch of flies before they start cruising and showing themselves on the surface.

The essence of loch style fishing is, I believe, drifting the boat over likely areas when there are few or maybe no fish showing on the surface. This came about because the style of fishing originated on brown trout lochs and the angler was invariably tempting fish up from deeper water. Nowadays this technique has been modified to waters that have large numbers of free rising rainbows, as well as the browns, and this gives today's loch style angler two bites at the cherry. Firstly the chance to cast to any fish that rise in front of the drifting boat, and secondly a proven method of searching the water for alert trout that are not showing at all.

Over the years at least 60 per cent of the fish I have caught by this method were 'out of the blue', so I have in effect risen a fish that would not have shown unless my flies persuaded him they were worth a taste.

At the beginning of the month the warmer part of the day will still be the most active time for the trout, and you are more likely to find a hatch during the middle of the day than at last light. The hatches when they come, are still likely to be buzzers but from now and all through the rest of the months, the colour of the artificials can become an increasingly important factor. During this month I still favour a sinking line, especially when there are very few fish showing on the surface; in fact, until the middle of May I would recommend a fast sinking line, except when a real rise gets under way, then I put up the floater with a sigh of relief. For the last part of the month, a slow sinking line used during the times when there are few fish showing is a worthwhile investment.

Now back to some reliable artificials for early May, a Wickham's, a Black Buzzer, and an Alexandra are safe bets for your first few drifts. I prefer a leaded buzzer on the point, with the Alexandra in the middle and the Wickham's as a top dropper.

The most likely part of the retrieve for a take is as the flies start to ascend, and watch during those last two pulls, just before the top dropper breaks the surface, as a flash of silver near the bottom two flies will often result in a trout coming up the cast and snapping at the top dropper.

By the middle of the month we hope for some settled warmish weather and the choice of artificials becomes increasingly more critical. Although I see few sedges appearing on the lake until mid June, the bushier loch flies start to play an important part on the cast. My first choice for the top dropper is a Soldier or Red Palmer, closely followed by a Red Tag. For the middle fly I go a little wild and choose a bright, cheerful fly the trout may not have seen many of — like a Morning Glory or Cow Dung. The point fly, being the easiest to change, I vary after a refusal from a moving fish or two that I know I covered properly. My first choice will be a buzzer imitation like a Mallard & Claret or a Williams. Should I take a couple of fish on either of the other two flies on the cast, I will sometimes try a second one on the point. It's surprising how often this results in rising and hooking more fish.

By the end of the month, the floating line will be on the rod more than the sinkers, especially if the fish are tending to stay near the top much of the day.

Today's most successful loch style fishermen all seem to use very long casts (by casts I mean the nylon below your leader), and the length most favoured seems to be just under double the length of the rod.

While it can feel a little ungainly when first used, a really long cast has a number of advantages.

The three flies can cover a much greater sequence of depths and if you have an eighteen foot cast you will have over seven feet between your point fly, the middle and the top dropper, which leaves four feet from the top dropper to the fly line. Fished fairly slowly this enables the point fly to fish two or three feet under the surface. The middle fly will be a foot or eighteen inches under, and the top dropper just below the surface. Towards the end of the retrieve, the top dropper can be dribbled along the surface in a most tantalising manner, while the other two flies are still well down.

The important thing for May is to stay flexible, and take advantage of whatever favourable conditions you run into. I had an amazing afternoon a couple of seasons ago when a fair number of large hawthorn flies hatched upwind from the lake and blew onto the water. The trout seemed to take every one as it landed onto the water and attacked my artificial with such gusto, many of them were hooked too deep to be returnable.

Towards the end of May, we are all praying for Summer to get really into its stride, and if you're lucky enough to be fishing on a soft, warm grey day, which, despite the weather we had in May 1981, can happen, you could enjoy one of the first super days of the season.

On such a day the trout feed busily between 10 am and 2 pm, go off until about 5 pm and build up to frantic evening rise around 8 pm. Now you have the best of both worlds, with hungry fish at their first big feed and perfect conditions for loch style fishing.

Normally I find nymphs do not work as well as winged and hackled flies in these conditions, but, as I mentioned earlier, the colour of the artificials, especially the body can start to become important.

Red bodied flies made with seal's fur seems to be a reliable colour for the point, and a Mallard & Claret tied with a bright red body rather than claret is a favourite variant of mine.

If you see a number of fish feeding on the surface and are certain you have covered three or four accurately with no response from the fish, don't hammer away at them with the same team of flies.

Firstly change the point fly from a Mallard & Claret (for example) to a bright bodied fly like a Silver Invicta. If you still get no response change down a size and fish it very slowly past the next fish to rise.

To ensure you cover the fish accurately, estimate the distance the fish is moving between rises carefully, and also the depth at which the rising fish is actually feeding. Now your next cast can position your flies where the fish can't help but see them, and you should only need to twitch them to get a response.

In between casting at moving fish you can 'fish the drift' by searching the water in a series of casts than fan out to cover almost 45° in three casts. I mention this again this month, having already covered it in April, as it is very relevant all season through.

Boat fishing – lures   BOB CHURCH

From May onwards, with the water warming up, drifting will produce far more sport than anchoring. Trout are now far more active and are likely to be found at all depths because there is greatly increased activity on the part of the aquatic insects upon which they feed. Drift fishing is a searching method whereby great areas of water are covered. It can be used to take trout which are surface feeders, trout feeding in mid water, or even those that are hard along the bottom. Even when fishing generally seems poor there is always the chance of getting a few trout on the drift. So many are being shown the fly or lure that there are always some that will make a mistake and get hooked.

There are two main ways in which to drift a boat, hence the choice of two different styles of fishing. The traditional style of fishing from a broadside drifting boat using small wet flies to rising trout is dealt with elsewhere. We are more interested in fishing in mid water, or right down deep on the bottom, so you need to have the boat drifting bows first down the wind. Select your drift by rowing or motoring up wind. But make sure, if you are in a motor boat, that you do not go roaring over the area onto which you will be drifting. Position the boat ideally about 80 to 100 yards from the bank, with the wind or breeze blowing parallel to the shore. A slow drift can be achieved by removing your anchor from the shackle and allowing the light chain to trip gently along the bottom. Attach a G clamp at the central stern position and pay out sufficient rope to achieve this. Put in a half hitch and loop over G clamp.

If there is a good wind blowing you may also use a drogue from the same G clamp position. This will slow you right down, allowing a normal fishing speed even though the waves are racing past.

For this deeper style the angler in the stern will cast out across the wind on one side of the boat, and the man in the bows casts similarly on the other side. In this way an extremely large area is covered. It pays to experiment with different line densities, i.e. slow and medium sinkers, fast sinkers like the lead impregnated types, and even heavy lead core. One of these will enable you to get to the trout's main feeding depth on that day. (Incidentally, don't try fishing a sinking line from a broadside drifting boat. All you will be doing is running over an ever slackening line, giving no control and poor presentation.)

A straight 4 yards of 7 lb breaking strain nylon is all that is required for a leader, and I advise just a single lure. Use No. 8 or No. 6 long shank hooks. The patterns I would try with confidence are: Jack Frost, Ace of Spades, Missionary, Sweeney Todd, Viva and my old standby the Black Chenille lure. The Viva is virtually a Black Chenille, but with a fluorescent green tail. On some days that tail coloration can make all the difference, but as to why, I can only guess.

You will notice that the lures I have suggested are basically white or black in their coloration. Without doubt these have proved most effective during April and May for at least two decades. I see no reason why this situation should change. I can also assure you that these lures work on all waters where trout are present.

On many of the big reservoirs it is a fact that the rich bottom feed keeps the trout deep down for most of the time, hence the success of the sunken lure. As May begins, the trout angler finds his options are complete by the opening of the big two, Rutland and Grafham. There is a special attraction for most of us to fish these two giants, for good results at either give us more satisfaction than elsewhere. Both waters have the natural capacity to grow small stock fish on fast. Grafham packs fat on rainbows mainly on a daphnia diet, while Rutland's bottom feed builds up the weight on brownies in double-quick time.

Obviously these waters have a lot to offer the boat fisher, so let's consider some of the 'hotspots' and regular 'taking areas' on both waters, and how we should boat fish them early on.

Like as not, when taking out your boat at Grafham, the wind will be blowing from the west, i.e. from left to right as you stand at the fishing lodge. This is perfect for a long searching drift. Get the boat positioned 100 yards out from the jetty and drift bow first with aid of a chain or drogue.

Each angler should be using some kind of sinking shooting head. You will pass just in front of the moored yachts, along the front of the sludge pits and into the bay, Gaynes Cove, finishing up in the right-hand corner of the dam. For many years now, this has been the route taken by stock fish when they are released at their weekly intervals. However don't expect to find just stockies, for some of those big brownies favour the area just out from the sludge pits.

Continue searching with sinking shooting heads on systematic slow drifts into the dam by using the drogue from the central stern. Work your way along the dam until you get to the far side. Now row or motor up-wind along the north shore to the far point of Church Bay. Use the chain again to drift across the bay, keeping about 100 yards out, and then drift back to the left-hand corner of the dam.

By now, which will be around lunchtime, you ought to have a pretty good idea where the biggest concentrations of fish are likely to be. If the results have been quite good — and I am expecting that to be so, but perhaps with only an odd big fish — let's try a few big fish 'hotspots' at the west end of Grafham.

Motor back up the wind but stop off to anchor at the aerator tower. This you should do by securing your position some 30 yards upwind of the tower. The reservoir bed is some 30 feet down, so a lead core shooting head can be used here. They have proved most successful in the past.

Try something outrageously big, like a white Marabou Tandem Muddler. If this does not produce fished normally, try a few retrieves at a very fast stripping rate but take care not to pull the fly out of the water too quickly. Often fish follow and take at the last second.

Move on to drift over the great shallow area that appeared as a large island during the drought in 1976. This lies some 250 yards out from the bird sanctuary marker buoys on the hut side. In many places you will find around 12 feet. Again work it by chain or drogue, drifting with slow or fast-sink shooting heads. (You will notice we have completely ignored the central main deep body of the reservoir.)

At Rutland the two main fish-holding and fish-catching areas are at the far end of the north and south arms. This was so for the first three seasons and I am convinced it will continue for some time as these rich shallow areas hold the most food.

I shall choose to go to the far end of the South Arm on my first trip right into Egleton Bay. From there using the built-in rudder to control the direction of my drift (placing a piece of thick foam rubber under the tiller arm to give me better control), I will aim to go into the big bay on the far side of the Old Hall. This should take me over the shallow, submerged Brown's Island, always a fish-holding spot. I will try this drift several times. At least one of us will be on a lead core, fast-sinking head for early season. One will use black based lures, the other white. If they don't work we will try Goldie, Nailer or Muddler Minnow. As the evening draws on, watch out for hatches of buzzer around Lax Hill. A lot of adult flies are also blown down from the spinney above. This is a very good area for rising fish.

Bank fishing – imitative patterns
BOB CARNILL

May is without doubt the most significant month of the season in the calendar of the 'true' fly fisherman. For not only is the weather turning more and more conducive to the sport with each passing day, but the hatches of chironomids (buzzers or midges) too, seem to mark time with this improvement by becoming increasingly 'heavy' as the month progresses. Given a steady south-westerly wind and a nice broken cloud formation, good rises of trout can almost be guaranteed right from the beginning of the month, and the beauty of May rises is that given the right conditions they can sometimes last the whole day through. However, the wind is apt to swing round to the north occasionally during May, and this, unfortunately, has the ability of killing the surface activity 'stone dead', forcing the angler once more to search the lower levels of the lake for his trout.

At the beginning of the month the 'main' rises will be to chironomids. Both the pupa and the adult fly are taken avidly by the trout — but more often than not the trout will feed exclusively on one, and ignore the other. It is, therefore, essential that the angler is able to recognise the different rise forms, in order to plan his tactics accordingly.

If the rises take the form of a sub-surface upthrust of water which doesn't actually break the surface, but instead has a 'flattening' effect on the surrounding ripple — then this is a positive indication that the pupae are being intercepted just below the surface. I usually tackle this sort of situation with a 12 to 14 ft leader with three buzzer pupae imitations of different colours. For my part, I always use my own version of the chironomid pupa — the Poly Rib, but there are numerous other patterns also available. My first choice of colours would be black, bottle green and claret, all dressed on size 12s. However, after taking and spooning my first fish of the day, the colour and size of my artificials in use may well be reorganised, depending on the outcome of the stomach contents. I find that the most productive method of fishing this kind of rise is to choose a bank with the wind running parallel to it, or if possible, slightly on to it at a shallow angle. The cast is then made in the general direction of the activity and the flies are allowed to 'settle in'. After the pause the flies are recovered using a moderately paced figure of eight retrieve. Once the correct depth and speed of retrieve are found — sport can almost be guaranteed.

If, on the other hand, the rise forms present a leisurely 'head and tail' view of the trout, then this will mean one of two things. First, it could be that the trout are taking the pupae as they hang just under the surface prior to breaking through the surface film, or it could be that the pupae are actually being taken whilst in the surface film prior to, or in the act of 'emerging' or 'hatching'. For this kind of rise it is essential that the artificials do not fish too deep in the water — an inch too deep can make all the difference between success and failure.

I find that three buzzer pupae on a greased-up leader, with the droppers thoroughly degreased, is an effective way to fish this kind of rise. The artificials should, whenever possible, be cast into the path of a rising trout, and if possible 'across' the ripple. The flies are *not* retrieved, but allowed to drift round on the wind. The indication of a take is usually a positive drawing tight of the line, which must be tightened into. Should no takes be forthcoming, but there are obviously feeding fish in front of you, it could be that the length of your droppers are at fault. By shortening or lengthening the droppers it could make all the difference.

Another excellent method of tackling trout which are nipping pupa from the surface film, is to mount a trio of John Goddard's Suspender Midge Pupae and fish them in the same way as described above. However, it sometimes helps greatly with this pattern to give the line an occasional tweak. This has the effect of making the pupae tilt up onto a horizontal plane — a movement which can sometimes prove irresistible to a passing trout.

There are two other rise forms associated with the buzzer, both of which are to the adult fly. It will sometimes be noticed that a particular rise pattern is a little faster and somewhat noisier than the usual buzzer rise. This type of rise is nearly always attributed to the trout taking an adult fly from the surface as it rests, prior to making its maiden flight. It is as though the trout realises that the fly could take off without a second's notice, and so seizes its prize accordingly. The most rewarding and pleasurable way of taking these 'risers', is to cast a single size 14 or 12 dry Grey Duster to a selected trout.

The other type of rise is to the spent adult as it lays with outspread wings in the surface film. This rise form is a most delicate affair, causing but a slight dimpling ring in the surface. For this kind of rise I would mount a single, or a trio — depending on the amount of ripple or wave available, of my Adult Buzzers.

The fly, or flies would be cast to individual risers and allowed to settle into the surface. If a take did not occur 'on the drop', then the flies would be retrieved very slowly indeed, just under the surface. My choice of Adult Buzzers for the first two weeks of May would be Black Duck Fly (No. 12), Grey Boy (No. 10), and a Medium Olive (Golden Dun Midge) (No. 12).

If the beginning of the month is mild, there is a large terrestrial fly that sometimes gets blown onto the water in large enough numbers to stimulate a good rise of trout. The fly I refer to is the hawthorn fly. It is a fly that is easily recognised by its overall black appearance, its hovering flight and its long trailing back pair of legs. There are several artificials available to represent this fly, which can be fished dry, or twitched slowly just beneath the surface.

By the middle of May things are very much the same as described for the early weeks, the main difference being that there is normally a little more of everything. The buzzer hatches become more intense, and so too does the surface activity of the trout. Olive buzzers of varying shades now tend to be taking over from the darker species, plus a few of the gingery orange species coming into evidence — forerunners of the main hatches yet to come. Lake olives, too, are starting to put in an appearance — much to the delight of the trout. Shallow, weedy bays are the areas favoured by this species, and it is not a difficult task to spot a hatch of these delightful upwinged flies, for after hatching the duns drift before the wind like an armada of tiny sailing ships.

If you are ever fortunate enough to find yourself in an area where a rise is taking place to a hatch of lake olives, there are two ways to take advantage of it. The 'wet fly' approach, I find, can be particularly effective. A Lake Olive or PVC Nymph size 12 on the point, a size 12 winged wet Greenwell's Glory on the first dropper and a size 12 or 14 winged wet Gold Ribbed Hare's Ear on the top dropper, make a great combination. I like to position myself, whenever possible, so that I can cover the activity by casting down and across the waves. The flies are then retrieved with a medium to fast figure of eight. However, as with ALL wet fly fishing, it pays dividends to experiment with different rates of retrieve.

If the risers appear to be concentrated mainly on the floating duns, then one could do much worse than to mount a single size 14 or 12 dry Greenwell's Glory — hackled or winged, both are excellent patterns — and then proceed to cover individual risers.

Towards the end of May the buzzer hatches and rises are at their peak — and in a normal season can provide the angler with some of his finest sport of the season. Apart from the hawthorn fly, which is still about, there is also another terrestrial fly which is beginning to put in an appearance. Albeit a much smaller fly, the black gnat has the ability of distracting the trout away from their beloved buzzers, to indulge in localized, but frenzied feasting.

Swarms of black gnats can be found in 'dancing columns', usually over the water, but not too far out from the margins. Every now and again a fly, or even a couple, will drop onto the surface of the water, as though locked in combat — only to be quickly snapped up by the waiting trout. A size 14 dry Black Gnat mounted on a fine leader point, is all that is required in order to ensure some fine sport. The fly should be cast directly below the column of dancing flies — or, if there is a ripple on the water, slightly downwind of the column.

A wet fly can also be used to good effect at this time, for it seems that once the trout has the small black fly imprinted on its mind, it's not too fussy whether the fly is 'on' or under the surface. An excellent pattern to use for this purpose is a size 14 Black Duck Fly (Adult Buzzer), and another is a size 14 Black & Peacock Spider. The fly should be cast into the centre of the activity, and twitched slowly back, just under the surface.

Bank fishing — lures SYD BROCK

May is usually a more settled month as far as the weather is concerned, and so the fish move more freely. This is one of my favourite months.

I know the general rule is to fish partly into the wind as the goodies are blown over to that particular shore, but I feel that this is not quite so necessary when lure fishing with sunk lines. I would rather fish with the wind slightly left to right and get extra distance, for by now the fish have learnt that it is dangerous close into the bank, and if you can reach those wind lanes which blow up from time to time, they are always full of feeding fish. It is the time when big fish do move up in the water on occasions as the temperature begins to rise .

Once again I stay with my fast sink line on one rod, but now I introduce my favourite pattern, the Black Ghost. I have used this lure for years on many waters and it is deadly fished fast, once again taking into consideration just what water I have in front of me. Long casting is the rule now for me, the more water I cover the greater my chances are. Now I introduce my fry imitator, the Mylar Minnow; this lure has accounted for brown trout up to 10 lb. The beauty of this lure is that it can be fished slow with occasional quick jerks to represent an injured fish. It can also be fished on a floating line with a long leader, say 12 ft, when those harried shoals of fry appear. Generally the trout attack the shoals by passing straight through, thereby injuring many fry which just twitch about on the surface; then the trout just pick off these easy targets. In these conditions just twitch your retrieves in 6 inch pulls across the surface. Most other lure imitations, with the exception of the Sinfoil's Fry, are so unlike the real minnow that the trout ignore them.

This is also a time for certain activity along the shoreline which might appear, at first, to be fish chasing minnows. A careful check might surprise you, for it can be tadpoles the trout are after. Some waters produce an abundance of these, and trout love them. My answer to this situation is to use a slow sink line, a 6 ft leader, and a lure that I call a Tadpolly. Slow, even retrieves just below the surface in the shallows can produce fantastic sport. I never let one method be the dominant way of lure fishing. You must never ignore the signs which appear, such as rising fish, but can capitalise upon them to a certain degree because rising fish are feeding fish and with just a quick change from a larger lure to a small lure you can pick off those surface feeding fish pretty smartly by retrieving as soon as your lure lands on the water, giving the trout only a fleeting glimpse. This method can also be deadly, especially when trout are rising to very small fly life such as early hatches of caenis, as it offers an acceptable alternative whereas trying to present an imitative pattern is often unproductive.

For myself, May is the month of the Whisky Fly fished on a slow sink line with a 7 – 8 ft leader. Time and again it has proved to be a day saver; even when the browns are in a non-taking mood it can sometimes take the odd fish on the bottom or one or two rainbows from near the surface.

However, most methods work well in May, and it can be one of the best months of the whole season.

If all other methods are ignored try the diver technique, which is a Muddler or White Pearly tied on a longish leader of 12 ft with a fast sink line. As the line sinks the buoyant lure will be left floating on the surface. In very deep water, as the leader is tightened by the sinking line, the buoyant lure starts to dive towards the bottom. This can produce some really hard takes and is an alternative to the deep straight line retrieve. Because of the lure's buoyancy, when the retrieve is started, the lure fishes just off the bed of the lake. During retrieves it is a good idea to stop every now and again to allow the buoyant lure to ride up in the water.

6 June

The weather

According to statistics, June is not only the driest and sunniest month of the year, but fewer gales are to be expected, although during the past few seasons the weather has been very mixed, so the angler must take it as it comes. During the early part of the month the unwelcome north-easterly winds from the previous month may return, but if we are fortunate, light westerly or south-westerly winds may take over fairly rapidly, bringing warm, sunny days and the possibility of heatwaves, which, of course, are not exactly welcomed by the stillwater angler. While this can be a very pleasant and enjoyable month for the fly fisher, it can also be extremely difficult when we experience those windless days when the sun shines down from a brassy sky, and the surface of the water is like a mirror, except, of course, for those fly fishers on small, clear stillwaters where these conditions present perfect visibility with the chance of locating a really big trout. At this time of the year we can also expect thunderstorms, particularly after these long, hot spells, and the accompanying cool rain will often revitalise the water and bring the trout back on the feed.

Boat fishing – imitative patterns
JOHN GODDARD

While May is probably the most productive month of the season, June is undoubtedly the most interesting, although at the same time it can also be the most frustrating, as this is the month of many changes. In an average season, the water temperature is likely to reach its optimum, and during hot sunny weather the fishing during the day is likely to prove difficult to say the least. Also, during this month many species of insects will disappear, and many new species slowly begin to take their place.

The heavy early morning or late evening hatches of chironomids (buzzers) are now beginning to tail off, but the odd spectacular surface rise may still be anticipated under calm conditions, when a team of Suspender Midge Pupae fished on a floating line from an anchored or slowly drifting boat will still pay dividends. On those evenings when there is less surface activity I find an excellent compromise is to mount a weighted Midge Pupa on the point, an unweighted one on the first dropper, with a Suspender on the top dropper. This combination retrieved very slowly with frequent pauses will take trout at all levels in the water.

From late May onwards when good hatches of buzzers occur, the trout will often switch from the pupae hanging under the surface film to the adult either emerging through the film or taking off from the surface. There are several effective adult

66

midge patterns available to represent the naturals at this stage, and one of these should be fished on the top dropper and retrieved very slowly or in short jerks with long pauses in between. The pattern of one's choice may be fished in the film or lightly treated with a floatant and fished as a dry fly on top of the surface. It can also be important at times to match the body colour of the adults hatching at the time; if you are unsure, however, try fishing a team of three in different colours until the killing colour is established.

During the early part of the month at least, tadpoles will still be much in evidence in the shallower areas, so an artificial such as my own Tadpolly, mounted on the point and retrieved at a slow to medium pace in mid water will take some nice trout. Various upwinged flies are now more in evidence, for in addition to the hatches of lake olives that started in May, hatches of the even more common pond olive are now likely to be encountered on an increasing scale on those waters that support them. The main emergence of these upwinged flies is most likely to occur during the day between eleven and three o'clock. Where these are observed hatching, with the odd trout swirling or rising to them, it is both pleasant and sometimes productive to fish a dry fly such as a Lake Olive or my own Super Grizzly, which is an excellent general pattern. Should the trout not be rising to the emerging duns, anchor the boat in water not exceeding six feet in depth and try fishing a weighted nymph, a small Pheasant Tail or PVC Nymph. Fishing in the sink and draw style on a long leader is usually most effective. Sometimes at this period of the year, if you are lucky, you may encounter in the early evenings a fall of pond or lake olive spinners to which the trout will rise. When this occurs it is a good plan to concentrate on bays into which the wind is blowing, as it is here where the largest concentrations of spinners are likely to be found being blown in by the wind. These spinners may be a little difficult to see as they lay flat in the surface film, but the trout, once they start feeding on them, do not have the same problem; they will pick them off the surface with a slow sipping rise. Your artificial, an Apricot or Pond Olive Spinner, should be cast to or in front of a rising fish, and if not taken within a few seconds, re-cast when another rise is spotted.

By the middle of the month, on many waters, particularly on calm, warm days, huge hatches of caenis, better known as the angler's curse, are likely to be encountered. These tiny, cream coloured, upwinged flies create considerable problems for the fisherman. Apart from their small size and great concentration on the surface, one is never really sure whether the trout are feeding on the emerging nymph, the hatching dun or the returning spinner. The trout, when feeding upon these, invariably move in a straight line, rising repeatedly after gulping down two or three at a time. At this difficult time I have had most success with my own Last Hope pattern, and this must be cast very accurately if one is to succeed, two to three feet directly in front of a rising fish. It can be fished dry to represent the hatching dun, or fished wet in the surface to represent either the emerging nymph or returning spinner. Once the trout start feeding upon caenis they become preoccupied and will look at little else, but they can sometimes be tempted by a complete contrast in pattern size. In this respect the Persuader, a large, general nymph pattern, has often provided a nice fish at this time. It should be fished just below the surface at a medium fast pace, and presented so that it is retrieved at an angle immediately across the front of the trout.

During this month we are likely to experience many sunny days with intermittent cloud, and as these conditions are usually accompanied by a steady breeze, we have all the ingredients for very pleasant drift fishing during the day. I usually try several short drifts in likely looking areas until I find the fish. I will then keep fishing this same drift all the time I am getting results. During June I favour a Red Palmer on the top dropper, and in the early part of the month I find that this, used in conjunction with a Green Midge Pupa mounted on the middle dropper and a red Midge Pupa on the point, is often very effective. A good alternative is to replace the midge pupae with a Collyer's Green Nymph and a Brown Nymph.

Towards the end of June we are likely to observe increasing numbers of sedge (caddis) flies hatching, particularly in the late afternoons or evening. By July these will have become a staple part of the diet of trout on many waters, but at this time of the season, before the really heavy hatches have started, the trout may not be fully onto them. However, from the middle of the month onwards, I often have considerable success drift fishing with artificials that represent them. An excellent combination in conjunction with the Red Palmer on the top dropper is to fish an Invicta on the middle dropper and a Stick Fly on the point. In shallow water up to four or five feet in depth, I prefer an unweighted Stick Fly, but in deeper water a weighted pattern seems to produce more fish.

Should you experience one of those hot, sunny, windless days which are often only too common at this time of the year, your best chance of taking the odd trout, which are notoriously difficult to catch under these conditions, is to anchor the boat, and fish tiny nymphs close to the bottom, while a weighted Stick Fly, retrieved slowly, is a good alternative.

Finally, it is important to appreciate that, from now on, throughout the rest of the season, evening rises are likely to vary tremendously according to the particular species that may be hatching at the time. It is also not uncommon to find, on some evenings, that the trout will switch rapidly from species to species, sometimes changing their diet as many as four or even five times during the course of an evening.

Boat fishing – traditional JOHN KETLEY

If I had to choose any one month to fish loch style, it would either be June or September, with a slight preference for early June as the fry are not yet featuring on the trout's main diet.

Even our British summer has usually settled down enough for the fish to behave rather more consistently and the fly hatches last long enough for an angler to find a team of flies that will catch fish after fish. Most large stillwaters don't allow their boats out until after 9 am, but it still leaves twelve hours of fishing in the day, so you can be selective if you wish, and fish when fish are showing on the surface, or flog away all day as I used to, until 'tennis elbow' caught up with me.

Floating lines should be the order of the day, and I must admit a preference for weight forward lines, rather than double tapers. I doubt there's any great difference in the delicacy of presentation of a team of size 10 artificials, but there is an additional few yards in the distance I can reach *quickly*, with a weight forward. The speed with which you can cover a fish showing on the surface often proves to be a major factor in catching it.

For this reason I recommend you to fish in a rather schizoid manner, with half an eye on the flies you're retrieving and half an eye searching the water in front for signs of moving fish. This is not as difficult as it sounds and most experienced anglers develop the skill naturally.

Should you be in mid retrieve and see a fish move some yards to the right of your flies, a powerful rod and floating line make it quite possible to lift the line, without any violence and place your flies neatly where you believe the moving fish will have reached. Perhaps one of the greatest exponents of this art is Bob Draper of English International fame, who can, and regularly does, lift 25 yards of line off the water, to re-cast to a moving fish yards from his original cast. Such prowess is beyond most of us, and demands a very powerful rod around eleven feet long, not to mention arms like a blacksmith. Nevertheless, I refer to my fishing friend Bob to illustrate the point that such manoeuvres are valuable fish catchers and well worth developing for all drifting boat enthusiasts.

One of the exciting aspects of early June is the diversity of artificials that fish will respond to, and there is no need to be too conservative in your selection of the day. Any bushy bodied fly is a great choice for the top dropper, as it gives you an opportunity to dribble it along the surface towards the end of your retrieve. In fact many loch style anglers try to fish the whole of their retrieve with the top dropper bouncing on the waves and the longer your rod the easier this is to do, for obvious reasons. For the sake of brevity, the contributors to this book have agreed not to give a long list of artificials, so I am tending toward describing flies by their action, rather than pattern. But proven bushy bodied flies like the Zulu and Grenadier will allow you to work the top dropper to its maximum advantage.

There will be days when the dribbled dropper seems to rise lots of fish that splash at the fly, but don't get hooked. To counteract this demands a form of discipline that is opposite to our natural reactions to strike as the fish appears. When the fish rises suddenly and splashily at the top dropper fly, but you feel no tug on the line, immediately lower the fly a foot or so into the water and allow it to sink.

The fish is, more often than not, still there and he will take it as neat as you please as he heads for the depths again. So, just hold on until you feel the rod dragged down, and you will find he is hooked perfectly in the scissors.

There is a second benefit to this lowering of the fly and waiting that few anglers give themselves the opportunity to experience. A fair percentage of trout that splash at the top dropper, but don't get hooked, take the middle or the point fly on their return to deeper water, if the flies are just hovering in the water.

By the middle of June, there should be some sedges hatching off and being taken by cruising trout during the daytime, whereas they may ignore sedges in preference to buzzers in the evening. These daytime cruisers are only a foot or so under the surface and work their way upwind, taking the odd sedge right on the surface. If it's a windy day, there is usually a fair splash as they smash at the naturals. In such weather you may well find that 'scum lanes' form across the lake; these, like the larger and smoother wind lanes I refer to later, are the sort of places to search for cruising trout. 'Scum lanes' are those white frothy lines that form when the wind is fresh but steady, and any floating matter in, or on, the surface tends to be pushed into the lane.

If you watch carefully, you will often see trout working their way up such a lane and rising every few feet as they either suck down a natural, or occasionally 'bat it' with their tail. This is the time to put on two bushy sedge flies, a Soldier Palmer or Grenadier on the top dropper and something a little brighter on the point like my own Allrounder. I created the Allrounder to perform, as its name suggests, more than one function. Firstly as a sedge pattern for top dropper work, to bounce nicely from wave to wave and dribble almost stationary just before the lift off. During the high summer months I find this a really killing pattern fished this way in a good breeze. Secondly, this is the time the 'needle fry' start to appear in numbers and once the trout start on them they seem to alternate between available sedges and little clouds of fry. I like to scoop my first fish, and if I see any fry in the stomach content I put an Allrounder on the point and fish it in short sharp retrieves. The design of the fly with its bushy front hackle makes it rise up in the water at each pull until it almost breaks the surface. The barred teal wing and gold mylar body gives it a great deal of 'flash', while the fully hackled body removes the lure look that so often results in more follows than takes. Later in the book you will find a full dressing guide for the Allrounder, but there are two modifications, that have proved to work better on certain occasions, that I will cover here. When the lighter winged sedges are fluttering around the surface, I find a hen pheasant tail wing more effective than the teal, and on cloudy days a silver body appears to have the edge over a gold body.

Towards the second half of June you may find the weather becomes very bright, with only a gentle breeze to ruffle the surface of the water. This is the time the loch style fisherman goes back to his sinking line and fishes a foot or two under the surface. The Scots have proved the advantage of the sinking line all through the season and I find many Irish traditional lough anglers also favour a slow or medium sinker without exception from April to October.

The main advantage of the sinker is the lack of line disturbance on the surface, for a floating line makes a hideous herringbone pattern on the surface every time it is pulled.

The sinker's primary disadvantage is the difficulty of a quick lift off and recast to a moving fish; but there is probably less opportunity for this manoeuvre when only wild brown trout are present. On England's large stillwaters with their high rainbow content, the quick covering of a free rising rainbow a few yards from your original cast can double your bag. For this reason I favour the floating line on June days, unless there is not enough wind to disguise the line's pattern on the surface.

Although I have mentioned cruising around in your boat looking for moving fish in previous months, it is perhaps more important in June and July than any other time. Spend the first half an hour of your day moving around looking in likely areas for signs of moving fish. Don't stop as soon as you see one, wait until you see three or more, then take the boat fifty yards upwind and drift down on to them.

When you have had a successful drift over a long stretch of water and finally either run out of moving fish, or reach the bank, do be careful how you take the boat back to the drift. I'm often surprised at the number of boats that motor directly up the path they have just successfully drifted over.

The obvious answer is to return to the start in a large semicircle, especially in a motor boat, as it's no effort.

Boat fishing – lures BOB CHURCH

As the summer progresses, so does the effectiveness of using the many Muddler Minnow variations that are now so popular. Let me tell you of some of my 'Muddlering' methods, which are a must in my approach to fishing stillwaters.

Rainbows become fatter and fighting fit with each summer day that passes, and by June will attack a surface lure fished on a floating shooting head and stripped back fast against the waves. Because of the Muddler's large buoyant deep hair head it skips and pops from wave to wave, creating quite a disturbance. Rainbows pick up the movement from deep down and will often come up to follow, then attack.

I have introduced many anglers to this summer technique, and once adopting it they all say it is the most exciting of tactics bcause so many fish actually follow the lure, although not all will take. For this style allow the boat to drift broadside on with or without a drogue according to the wind's strength. In a big wind and wave a size 6 Muddler is fine. For a medium wind a size 8 is best, and for a light wind a size 10 is preferred. This method could be classed as hard work, because you are forever casting and stripping back — so use it sensibly. I find a No. 9 or 10 visible shooting head allows me to pinpoint where my lure is at long range, and this weight of line also permits a comfortable 40 yard downwind cast.

Last season, in June and July, there were quite a few occasions when the standard Muddler pattern either failed or produced slow results. A change to a size 8 orange Marabou Muddler then gave me quite astonishing results, especially at Rutland.

For those difficult bright days when we know for sure that most fish are lying deep I often get a fish or two on a pure White Muddler. If I am boat fishing in deep water I will use a fast-sink shooting head. The buoyancy of my Muddler will help when retrieving, so I am not forever catching bottom weed or debris. For shallower water I use a slow-sink head. Also for those bright sunny days try the set of black lures again, Black Chenille, Ace of Spades, Sweeney Todd and Viva. All remain very good when fished below the surface.

By mid-June the temperatures are still rising in the largest waters. When they reach 62 to 64°F which usually coincides with this time, orange coloured lures often produce excellent results.

Perhaps the most famous orange lure of them all is the Whisky Fly and its variations. By this time of the year the rainbow trout become very aggressive, particularly towards such lures, but speed of retrieve now becomes important, so a fast or very fast retrieve often produces the best results.

These warmer temperatures usually mean that lots of algae particles are suspended high in the water, and so long as these are the larger kind, lots of rainbows will be up close to the surface, particularly if it is a perfect day with a steady westerly wind and grey rolling clouds. Let me give you an example from my diary. On two successive Grafham boat sessions I fished in the conditions mentioned, 62°F and plenty of algae. The rainbows went crazy for orange lures and I had a good limit bag on both trips, as did many other anglers.

Obviously the word got around about the effectiveness of orange based lures, and the catch rate in general stayed very high. Then came a two day period of heavy rain and the weather cooled down. The following day saw me fishing again, but the algae had all gone, leaving gin clear conditions; such rain nearly always has that effect. I tried a Whisky Fly and several other orange coloured lures which had worked so well previously, but without a sign of a take. Yet as soon as I changed from a slow sink to a fast sinking line and a size 8 Black Chenille I began to catch some good fish, both browns and rainbows. Just to make sure I switched to orange colours again later in the day, but with nil results.

To sum up, I find that in higher water temperatures rainbows will lose a lot of their caution and are willing to chase a fast-retrieved orange lure, fished in the top 6 feet of water. The faster-than-normal retrieve seems to be the key to success, for the rainbows don't have time to inspect and reject the lure as inedible.

I don't believe they take these gaudy orange inventions for small fish. I think their attack is triggered off more by a natural aggressiveness towards smaller aquatic animals. In this case and under these special conditions, orange proves to be an irresistible mouthful that really brings out their predatory instinct.

Up to now all I have mentioned is the word 'orange' and a single pattern — the Whisky Fly. Apart from that one a few excellent alternatives incorporating this colour are Church Fry, Orange Marabou Muddler and the Dunkeld lure. There is one other gaudy artificial that kills equally well at this time. It is the top American pattern Micky Finn, although this is basically yellow and red.

I advise drift fishing for the whole of this month. According to the wind's strength use either the chain or drogue, or at Rutland the built-in rudder which up to a point allows you to control the direction of your drift. A single lure should be fished on a 4 yard leader of 7 lb breaking strain nylon.

Side casting across the wind by each angler will again be the best tactic, and finding out the taking depth and colour early in the day's session will be important.

For this reason one angler should be using a slow-sinking shooting head, such as a Wet Cel 1, the other a medium sinker like a Wet Cel 2. Soon it will become obvious who is getting the most offers, then both men can use the same line.

If you use too fast a sinker when fish are in a mid water feeding position your lure will be dragged down quickly through them and they will ignore it. If, however, you are using the correct slow-to-medium sinker, your lure will sink slowly to the depths and may well be taken by trout merely on the drop, without any retrieving.

You have heard me mention shooting heads quite often in this chapter so, naturally, there must be a good reason. The extra distance that all practised casters can achieve with a shooting head over a full fly line is quite considerable. This extra distance most certainly gives you far more chance of catching fish in all boat lure fishing situations.

Thus I must advise those who have yet to try the method to do so. And to those who have tried and failed because of tangles, etc. I can only say try again. To eliminate this problem first of all build up the diameter of your reel with some old backing before winding on 100 metres of special shooting head backing. And if you use one of the special nylons produced for use with shooting heads, make sure you stretch it as you pull it off the reel ready for use. On the other hand this will not be necessary if you use one of the new hollow core braided nylons now available, as these are soft and limp and not so prone to tangling.

Bank fishing — imitative patterns
BOB CARNILL

The weather is always the governing factor to successful trout fishing, and any sudden changes in an established weather pattern can be expected to effect the sport — sometimes the sudden change can be detrimental, and at other times it can be very beneficial. June is a month that is apt to suffer the consequences of the extremes in weather. A mild south-westerly wind at the beginning of the month can suddenly be replaced by a bitter, raking north-easter — then by the end of the month the trout fisherman could find himself basking in a climate that would be more fitting to the Mediterranean. With the possibility of such extremes occurring within the space of a few days, or at the most a few weeks, the angler must exercise a high degree of adaptability if he is to take trout consistently throughout the month.

The beginning of June, given the right conditions, follows on in much the same vein as the end of May. Chironomids still form the staple diet of the trout, with the lake olives and black gnats putting in an occasional appearance to add a little variety. The hatches of buzzer now are predominantly olive, but ginger (red) buzzer are definitely on the increase. June is also the month when the 'summer feeding pattern' begins to establish itself. Even though good rises can be experienced at almost any time during the day, it will be noticed that morning and evening rises, weather permitting, can be relied upon — a trend which will become even more pronounced in the weeks ahead.

A trio of buzzer pupae are still good medicine for the early weeks of June, but what size and colour of artificial to mount is always a gamble until the stomach contents of the first trout of the day are examined. For this particular period I tend to choose lighter coloured patterns than in previous weeks — a typical example to start the day with may well be as follows: Pale Olive, Orange & Copper, Light Claret or Red. However, trout can be fickle creatures at times, and will on occasion, show a far greater interest to a darker imitation even when feeding predominantly on paler naturals. Experimentation with various colour combinations can, therefore, occasionally be more rewarding than reading the stomach contents. There is, however, one pointer that should never be overlooked or ignored when examining stomach contents, and that is the size of the naturals being taken by the trout. Quite often they will concentrate on *a* particular size, and will totally ignore anything else that is either larger or smaller.

The method of fishing the pupae must be dictated by the type of rise in progress at the time. Sub-surface boils mean that the trout are intercepting the pupae several inches below the surface, and the artificials shoud be fished accordingly. 'Head and tail' rises, on the other hand, means that the pupae are being taken either just under, or even in, the surface film. A greased-up leader with the droppers thoroughly degreased, is the way to tackle these kinds of feeders. The cast should be made, whenever possible, across the wave, or ripple, and allowed to drift round without retrieving. The takes are detected by a positive drawing tight of the line — which must be tightened into. Another way to tackle these 'head and tailers', is to mount a trio of Suspender Midge Pupae, and fish them as described above, but with this pattern it pays to give the line an occasional tweak. This has the effect of momentarily tilting the pupa up onto an horizontal plane — a movement which can sometimes prove fatal to a passing trout.

Should a good 'blow' occur, one of my favourite techniques is to fish the 'drowned' Adult Buzzer. There are several types of location which lend themselves to this style of fishing; each one, however, should be fished according to its own particular requirements. For example, a wave breaking onto a shoreline at a long shallow angle will turn spent, hatching and freshly hatched buzzers under the surface and then carry them along in a sub-surface current — much the same as would a river or a stream. This kind of location calls for similar tactics as one would employ when fishing a team of wet flies in a river or stream, i.e. casting down and across the current, and then letting the flow of the water do the work, the flies being retrieved only when the fly line is hanging straight downwind.

If there happens to be a point overlooking a bay, on the type of shoreline described above, then this is an ideal position from which one can take trout 'on the drop'. The current of water that has, up until that time, been hugging the shoreline is suddenly, on reaching the 'point', discharged out into the bay whereupon it begins to disperse. Any 'goodies' that the current happened to have been carrying now begin to drop out into the deeper water. It is there that the trout will congregate to take advantage of this steady supply of drowned food — and it is there also, that the angler should position his flies.

In order to get one's flies into the correct fishing position, the cast should once again be made across and down the wind. The fly line is then allowed to come round on the wind until it is in position over the 'dispersal area'. The dispersal area is easy enough to recognise, it is slightly to the windward side of the lighter ripple or wave of the bay. Positioned correctly, the angler is then able to let his fly line hang straight down the wind, thus allowing his flies to drop steadily down through the water. If no takes are forthcoming, the length of the cast should be gradually increased until the hot spot is located. It may also be necessary to use a weighted fly on the point should the trout be lying too deep for an unweighted fly to reach them. The takes can quite often be sudden snatches when 'hanging on' straight down the wind. It is therefore essential that an angle is kept between the rod tip and the fly line, in order to absorb some of the initial power of the take. The Adult Buzzers I use at this time of year are Medium Olives (Golden Dun Midge) in sizes 12 and 10, and my large Ginger (large red) Adult Buzzer, size 10. The latter pattern is an exceptionally deadly pattern from now until the middle of summer.

The middle of June brings about a change, or at least a variation, in the diet of the trout. There are several different species beginning to put in an appearance, which, along with the buzzer, are all welcomed and taken freely by the trout. This surfeit and variety of food has, however, its headaches for the angler. For not only do the trout become more choosy about what they dine upon, it also becomes increasingly difficult to isolate that particular item — especially when as many as three different species are hatching or are in evidence at the same time. And as if to add insult to injury, the trout are renowned at this time, particularly in the late evening, for swapping over from one species to another without any indication or warning — except perhaps for a slight difference in the rise forms. It is, therefore, a sound policy for the beginner, until he has gained sufficient experience, to work to a 'rule of thumb' guide at such times.

A typical mid to late June evening may well start with a prolific hatch of caenis, with the trout at first feeding avidly on the ascending multitudes of minute nymphs. The period of time spent by the trout feeding on the nymphs is usually quite brief, for it is not too long before their attentions turn to the hatching and freshly hatched caenis duns. The rise to the duns may also last for half an hour or so, but it is quickly followed by another rise, this time to the spent caenis spinners. This is an unmistakable rise, whereby the trout barely ever leave the surface as they patrol half out of the water, sucking down the 'soup' of dead and dying spinners. It is at this point that the next switch in the feeding pattern can be expected. The adult sedges that hatched earlier in the day, or possibly the previous evening, are now returning to the water to lay their eggs. The change in the rise forms as the switch takes place are very distinctive from the caenis rise. They usually start by 'slashing' at the sedges as they flutter out over the surface, but later settle down into deep-bodied slurping rises, as the trout suck down the spent adult flies. And as if to complicate things a little more, quite often a hatch of sedge can be expected at this time. By now the last light of day has almost gone — and to the uninitiated it would appear that things are about to come to a halt — but believe it or not, there is still one more course of the feast yet to be served. Late into the June evening a hatch of large buzzers is commonplace — a fact well known by the trout, but a point missed by many an angler.

In order to take full advantage of a typical June evening beanfeast, one must prepare one's tackle and strategy in advance, in the hope that all the species will show up — because if they do, then there will be precious little time to spare in the fading light of evening to fiddle about with new leaders, droppers and fly pattern changes. That is why I would strongly advise the beginner to stick to the 'rule of thumb' guide I am about to explain.

Ideally, the angler requires two rods for the evening period. However, one rod will suffice, provided that two spare leaders are made up beforehand, complete with the appropriate flies, and then stored on easy to unwind leader (cast) carriers. See Tip No. 1 on page 36. On the first rod a trio of caenis nymphs are mounted on a fairly light leader in readiness for the first rise. I always dress my nymphs on size 14 hooks, as the larger hook helps the artificial to sink more readily and it also offers a better hook hold. The second rod is set up for dry fly work. A knotless, tapered leader, of between 9 and 12 ft, with a tip size of approximately 3x, is ideal for the job. To the tip is tied a size 16 artificial to imitate the freshly hatched dun (the Last Hope is an excellent pattern) which is then given a good dousing in *Permaflote* and left to dry. I also like to give my leaders for dry fly work a light application of Mucilin, particularly so when using such a small fly.

The spare leaders need only be about 10 ft in length, as they will be used during the fading light. for my personal preference they should have two droppers, and taper to a 5½ lb point. But tip strength should always be governed by the size of fish one can expect to catch in a given fishery.

On the first leader there should be mounted two sedge pupae, one on the point, the other on the first dropper, and on the top dropper a winged wet sedge (or an Invicta). The second leader should carry two size 10 black (or some other dark coloured) buzzer pupae, one on the point, the other on the first dropper, and on the top dropper a size 10 Ginger (Large Red) Adult Buzzer. And finally, to complete the preparations, a few dry sedge patterns should be selected, given the *Permaflote* treatment, and then, when dry, popped into a handy container ready for immediate use.

The caenis can be expected to hatch any time from round about tea time, up until early evening, so this is the period when the angler should be fishing his team of caenis nymphs. Even when the hatch is well under way and the trout's attention is turning to the floating duns, one should not be in too much of a hurry to swap over to the dry fly rod — experience has proved to me that the nymph fished just under the surface is far more productive than the dry fly. However, as soon as the offers or takes to the nymphs cease, then this is the time to try the dry fly — but do not expect too much in the way of fast sport, the caenis is not called the angler's curse for nothing.

While fishing the dry caenis, a keen watch must be kept for the appearance of the first sedge. As soon as they start to fly out over open water, this is the signal to change one's flies and forget the caenis — even though the trout may be moving to them all over the place.

A dry sedge replaces the dry caenis, and the spare leader with the sedge pupae and the winged wet sedge, replaces the caenis nymphs. As soon as the fly change has been made, the angler should begin to fish — nothing is gained by waiting for the rise to the sedges to start. I nearly always start by using the team of wet flies and then, depending on what response I get and the surface activity at the time, either stay with that method or go over to the dry sedge. It is strange how some evenings will produce better results to the dry fly, and how others, under an identical set of conditions, will fish better with the wet — it is up to the individual therefore, to sort this one out on the evening. In any event, as the light starts to go, the team of wet flies is always the best proposition.

In the fading light it is always difficult to see whether or not a hatch of buzzer is taking place. However, if one has been enjoying sport to the wet sedge patterns, but suddenly it comes to a halt — even though the trout are still rising, then it is odds on that this is in fact the cause. A quick swap over to the leader carrying buzzer pupae is usually all that is needed to bring about a response from the trout. Many's the time I have taken trout during the last minutes of the evening, whose stomach contents have revealed, on spooning, a tangled mass of adult and hatching sedge at the bottom of the marrow scoop, and at the top a writhing mass of live, freshly taken buzzer pupae — confirming the switch better than words can convey.

There is another species of aquatic life I have yet to mention that is of importance to the trout fisherman from the middle of June onwards, and that is the damsel fly nymph. Because of its size rather than its numbers, this large nymph is a blessing in disguise in more ways than one. After the morning rise to the buzzer, things are apt to slip into something of a 'siesta-like' situation, particularly so during hot, calm conditions, when nothing seems to hatch, and nothing seems to stir. It is under conditions such as these that the damsel fly nymph prefers to put in its appearance. At any time between mid morning and mid afternoon the damsel nymphs are likely to make their shoreward migration. Unlike most aquatic insects these nymphs do not hatch, or emerge, in the surface film of the water, but instead need to climb out of the water by means of emergent rocks, plant stems, etc., in order to transform.

Once the shoreward migration begins, the nymphs leave the lake bed and swim up to the surface, whereupon they make for the margins by swimming just below the surface with vigorous lashing, almost eel-like movements of their entire bodies. It is during this sub-surface swim that the nymph is at its most vulnerable to attack from below, and it is this period of the perilous journey that the trout fisherman should endeavour to imitate.

There are many artificials which imitate these large nymphs admirably — most are dressed on long shank hooks in sizes 8s and 10s, others are dressed on normal shank hooks with a hinged rear half of the abdomen (Damsel Wiggle Nymph) in an effort to stimulate the wriggling action of the natural insect. The artificial nymph is best fished as a single fly on the point of a fairly long leader — and if possible in the immediate vicinity of reed beds or other emergent water plants. The long leader serves to put as much distance as possible between the wake made by the end of the fly line, and the nymph swimming just below the surface. A tip worth remembering is, the calmer and brighter the conditions, the longer the leader should be. I find that a medium paced retrieve in the form of long draws on the fly line is the most effective method of fishing the damsel nymph — however, there is still plenty of scope left for experiment with this particular nymph.

The colour of the natural insect can range from drab brown to brown olive, and from olive to bright green. The overall length of the various species can range from 20 mm to 32 mm. *Enallama cyathigerum* is reputed to be the most common and widely distributed of the species in Great Britain. This nymph is bright green in colour, with an overall length of 20 mm and it is in evidence from mid May until mid September. A few artificials to represent this particular species are bound to earn their keep, but it is good sense to have a few of the more drab coloured nymphs represented also.

Bank fishing — lures SYD BROCK

June can also be a really good month for fishing. My idea of ideal conditions is occasional rain, a fairly light westerly wind and overcast skies, which is often the weather experienced in this month, so my advice is to choose your day's fishing carefully.

By now the trout have got a taste for fry and could be feeding freely on them in the shallows, but because many standard lures have now passed across those trout I change my lures. The one that seems to work well is a White Pearly Lure size 8, with big eyes. Because the Pearly floats and is a very buoyant lure it can be fished right in and along the shallows on any form of sinking line. I use a fast-sink line and a short cast of 7 ft, making the lure work well at all depths; by attaching a long leader of 12 ft it can be fished using the diver technique. Because of its pearl head it is a really good fry imitator with big eyes which, in most cases, are the most striking feature of small fry as they dive away to the safety of the weed beds. I use this form of lure in three different colours, black, orange and white, and therefore if unsuccessful with one colour I try another until I find the one that's wanted, usually size 8 or 10.

Another method with the same lure is to use a floating line and longish leader of say 12 ft and add a little floatant to the feathers of the lure and cast to rising fish, not retrieving straight away but watching for fish to move nearer to the lure. This method has produced fish while static, just floating in the surface film, but it may be necessary to alter the lure from a size 8 to 10.

During early mornings and late evenings I will again use my Mylar Minnow twitched across the top on a floating line to represent an injured fish and to test this lure to its fullest I will then change to a fast-sink line and seek out the fish feeding between mid water and the bottom.

Towards the end of the month I will be teasing the trout with different patterns. My slow-sink line will gradually be more predominant — I will use the Black Ghost (size 8) on a fairly fast retrieve at most depths, also the Whisky Fly (size 8) between mid water and the surface film, but I will also introduce the size 6 Streaker, with its brilliant flash of colours. This I usually fish at all depths, but generally find it more successful when fished on a fast sink line with an 8 ft leader just off the bottom. The retrieves should be as long as possible, almost continuous for best results. Another lure I introduce about now is the scarlet coloured fly I call a Ruby. I have had outstanding results with this lure fished on a slow-sink line when all other lures have failed. I am not sure but I believe it to be the only scarlet lure I have seen. The method I use is to attach a Ruby to either a sink tip line or a slow sink line with a leader of 10--12 ft and retrieve it in short, smooth retrieves just under the surface; from experience I usually find it will take fish when they are getting a little difficult to catch.

As June draws to an end, unless you are fishing a 'put and take' water where stocking occurs every day, bank fishing is best during early mornings and late evenings, and sometimes between the hours of 11 am to 2 pm. There can occur a sudden frenzy with fish freely feeding, only to die out within half an hour of the activity starting. This is a sure sign to try one or two experiments with a change of lure.

Very often I have tried to experiment with different coloured lures to suit the weather conditions, such as a white lure on a dark overcast day, and then reversing tactics, but I have found there is no hard and fast rule, and very often it can be that the most effective pattern is the one which we thought to be absolutely wrong. There are several lines of thought on this subject but my own belief is that if your favourite lure just happens to be white fished on an overcast day, more often than not the truth is that you have complete confidence in that particular lure, and therefore you tend to fish it correctly, which will, in turn, bring success.

Another method starts to come to the fore now, that is the use of the black or white Muddler, or black or white Pearly, in what I term as the wake method — a floating line with a long 10–12 ft greased leader. This is cast right out into the ripple and retrieved with long even pulls. This produces some of the best action in trout fishing, for the angler can see quite clearly the trout chase the lure which is causing a wake across the surface. So much does the trout try in its frenzy to take the wake fly, that it appears to hump out of the water with its back clearly visible. Now, at this point, most fly fishermen make the big mistake of striking too early, and although I know it is extremely exciting, the best method is to look away and wait for the take before tightening into the fish.

7 July

The weather

This month can often be the warmest of the year, and also the wettest. Westerly winds seem to predominate, and these will sometimes bring periods of heavy rain which will often last for several hours. In some years we are likely to experience several very hot, sunny and humid days, and these are invariably followed by heavy thunderstorms. These are most likely to occur in the southern part of the country. So far as the stillwater fisherman is concerned, this can be a difficult month, as we are likely to have very heavy rain at times, as well as hot muggy days with little wind, and neither of these conditions are conducive to good fishing. In addition, by this time of the season, if we have had a lot of hot weather, the water temperature is likely to reach a high level, which seems to make the trout lethargic and less likely to feed, particularly during the day. The best fishing during July is to be expected either in the very early morning just before or after sunrise, or again in the late evenings. However, if you are fishing during the day, it is worth noting that the peak feeding times occur very close to one o'clock and again at five o'clock. Now this may sound like an old wives' tale, but I do assure you it is not. Over the years I have caught more trout between one and two and between five and six, then at any other time during the day. It is also worth noting that on those very early morning sessions which prove to be unproductive, the trout will often come on the feed for a short period around nine o'clock.

Boat fishing — imitative patterns
JOHN GODDARD

While this can be a very interesting month, it can also be extremely difficult, particularly if June has been warm and sunny. This will mean that the water temperature will have reached its optimum very early in the month, and the trout may be disinclined to feed during the day, unless the weather is dull and breezy.

In the early part of July, we are still likely to experience some very heavy hatches of caenis in the early mornings or evenings. These tiny, pale, unpwinged flies often hatch in such enormous numbers that you can become smothered in duns transposing into spinners which they can achieve within minutes of hatching. The trout, when feeding on the emerging nymphs, hatching duns or returning spinners, can be very difficult to catch, due to the sheer numbers of flies available to them on the surface. The trout usually rise repeatedly in a straight line, and accurate casting is necessary if any success is to be achieved. A small Last Hope or similar artificial should be used and this can be fished either as a dry fly to imitate the dun or as a wet fly to represent the emerging nymph or spinner. In complete contrast a large pattern fished medium fast just below the surface will sometimes tempt the odd trout. The pond olive and various other upwinged duns are likely to be observed this month, although hatches are unlikely to be on a scale that will tempt the trout to feed on the hatching duns on the surface. However, the trout will certainly feed upon the nymphs where they occur, so a small Pheasant Tail or PVC Nymph fished in the sink and draw style from an anchored boat will often give good results, and is a particularly useful technique to adopt, when drift fishing proves unproductive due to adverse weather conditions.

During July, hatches of the larger chironomids (midges) are likely to be sparse; on the other hand, hatches of some of the smaller species such as the small red or small brown midge are likely to reach a peak in this month, and on some waters hatches usually from midday onwards are often of sufficient density to bring on a surface rise. When feeding upon these the trout cruise just below the surface, taking both the ascending pupae as well as the adults hatching in the surface film. In calm conditions they rise in a very erratic manner, taking the flies off the surface with an audible sip, and it is often difficult to get within casting range without putting them down. As when fishing to trout feeding on caenis, casting must be accurate, and I have enjoyed most success using a single fly mounted on the point of a long leader, either my own small Hatching Midge or a Gold Ribbed Hare's Ear. In breezy conditions the trout feed upon these tiny midges in a straight line upwind, and are much easier to catch. Mount a Gold Ribbed Hare's Ear on the point and a small Hatching Midge on a dropper, and if you can find a wind lane, anchor the boat in this and wait for the rising trout to come to you.

Towards the middle of the month, hatches of the many species of sedge or caddis flies will be reaching their peak, and these as a source of food for the trout are second in importance only to the chironomids, so the emphasis on many artificial patterns until the middle of September at least will be orientated towards the sedge flies. Most species hatch during the afternoons or early evenings, so drift fishing during this period, if the weather conditions are right, provides one of the most effective methods of taking trout feeding upon them. One of the best fly combinations to use is to mount a G & H (deer hair) or a Richard Walker Sedge pattern on the top dropper, with an Invicta or Longhorns on the middle dropper, and one of my Sedge Pupa patterns on the point. The artificials on the point and middle dropper should be well degreased and retrieved just under the surface, while the dry sedge on the top dropper should be well greased so it is retrieved bouncing along the surface making a considerable wake which will attract the trout to your flies from a considerable distance. The same combination is effective whether the trout are rising or not, however, when heavy hatches, which usually occur in the evening, take place, and there is a corresponding surface rise; a very enjoyable and effective method is to anchor your boat and fish a dry sedge alone on the point. This can be cast to individual rising trout, and be given an occasional tweak to animate. Should this method prove unproductive, try skating the dry sedge as fast as you can retrieve it across the surface, as at times the trout seem to react more positively to this rapid movement. When drift fishing in the mornings at this time of year, I often concentrate on drifts across the shallower areas, and in conjunction with a dry sedge on the top dropper and a Dunkeld on the middle, I mount either a weighted or unweighted Stick Fly on the point.

Another important event in the stillwater trout fisherman's calendar during June, July and August with the peak hatches occurring on many waters this month, are the shoreward migration of the nymphs of the damsel fly. These large nymphs, which vary tremendously in colour from bright green to dark brown, are over an inch in length when fully mature and are eagerly sought by the trout. They usually emerge during the mornings, swimming towards the surface, and then towards the shore, just below the surface with a strong wriggling action. The rise of a trout to one of these nymphs when it is close to the surface is unmistakable, as it is a violent, slashing rise which can be seen from a considerable distance. There are many different artificials to represent these but my favourite is Cliff Henry's Damosel, closely followed by my own Damosel Wiggle Nymph. Either of these are very effective, particularly in the mornings at this time of the year, mounted on the point when drift fishing. These are also very useful patterns which may be used with confidence at any time during the summer.

Finally, during July and also August, always be on the lookout for trout feeding upon floating snails. At this time of the year on hot, calm days, the common aquatic snails that normally live on or close to the bottom, float up to the surface where they will hang, pad uppermost, at the mercy of the current. As these molluscs are a favourite food of the trout, when they can find them, they are naturally very vulnerable when floating on the surface, and as soon as the trout become aware of this surface migration they will feed on them in complete preoccupation and will look at nothing else. The rise form of trout when feeding on these is a typical head and tail rise, and one can easily be misled into thinking they are feeding on midge pupae as it is virtually impossible to differentiate between the two rise forms. In addition, floating snails in the surface are extremely difficult to see, unless you look straight down into the water. If you are alert enough to spot them and you observe trout rising, anchor your boat and mount an appropriate snail artificial alone on the point. This should be cast in the vicinity of the rising trout, and left without movement until a trout spots your artificial and accepts it. Takes are usually positive, and it will only be necessary to tighten on the fish. My favourite floating snail pattern is one developed many years ago by that observant and skilled fly fisher, Cliff Henry. This migration of snails to the surface is not a particularly common occurrence, but remember, when it does happen the trout will rarely look at any other artificial.

Boat fishing — traditional JOHN KETLEY

Over recent seasons I have noticed a steady change in our weather, in that winter has hung on until May and this is having a fundamental effect on our fishing. If this trend continues it may well be that what we normally think of as June fishing will not appear until July, and so on through the season. Nevertheless, I will assume in these sections on loch style fishing that our summers will go back to the weather patterns considered normal a few years ago. But, should you find that summer doesn't start properly until late June, then it may pay to fish May/June style until August.

In a normal season, early July will find the trout in many stillwaters starting to concentrate on the coarse fish fry at certain periods of the day. The main hatches of buzzers will diminish and it's quite possible no fly will hatch until late afternoon. As the month wears on this lack of fly life will probably become more noticeable, the only hatches of any significance being at last light. Happily the loch style fisher is not totally dependent on a hatch of fly and can ring the changes in all sorts of ways that will produce trout.

Let me first explain how I discover whether the fish are on the fry, as this is not always a simple matter. The neatest way is to catch a fish or investigate the stomach contents of someone else's fish and see if there are any fry present.

If this is not possible then look near the weed beds for signs of fry 'showering'. By that, I mean a sudden glittering explosion of fry as they leap out of the water like a silver fan or upward showers of mercury. This is a sure sign that perch or trout are attacking them. In lakes that have a fair number of mature perch, the trout often develop the interesting habit of letting the perch shoals 'round up' the fry into a cloud of silver two yards or more across. Then a number of individual trout will steam into the fry shoal gulping down as many as they can.

Even if you don't see the showers of fry, you may well notice some dead or mortally wounded fry floating on the top, although these are usually quickly gobbled up by either the trout or the perch. This sort of activity also attracts the gulls, who collect in very short order over such areas to steal their share of the wounded fry. So, if you see half a dozen gulls bombing a small section of water near a weed bed, you have another indicator the fry are being attacked.

It seems once the trout have got the taste for fry they will readily take one, or sometimes any of the fry imitating artificials, even if they are not at that moment feeding on fry. Which leads me neatly to the fly patterns I find most effective for fry time. The famous loch patterns like the Dunkeld, Alexandra, Peter Ross and Silver Invicta all do stalwart service and also catch trout all season through, although more recent innovations like my Allrounder, a size 10 Baby Doll and the small Muddlers have the edge on occasion, in my opinion.

When fishing for trout you have reason to believe are feeding on fry, remember that these little fish spend far more time static in the water than they do rushing about. The traditional loch style retrieve with its pauses after the cast and just at the lift, is a good basic method, but I have discovered a particularly effective method for the times you can see trout smashing into the fry.

I put one Allrounder on the point, with a size 10 Black Buzzer on the dropper and another silver-bodied light hen wing Allrounder on the bob. I cast these right into the boil where the trout has moved and let it sink for twenty seconds. If there's no take I then twitch them back with short, sharp retrieves, pause for ten seconds and lift slowly up, then pause again to let the top dropper lay on the surface before

I lift off and recast. If the takes come to the buzzer I put a second one onto the point in preference to the Allrounder.

The fry feeding phenomenon is very much a movable feast for the trout and may come any time in July, last a few days and be over. Alternatively it can start earlier or later and sometimes lasts for three or four weeks.

In my experience two kinds of nymph patterns work very well fished loch style during the latter part of July and into August; they are the Hare's Ear Nymph and the Midge Pupa.

The Hare's Ear Nymph tied neat and tidy, fished on the point, or tied bushy and rough when fished on a dropper, works well on cloudy but warm days when you see sedges fluttering about over the surface. I find this very ordinary looking pattern a wonderful standby that on certain occasions will take fish when very little else seems to work.

The midge pupae can make the trout extremely selective in their feeding and although I'm sure John Goddard will cover it in his section, I would like to mention three ways I have found to take fish in what can be terribly frustrating conditions.

The first thing is to recognise when the fish are feeding on midge pupae, and as always the easiest way is to catch one and examine its stomach contents. If this is not possible, you may be able to recognise the particular rise form as it is different from most other rises. The only other time I notice trout feeding with something like this movement is when they are feeding on daphnia. The trout appears to move in a random manner, often in little tight circles, then it suddenly bow waves up a wind lane for a yard, then turns about face and circles again and equally suddenly disappears. You seldom see any part of the fish, maybe an occasional back fin, or an inch of tail for a second as it turns and boils at these invisible (to us) little creatures.

One solution that works amazingly well is to take a large bushy Coch-y-Bonddu or even a Worm Fly and cover it liberally in floatant. Cast it directly in front of a moving fish and strip it back across its nose. The main problem with this technique is that it results in more follows than takes, but it should get you two or three fish when you have been 'through the box' to no avail.

The second solution I have adapted from experiences gained fishing International competitions on Loch Leven. This loch is often thought of as the original stillwater and the Scots have developed a series of very small flies tied on 'wee doubles' specifically for the famous Loch Leven trout. These double hooks may have a hooking advantage, but they certainly are heavier than a similar size single hook, and when fishing size 16 flies I find they tend to skate on the surface unless they are on doubles, or given added weight. These small double flies in a number of patterns can prove a very satisfactory answer when the fish are feeding on midge pupae, and are commercially available from some tackle shops.

Taking this experience I now add a little lead to my size 16 and 18 single hook flies and find they stay just under the surface without skating. A simple Midge Pupa pattern tied this way and fished loch style over fish feeding in this particular manner can really solve the problem. I put on three slightly different colour patterns, a green size 16 on the point, a brown size 16 on the middle and an orange and brown on the bob. Then cast to the moving fish, give the flies a second or two to sink and retrieve slowly with a lift on the rod.

Most English stillwater anglers may look a bit doubtful when they first tie on these minute flies, but the trout see them all right, I promise you.

Boat fishing — lures BOB CHURCH

Although we may have found daphnia in the stomach contents of trout (mostly rainbows) from early season onwards, it is July when it reaches its peak. Most fertile stillwaters I fish have daphnia blooms and it seems incredible that such a tiny animal can be a major source of rainbow food, yet the facts from a survey carried out at Grafham in 1974 prove it beyond doubt.

With water temperatures being at their highest, this tiny crustacean, a member of the plankton family, are now reproducing in their billions at a fantastic rate. Rainbows just swim along taking them in like soup. The nutrient value must be very high as demonstrated by the Grafham rainbows' fast growth rate.

The clouds of daphnia are constantly moving up or down from the surface to the lake or reservoir bed. This movement is governed by the amount of light, for early in the morning daphnia are high in the water. As the morning wears on it slowly sinks to greater depths until around noon with the sunlight at its peak, daphnia will be at its deepest. By late afternoon once again it will rise to mid water and as evening approaches it will move closer to the surface. The exception is in very dull weather when they are likely to be seen in abundance close to the surface throughout the day.

It would be natural to assume that when rainbows are preoccupied with daphnia, one should try to tempt them on a small hook pattern. In fact the opposite is true, for at this time rainbows seem to throw caution to the wind and will often attack lures with gay abandon. It is important that you understand about daphnia and their up and down movement because this will help you choose the right type of line. Unless it is bright and sunny I favour at least to start with a slow sinker, and find that No. 6 long shank lures score better than smaller sizes.

The patterns I favour at this time are Nailer Fly, Orange Muddler, White Muddler, Black Chenille, Goldie, Concorde (with its unique shape) and the fluorescent green Leprechaun. The Leprechaun can be an absolute killer on its day and I find this is usually when there are a lot of suspended green algae particles in the water.

On the larger exposed reservoirs July's continuous westerly winds help you find the fish. The wind and wave action set up a surface and sub-surface current which in turn will push the vast daphnia blooms to the windward side of the reservoir. So try short drifts into this shoreline, say from 300 yards out. If you find a dense concentration of fish you can always anchor on the upwind side of them.

Although hot orange is such an important colour to incorporate in our lures during high summer, so too is fluorescent lime green. From the mid 1970s onwards following Peter Wood's Leprechaun lure discovery, this colour has crept into many patterns. I have already mentioned Viva. Another good variation is a fluorescent green backed Baby Doll. The unusually named Christmas Tree has been around since Rutland opened and it is a great favourite there. A Sweeney Todd with a fluorescent green throat instead of magenta is also a very useful variation. I can vouch for the success of adding fluorescent green to lures and they have caught trout from a wide range of waters including Loch Garry in the north of Scotland, and Lough Mask in the west of Ireland, as well as all the English and Welsh reservoirs. If you arrive at your favourite water and the algae is particularly bad, then this is the ideal time to try one of the fluorescent green lures.

As in June, July is perfect for all surface Muddlering methods incorporating a floating shooting head and drifting the boat broadside to the wind. A very similar technique is to use an American popping bug instead of the Muddler. The bugs were originally used to catch large and small mouthed black bass in the States before becoming popular with trout fly fishers over here. These popping bugs have worked very well with Rutland and Grafham rainbows. They float of course after being cast downwind and should be retrieved in short sharp jerks against the waves; the hollow concaved head gives off a series of bubbles and a loud pop each time it is moved. This action causes fish to investigate, and takes can often be savage.

Of course July is a peak time for food availability as the sedges are also at their peak. Trout, both rainbows and browns, tend to eat quite a lot of sedge larvae and this means fishing on, or close to, the bottom in water from 8 feet to 15 feet in depth. A sheltered weedy bay is usually a good spot. The sedge larvae, or as Midlanders call them caddis grubs, build themselves a protective house which safeguards them against predators. Often this protective cover is made of twigs or vegetation, so this leaves a dark, drab inch-long shape crawling about the bottom.

To fish this situation I would anchor and fish with a floating or sink-tip line and long 5 yard leader. The two lures I have caught lots of trout on at this time are the Worm Fly and the ever faithful Black Chenille, both on No. 10 or 8.

During late evenings, particularly in the last two weeks of July, there will be a lot of surface activity with trout rising to the hatching or adult sedge flies. At this time a No. 10 standard Muddler Minnow can tempt a lot of trout into making a mistake if it is fished slowly across the top as a wake fly. Perhaps it is taken for a pair of adult sedges locked in mating.

Bank fishing — imitative patterns
BOB CARNILL

Each and every month of the fly fisherman's season has its own individual character, and given anything like normal weather conditions, these individual characteristics can be relied upon to present themselves — sometimes they are for the good of the sport, but at other times they can make things most difficult. July is a month possessing both of the above-mentioned traits, starting off by following in the footsteps of June and giving the angler some first class sport, but gradually, as the month progresses, so the water temperature rises. The end result is lethargy, particularly amongst the brown trout population, and a distinct preference for early morning and late evening feeding.

I have always looked upon the middle of July, under normal seasonal conditions, as being the start of what is often referred to as the doldrums. The doldrums usually occupy a period of approximately four weeks — in other words from about mid-July to mid-August — and it can prove to be a most testing time for the daytime fly fisherman. Any trout that are available will have to be 'fished' for, using forethought and stealth — as opposed to 'fishing the water' or, as some would call it, 'chucking and chancing it'.

From the beginning of July onwards I try, whenever possible, to be at the water's edge just before first light. There is something very special about hearing the trout moving before they can actually be seen, and to feel that sudden stopping of the line followed by the splash of a hooked fish are ample reward indeed for having had to leave a warm and comfortable bed in the middle of the night.

These very early morning rises are nearly always to buzzers of one form or another. Sometimes the rise is to a hatch of fly, at others it is to the spent adults still floating in the surface film from the previous evening's egg-laying missions. More often than not I will start the morning by fishing a Buzzer Pupa on the point, either red or pale green on a size 10, and on the droppers a size 10 Ginger (Large Red) Adult Buzzer. The flies are fished just sub-surface with a slow figure of eight retrieve. A good alternative to the Ginger Adult Buzzer is the Ginger Quill or a winged Greenwell's Glory. I always dress my Greenwells with a small tag or tail of DRF phosphor yellow nylon under the tail whisks, which makes the fly even more deadly, especially in low light conditions.

Bays, inlets and creeks are areas well worth a try in the early hours of the morning, particularly so if they happen to have been the lee shore of the previous evening. The trout at this time of day are sometimes in very shallow water, therefore the margins should not be ignored or neglected in one's haste to fish further out.

The daytime fishing during the first half of July can range from excellent to hard going — it all depends as always on the weather. Flat calms with the sun blazing down out of a cloudless sky are without doubt the most difficult conditions that one is likely to meet with — under such conditions a trout caught is a trout earnt. By nature, I am a roving type of fisherman — that is until I find what I am looking for — and time and time again I have proved that this 'walkabout' approach during these conditions can quite often help put a trout or two in the bag that otherwise might not have been there. There is little point in standing in one spot and flogging a dead horse — far better to take a slow rove along the bank on the look-out for the odd riser, and then to show it your fly just once or twice, any more than that is usually a waste of time. A single fly on a long, knotless leader is the best approach, more than one fly and its accompanying knots can sometimes create too much

87

surface disturbance. The choice of fly for such difficult conditions is by no means easy — let alone cut and dried. It is up to the angler, therefore, to be prepared to experiment, and if need be to solve the problem by a process of trial and error. Whatever the pattern chosen, it should be borne in mind that it must have the ability to penetrate the surface quickly — having to twitch the leader in order to induce the fly or nymph to sink can only serve to lessen one's chances of success.

The choice of patterns that I would first consider, and in fact try, would be small (size 14s and 12s) imitations of nymphs and pupae which the trout have recently been familiar with, and indeed been feeding on. That good old standby the Buzzer Pupa just has to be amongst the first to be considered. There are several proven patterns which readily spring to mind. John Goddard's Hatching Midge, Geoffrey Bucknall's Footballer and my own Poly Rib have all stood the test of time, having accounted for vast numbers of trout over the years.

A Sedge Pupa, too, can quite often work the oracle, especially when fished in and around weed beds. Imitative patterns for the sedge pupa are legion, but those which I would strongly recommend are the Amber Nymph (Bell), the Orange, Green, Brown and Cream Sedge Pupae (Goddard), the Longhorns (Walker) and last but by no means least, a pattern given to me by the late Jim Sharp of Nottingham, which was reputed to have originally come from that other late, great angler, Cyril Inwood. This pupa has a brick-red seal's fur abdomen ribbed through with oval gold, the thorax is green drake seal's fur with wing cases of hen pheasant primary. For the legs and antennae, a few long hot orange cock hackle fibres are tied in underneath the shank just behind the eye, to reach a little beyond the hook point. The effectiveness of this pattern needs no further recommendation — if it came from the Sharp–Inwood stable, then it has to be good.

Quite often a small dry fly will do the trick with these solitary risers. I tend to favour a fly with a rich red-brown tone, either a small sedge or a small dry Wickham's fancy.

Whether the daytime conditions be calm or windy there is one other pattern that should not be overlooked, and that is the Damsel Fly Nymph. Fished on a floating line and a long leader in the vicinity of weed or reed beds, with long steady draws on the line, this nymph can very often bring about some exciting and memorable sport.

No matter what the trials and tribulations of the day, the July evenings are something to look forward to. July is without doubt the month of the sedge, and the evening angler could do far worse than to plan his approach accordingly. However, before the main rise to the hatching or adult fly begins there is quite often a caenis hatch and the subsequent rise to contend with. I usually fish a team of Caenis Nymphs of my own design for most of the rise, only rarely bothering to try the dry or spent patterns. My main concern during a caenis rise is to watch for the first sedge of the evening to appear out over open water. When this happens I settle down to fish and enjoy what must be one of the most exciting facets of our sport.

When there is a large concentration of sedge out on the water — as is quite common throughout July — it sometimes pays dividends to stand and observe the surface activity before actually deciding on one's line of attack. It is strange, but some evenings the trout seem to concentrate mainly on the ascending pupae — taking them just sub-surface, and in doing so throw up heaving boils of turbulent water to the surface. These upthrusts have a flattening effect on any surface ripple that there may happen to be, making this rise form instantly recognisable and easy to see even at a considerable distance. The best medicine for this situation is a team of any of the aforementioned Sedge Pupae, fished just sub-surface with a medium paced retrieve.

However, if the rise forms indicate an actual breaking of the surface, with the trout's neb or even its head showing above the surface, then this is a good indication that the pupae are being taken whilst in the surface film, and most probably in the process of hatching. I have always had great success with a single Invicta or my Fiery Brown Sedge during this kind of rise — it is important, however, that the fly does not fish too deep at such times. A light application of grease to the leader, up to within a few inches of the artificial, will make the fly bulge enticingly just under the surface even with the slowest of retrieves.

After hatching, the sedge fly prepares for its maiden flight, with wings quivering violently it 'skitters' across the surface of the water carving quite an uncertain course and throwing out a considerable disturbance. Such actions are an open invitation to any trout cruising within the immediate vicinity, and can often prove to be the undoing of many a sedge as it is snatched from the surface with a vicious slashing rise. There is, to my mind, only one artificial to fit the bill for this kind of situation, and that is the wonderful creation by Messrs Goddard and Henry — the G & H Deer Hair Sedge. Due to its overall silhouette, its floatability and its wedge-shaped form this fly, when retrieved across the surface, creates such a realistic impression that it is hardly surprising when trout come crashing after it.

Another rise form that can quite often be confused with the rise to the skittering sedge is the chasing, and quite often leaping, rise to the adult fly as it flies low over the water on what appears to be an egg-laying flight. During this low-level flight, the female continually flops onto the surface of the water and off again, sometimes in very quick succession. This action brings forth a spectacular response from the trout by producing a series of arching and leaping rises as it chases after the fly. The only chance that one has of imitating this kind of action is to skate a stiff-hackled artificial fast across the surface. Richard Walker, in all his wisdom, recognised the need for such a pattern and so brought forth the Walker's Sedge, a specially designed, custom-built fly — and what an effective fly it has proved itself to be.

There are two other rise forms that are worthy of special note, and both are to the static sedge fly as it sits on the water prior to its maiden flight. The first is quite a confident and clean cut rise, very much the same as the rise to the hatching sedge, but with a little more shoulder showing above the water. It was for this kind of rise that the vast majority of the dry sedge patterns were created. To fish this kind of rise is perhaps the least demanding so far as physical effort is concerned, but by far the most demanding when it comes to accuracy and presentation. In order to be most effective, the fly must be cast delicately ahead of the rising trout in such a position as to be on a collision course with it. If the trout accepts the fly, then the angler must allow enough time for the trout to turn down with it before attempting to set the hook. An all too common mistake made by the uninitiated is to strike the instant the fly is taken; this kind of reflex action nearly always results in failure to make contact with the trout.

The other kind of rise to the static sedge is what could best be described as the 'tail slap'. This is a rise form that is by no means common, and I cannot for the life of me think why it should happen at all, but occasionally the trout will rise from directly beneath the sedge and with a quick turn of the body will bring its tail down with a slap on the unfortunate fly. It would appear that the object of this exercise is to sink the fly beneath the surface, where it can be taken leisurely from the sub-surface turbulence. There have been a number of occasions in the past when I have been able to cash in on this kind of rise by using a leaded version of my Fiery Brown Sedge. The method is to aerialise the fly line in anticipation of the next rise to occur within one's reach. The instant the rise takes place, the fly must be dropped accurately into the boil of the rise. There then follows a brief pause to allow the fly to 'drop in', this is immediately followed by a steady draw on the fly line. If a take is to be forthcoming, it is usually within the first foot or so of the draw as the trout turns back into the turbulence to pick up his spoils.

From the middle of July up to the end of the month the morning and evening rises provide the best and most consistent sport, but that doesn't mean that the daytime fishing should be avoided. On the contrary, there is some interesting and challenging sport to be had during the heat of the day — provided one knows what to look for. For it is now that the coarse fish fry — which, by the way, hatched out during the early weeks of June, are beginning to be taken seriously by the trout. During bright sunny weather the fry congregate close to the surface, particularly around weed beds, in their millions, and despite the bright sun and the high temperature of the surface water, there are always a few trout that seem to spend most of the day harassing the fry shoals.

Most anglers tend to look upon these fry-bashers as only fair game for the lure — but this is by no means the case. With a little observation and forethought by the angler, they are just as liable to fall to an imitative insect pattern as they are to anything else. One has only to stand and observe fry feeders for a short while to realise that the attacks on the fry are not 'willy-nilly' affairs. Whether they be in open water or around weed beds, there is nearly always a pattern to the attack. After only a short observation the frequency of the attacks and the pathway, or beat, used by the trout will begin to reveal itself. Once this pattern is recognised, the angler can then use it to his advantage by positioning his artificial in the right place and at the right time. There are two avenues of approach open to the angler who chooses to fish imitative patterns for fry-feeders. One is to use a pattern which, when retrieved in a particular manner, will loosely resemble a darting fry. For this kind of approach the artificials I would choose would be a Pheasant Tail

Nymph dressed on sizes 8 and 10 long-shank hooks, or a Persuader of a similar size.

The other technique is to use a smaller and much closer copy of a natural food form with which the trout is familiar. This technique is particularly effective when used for trout that are hunting fry around the weed beds. Over the years one thing I have proved from the scores of autopsies I have carried out on fry-feeders is that any naturals disturbed or dislodged from the weed during their attacks on the fry are very often taken by the trout. It is nothing unusual to find corixa, small diving beetles, chironomid larvae and sometimes even a few chironomid pupae intermingled with the fry. These naturals are, however, generally overlooked by many fishermen when the spoon is withdrawn packed solid with fry. The sight of so much fry is usually enough evidence to convince them that the trout are completely preoccupied, and the contents of the spoon are quickly disposed of. However, if they were to drop the contents of the spoon into a jar of water and give it a stir, they might be surprised at what they find. It might be worth mentioning at this point, if only to instil a little confidence in the method, that in August 1980 I had the great thrill and pleasure of taking the largest rainbow trout of the season at Rutland Water. This absolutely perfect hen fish of 8 lb 1 oz was taken from the far side of a weed bed on a very simple bloodworm imitation. Later, after the weigh-in, when the stomach contents were examined, this fish was found to contain both coarse fish fry and a mixture of partly digested invertebrate matter. Obviously a fish of catholic eating habits — perhaps that's what made her so pretty.

Bank fishing — lures SYD BROCK

July can be very humid, very hot, with occasional storms in between — a truly difficult month. Often during this month only very light winds occur — all waters seem to take on that glazed, settled look which all too often means fishing will be difficult, with the exception of fishing after a storm or heavy rain, but this period of good fishing does not last very long, so early mornings and late evenings are the times when you have your best chance.

During this month if any surface feeding fish are seen I would try for these with my floating line, long (12 ft) greased leader and a Brown or Black Muddler, or Black Lure, with long fast retrieves in the wake method.

This is also a time when the sedge appears, and although it may generally be thought not to be part of a lure fisherman's practice, I just cannot ignore them. The best fly for this I have found is the G & H Sedge, with its very buoyant deer hair body. The fly is best used when it is just left to float on the surface film in amongst the rising fish, or if this does not work, a slight twitch of the line now and again will very often produce a good take.

Early mornings and part of the mid day will see me still trying for those browns with a fast sink line and size 6 Black Ghost in deep water, or if I am fishing the shallows, slow sink line and Black or White Pearly, size 8.

This is a difficult month, so using these tactics I will interchange from black to white to orange, unless I get a definite take on one colour consistently. However, experience has shown that all too often, if you are lucky, you will get maybe one take and no more on each colour.

The unusual is very often successful during this month, so try those lures that tend to be put aside in favour of the more standard designs during the easier early months. I use a streaker of blue and sometimes red, fished at all depths on my fast sink or slow sink lines. Also during the day I will often fish with a size 8 Orange Pearly, with its staring black eyes, between mid water and the surface, with a leader of 12 ft. This very often produces a fish when all else fails.

If you are unfortunate and picked a day of almost complete calm, or one of those balmy days, it is often better to rest for periods watching and exploring the bankside with your polarised glasses. Very often you learn more this way than continual efforts can bring. A deep hole may be discovered, or stickling fish, and sometimes a big fish lying in the shallows will be your reward.

One lure I have found to be very successful during this hard period is a yellow lure I named Yellow Hammer, size 8. It is probably no better than any other lure in design, but it always catches one or two fish when fished on a slow sink line between the surface and mid water, although I feel any depth must be tried on these days, so I would also fish it fairly deep. I would also try the diver technique with a Black Muddler or Black Pearly (size 8 or 10), tied on a leader of 12 ft with a fast sink line; the action of the lure diving down from the surface is just a little different from any other action and could bring results.

Watch for those telltale signs of scattering fry. Although fish tend to be lethargic during this month, a sudden feeding frenzy can occur which may not last long, so I would be ready on my other rod with a floating line and a leader of 12 ft, and my Mylar Minnow which, when fished correctly — slow with occasional quick jerks — will bring those feeding trout up for an easy target.

Towards the close of the month I will have tried most lures, and in this way found the most successful method to suit each water. The variation during this month is almost mind boggling and in no way to be relied upon from year to year; which is a good thing in lots of ways, because it makes you think hard. It can be a shattering experience to fish for three days in a row and find each day quite different from the others.

8 August

The weather

The weather in August is likely to be similar to that of July, and if the westerly winds persist, with continuing depressions, long periods of dull weather with much rain may be expected. Anticyclones are just as likely, however, and will bring a few very hot days which are again likely to end in severe thunderstorms. Also, towards the end of the month, stronger winds are to be expected, with the distinct possibility of gales. In some years the wind is likely to turn around to the north or north east, and while the latter wind is not normally welcomed by the fly fisher, at this time of the year these north-easterlies usually bring clear nights with a substantial drop in temperature. This means that the temperature of the water also drops, which will bring the trout back on the feed. August is reputed to be a dead month for the fly fisher, and if the water temperature remains high it can certainly be difficult; also, by this time of the year, there are less trout to be fished for, and those remaining have become very wary. But for those fly fishers who know what they are about, August can be a very interesting month; there is usually less competition from other anglers, as fewer fish are caught during this month than any other during the season, and the fish that are there to be caught are usually in excellent condition.

Boat fishing — imitative patterns
JOHN GODDARD

Traditionally August is considered the most difficult and unproductive month of the season for the stillwater fly fisher. Personally I think the case has been rather overstated. Certainly the water temperature is still likely to be high and the trout disinclined to feed during the day in warm weather. In addition there will be fewer available for the angler to catch. Despite this I have had some excellent days fishing during this month, particularly on cool, wet or windy days after periods of hot weather.

During the early part of the month we are still likely to encounter good hatches of the small red or brown midges in the late morning or afternoon, and during hot sultry weather we may still be fortunate to find odd days when floating snails are to be seen. Full information on both of these are provided in the previous chapter. In the mornings Damosel nymphs may still be observed swimming shorewards just beneath the surface, so at least during the early part of the day at this time of year I find that an excellent combination of patterns for drift fishing is as follows. A Damosel Nymph on the point, a Dunkeld on the first dropper, with a well greased Red Palmer on the top dropper.

Throughout the month the sedge or caddis flies will still be much in evidence from early afternoons onwards, so for general drift fishing at this period of the day I often switch my team of three flies to a G & H Sedge on the top dropper, a Dunkeld or Invicta on the middle dropper, with an Orange or Cream Sedge Pupa on the point. Should one mostly be drifting across shallow water, exchange the Sedge Pupa on the point for a Stick Fly, which is the artificial equivalent of the larva of the sedge fly. In the late afternoon or early evening when the hatches of sedges intensify I tend to fish sedge patterns exclusively, and over the past two or three seasons I have had excellent sport with a new hatching sedge pattern that Brian Clarke and I developed originally for river fishing. This may be dressed in two basic colours, either orange or green, on a size 12 eyed hook, and I favour fishing the green pattern on the point with the orange pattern on the middle dropper and a G & H Sedge or small Red Palmer on the top dropper. The leader and both hatching pupa patterns should be thoroughly degreased and retrieved slowly on a floating line just in the surface film.

Now while either of these methods is good and will produce fish, to obtain the best results — particularly during this difficult month — it is really necessary to know at what stage the sedges are being taken by the trout, so one can fish an appropriate pattern accordingly. As the tyro, and even some reasonably experienced fly fishers, seems to have difficulty in recognising the various stages and how to present patterns accordingly, let us look in detail at a hatch of sedges during a typical August afternoon and evening.

The first indication that the hatch is under way will be the presence of various medium or small sized sedges crawling around in the boat, while you may also see the odd one in flight. These are most likely to be silverhorns, grouse wings or similar species which mostly hatch out via emergent vegetation in the shallower areas and then fly out over the water preparatory to mating. During this period, if conditions are reasonable, the trout will be feeding under water on the pupae as they commence their shoreward migration to hatch. Mount a team of Sedge Pupae in different colours and fish these slowly as far below the surface as you can on a floating line. If you are drifting too fast to do this, then anchor the boat but never in water more than about ten feet in depth. As the evening progresses and the hatch intensifies, swarming and mating will commence in flight, and many of these mating pairs will be blown onto the surface where the trout are waiting. The rise of trout to these is a splashy affair and in some cases the trout will arch out and almost clear the water. When this occurs mount a single large G & H Sedge alone on the point and fish as a dry fly with occasional movement. Later on many of the larger species of sedges will start emerging, and as most of these hatch on the surface in open water, the rise will start in earnest. Initially the trout will be feeding on the pupae preparatory to hatching just under the surface film, and the rise to these will be indicated by boils and swirls just under the surface often accompanied by the neb of the fish just breaking the surface. My favourite medicine at this time is an Invicta on the top dropper, with a pair of my own Hatching Sedges, the orange colour on the middle dropper and the green on the point. Both leader and flies should be well degreased and then retrieved slowly just beneath the surface. This team of flies will account for trout feeding either on the pupae just under the surface or those that are transposing into the adult, winged sedge fly on the surface. Should the trout be concentrating on the hatching pupa rather than the pupa itself, they will often rise in a straight line, tilting upwards every few feet and opening their mouth to sip in the hatching fly, which is an easy target at this time as it is completely immobile and unable to escape. Should it be a nice evening, and the hatch of sedges heavy, then the trout will eventually start feeding upon the adults on the surface as they are struggling to become airborne. Now is the time to present a single dry fly (a small Red Palmer or G & H Sedge will usually suffice) to individual rising trout. This may be tweaked occasionally to provide animation to attract the fish, but if this does not work try a Walker's Sedge or similar, and retrieve this as fast as you can over the surface across the path of any rising trout. When the trout are feeding on these adults the rise form is often violent as they seem to realise that the struggling sedge may take off at any second and escape.

During this month on many waters we are likely to encounter good hatches of the large green midge, but as this rarely occurs until very late in the evening when the light has almost gone many fly fishers fail to realise it, and miss the opportunity of a good trout or two. On a typical August evening if a good rise occurs the trout will be feeding mainly on sedge, and if you are lucky you will probably be taking the odd fish and getting sundry tugs and pulls. If, as the light is fading, the rise suddenly intensifies and the trout stop showing an interest in your flies, you can be sure that they have switched to the midge pupae or hatching adults. To cover this eventuality I always carry a spare rod in the boat, and at some time during the early evening make this up with a team of Midge Pupa or Adult Midge patterns in the appropriate colour ready for this late switch. Both leader and flies should be carefully degreased and retrieved slowly just beneath the surface.

August is traditionally the month for dapping with the live daddy longlegs, particularly on the Scottish lochs and Irish loughs. These large and ungainly insects hatch in large numbers some years, and are then blown onto the water where they make a tasty meal for any observant trout. Personally I rarely fish the artificial daddy, for unless you get a year with particularly heavy hatches adjacent to our southern waters the fish largely seem to ignore them. If you are going to fish a daddy, Dick Walker's pattern is one of the best, and I have found that, at least from a boat, it is best fished on its own on the point. It should be presented as a dry fly to represent the drowned insect floating on the surface, and so should be fished with little or no movement. Of course if you wish you may dap with this pattern or even various sedge patterns; this can be great fun for a change and is now gaining in popularity on many Midland and Southern waters. During the past two seasons I have been assisting John Ketley in some interesting dapping experiments, which he fully covers in his section on traditional boat fishing.

Two other terrestrial species, the black gnat and the heather fly, are also likely to be seen during August, and will bring on a good rise when they are blown onto the surface. The former is common and widespread throughout Britain, and when these tiny black flies are on the wing in large numbers an artificial of the same name fished as a dry fly alone on the point will often tempt the odd trout.

The heather fly is mainly confined to Wales and the Northern part of Britain and is particularly common in Scotland, where it is known as the bloody doctor. It is a large fly, very similar in appearance to the hawthorn fly except that the top part of its legs are bright red. These flies present a very juicy target for patrolling trout, and any standard Hawthorn pattern either fished dry or wet and retrieved slowly in the surface film will prove effective.

Finally, in late August and early September we are once again likely to observe some good hatches of lake olives, particularly on many Northern waters. If you are on the water when a hatch of these medium sized upwinged flies occurs during the day, try drifting over fairly shallow water with a PVC Nymph on the point, a Gold Ribbed Hare's Ear on the middle dropper and a wet Greenwell's Glory or similar on the top dropper. Alternatively, if the hatch is a good one and brings on a surface rise try presenting a single Super Grizzly fished dry on the point among the rising fish. However, should a trout accept your offering give him sufficient time to turn down with it before tightening. During a sparse hatch try anchoring the boat adjacent to weed beds and fish a single weighted PVC or large Pheasant Tail Nymph alone on the point in the sink and draw style. On dour days this month if sport is very slow try anchoring the boat and fishing a slow sinking line with a Persuader or Black Bear's Hair Lure on the point, with an Invicta or Dunkeld on the dropper. Retrieve these slowly, experimenting at different depths, and you may be rewarded with the odd trout.

Boat fishing — traditional JOHN KETLEY

Dapping

I have chosen to devote this August section to the gentle art of dapping, for two reasons. Firstly because there are more similarities than differences between stillwater fishing in July and August. Secondly, I feel that dapping can on occasion actually be a more effective way of fishing from a boat in our summer months. Perhaps I should add that as this section is designated traditional (that is to say, loch) style boat fishing, it is worth remembering that a considerable percentage of the loch fishing in both Scotland and Ireland is in fact dapping. The large artificials being favoured in Scotland and the natural daddy longlegs in Ireland. So in the hope that I have convinced you, gentle reader, that you ought at least to read a section on the art of dapping, let me hasten to add it will not necessarily cost you any important sums of money, or even waste prime fishing time.

There is not enough room in one section for me to go into the history of dapping, or even to write at any length about how it is practised today in Ireland and Scotland. Instead I shall report on my personal findings while dapping on English stillwaters over the last few seasons.

Starting with tackle, let me reassure you that you probably already possess enough of the major items at least to experiment with dapping the next time you

Alexandra	Allrounder	Blae and Black
	page 146	page 184

| Black Zulu | Bloody Butcher | Coachman |

Coch-y-Bonddu	Dunkeld	Gold Ribbed Hare's Ear
		page 184

Greenwell's Glory	Grey Duster	Invicta
page 158		page 158

Mallard & Claret

Orange John
page 168

Peter Ross

Red Palmer

Short Orange Partridge
page 184

Teal Blue & Silver

Teal & Green

Wickham's Fancy
page 180

Adult Buzzers
pages 142, 184/5

Black Duck Fly (note wings)
page 184

Alder Larva
page 144

Amber Nymph
page 185

Black & Peacock Spider
page 185

Bloodworm
page 185

Caenis Nymph
page 152

Cased Caddis
page 152

Collyer's Nymphs
page 185

Corixa
page 185

Daddy Longlegs
page 185

Footballer
page 186

Fiery Brown Sedge
page 154

Damosel Nymph
page 186

Floating Snail
page 156

Grenadier
page 186

G & H Sedge
page 156

Hatching Sedge
page 186

Hatching Midge Pupa
page 186

Hawthorn

Last Hope
page 186

Longhorns
page 162

Pheasant Tail Nymph

PVC Nymph
page 168

Mating Shrimp
page 186

Mayfly Nymph
page 186

Poly Rib C Pupa
page 170

Pond Olive Spinner
page 187

Persuader
page 187

Red and Green Larva
page 187

Small Hatching Midge
page 187

Walker's Sedge
page 187

Sedge Pupa
page 172

Stick Fly
page 187

Suspender Midge
page 176

Super Grizzly
page 187

Williams
page 182

Tadpolly *page 187*

Ace of Spades *page 142*

Baby Doll

Appetiser
page 146

Badger Matuka
page 148

Black Bear's Hair
page 148

Black Chenille
page 150

Black Ghost
page 150

Black & Orange Marabou
page 188

Christmas Tree
page 154

Concorde
page 188

Church Fry
page 188

Dambuster
page 188

Dunkeld Lure
page 188

Jack Frost
page 160

Goldie
page 188

Jersey Herd
page 188

Leprechaun
page 160

Mickey Finn
page 162

Missionary
page 164

Nailer Fly
page 166

Muddler Minnow
page 164

Mylar Minnow
page 166

Popping Bug

Orange Marabou Muddler
page 188

Pearly
page 189

Pearly Nobblers
page 170

Polystickle
page 189

Ruby
page 172

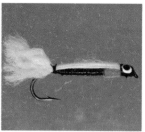

Special Baby Doll
page 174

Viva
page 189

Sweeny Todd
page 189

Squirrel & Silver
page 174

Whisky Fly
page 180

Yellow Hammer
page 182

White Marabou Tandem
Muddler
page 178

Worm Fly

Streaker
page 176

White Muddler
page 189

fish from a boat on a stillwater. Any rod over ten foot long will suffice. It may even be an old glass rod hanging in the garage, and now superseded by your latest carbon delight. It could be a coarse fishing rod more normally used for long trotting, the only important things being that it is fairly long and it has rings and a reel fitting. The day will come when someone develops a rod specifically for dapping and it will have, I hope, a number of refinements no rod currently available can match, but until such a development, start with whatever you have.*

Next you need the simplest of reels to house a short length of blow line. I call it blow line because that is its primary function, to be light enough, and yet wide enough to blow out in a breeze. There are a number of dapping lines on the market, most of which are in violent colours (which seems to me to be the opposite of what is needed), but it is so easy to acquire a 10 yard length of white floss or make up your own from strands of 3lb b.s. nylon that I won't waste any more space on the blowline.

Now all you need are some dapping flies, which poses rather more of a problem. My experiments have proved to me that English stillwater trout seem to prefer dapping flies tied on a short shank size six wide gape hook. While the detail of the dressing can vary considerably, the two essential factors are that it should be very bushy and dance well in the wind. Nevertheless, as my first objective here is to persuade you to try this fascinating aspect of boat fishing, you can start with just two flies something like the following.

Any large (size 6) well hackled Soldier Palmer, plus a Daddy Longlegs, a large Coch-y-Bonddu or a big bushy Zulu. The reason I suggest two flies is that my personal experiments have led me to believe that two dapping flies work better on our stillwaters than the single fly favoured in Ireland and Scotland.

The way to rig your dapping outfit is simplicity itself; just thread your white floss line through a longish rod, attaching the dapping line to a normal fly line for the early experiments. Next tie an 8lb b.s. 3ft leader to the end of the floss and then tie on a 'T' section of 6lbs b.s. nylon to the leader. This piece of nylon also needs to be 3ft long. Make one side of the 'T' piece 2ft long and the other 1ft.

Now you should have a reel with 10 yards of white floss dapping line, utilising the fly line as temporary backing, on a long rod with a leader that suddenly sprouts a left and right dropper, one a foot longer than the other. Put your bushiest fly on the short side and a different pattern on the long side. Next you treat both flies with a floatant, hold the rod vertically, pull enough line off the reel to allow the flies just to touch the water in front of the boat, and drift them out on the wind. By lowering and lifting the rod you will find you can keep one fly permanently on the water's surface, while the one on the short dropper skips and dances around in a most attractive manner. To cover a greater area of water, just lean the rod left or right and the dapping flies will zig-zag to your command. On very gusty days the bottom fly also acts as an anchor for the skipping fly, but will need occasional

---

* John Goddard has now developed such a rod. Designed specifically for dapping, it is 14ft long, with carbon top and middle sections and a glass butt section. The rod, marketed by Efgeeco Products, comes with an additional short handle to convert it into an excellent 10ft boat rod.

drying out with a tissue or salt crystals as it gets dragged under now and then.

So, let's imagine we are out on the water with the equipment working as predicted and sufficient wind to enable us to dance the flies some 15 to 20ft in front of our drifting boat. If the day is a little bright for ideal wet fly fishing, then my experience indicates it could well be an ideal dapping day, especially if it is also comfortably warm. Should there be no sign of rising fish, that again is often the time when dapping works best, so, you see, we are not even sacrificing good wet fly fishing time.

The choice of area to begin our dapping will be partly forced on us by the condition of the wind, but apart from one or two sheltered corners most of the lake is available to us, so we start our drift over an area where we have caught fish before; it is probably an underwater ledge where the depth reduces steadily from 15ft to about 6ft.

Suddenly, and I do mean suddenly, a fish casually porpoises over one of your flies, the fly disappears and your normal reaction whips the fly clean out of the trout's mouth. It is critical when dapping to let the fish take the fly down, out of sight, before you strike. The Irish have a ritual, I have heard, where they say on first seeing the fish, 'Mother of God, it's a trout', and then they strike, thereby building in a delay that enables the trout to take the fly down with him.

Personally I have trained myself, and it's not that easy, to wait until the trout has disappeared and I can see the leader sliding gently down into the swirl made by the fish. Then I just lift the rod in a steady upward sweep and more often than not meet that lovely solid thunk as the hook goes home in one very surprised trout.

By this time I hope you will be more confident about experimenting with dapping and we can move on to fill in one or two gaps in my earlier descriptions.

Naturally, dapping is not a miracle method of fishing, and you could well have little or no success on your first outing or two, but don't be disheartened. On a surprising number of days, dapping can catch as many fish as normal wet fly fishing, and the size of the fish caught dapping is often greater, in my experiences over the last few seasons.

I referred earlier to making your own dapping line, so let me explain how this can be done by anyone who can tie a few ordinary knots. Take about eight lengths of 3lb b.s. nylon, each piece about 10 yards long. Tie them together at each end and there it is! A dapping line that will blow beautifully in the wind, will dry off instantly if it gets wet, throws very little shadow and is virtually invisible against the sky. It will only cost you the price of a 100 yard spool of nylon, and you can make a posher job with the knots if you use super glue to make a loop at each end. Then loop it onto any spare fly line you have on a reel and attach your two dropper cast to the other end.

During my experiments with dapping I have come to believe the trout respond initially to the shadow thrown by the dapping flies more than the actual sight of them. The vast majority of fish I have risen have come from many feet down and with no hesitation they have *gently* engulfed the fly and headed down again in one smooth movement. So don't expect a great big splash when the fish rises, as it all happens in a neat head and tail.

This shadow theory is in no way diminished when one realises dapping is used as the favoured technique in both Scottish and Irish lakes when fishing for salmon and sea trout in crystal clear waters. These fish are mainly lying right on the bottom, and are known not really to feed in fresh water, yet these really large fish come up 6ft and more to take the dap.

Should you have a wife or friend who would like to join you on the boat, but is unable to cast a fly line, then fix them up with a dapping outfit and in next to no time they will get the hang of it. Alternatively, you may suffer from tennis elbow or just the disability of getting older and tiring more easily. Then break up your day by dapping some of the time and save the muscle work for the evening rise. It is also an excellent method of fishing for disabled anglers.

Boat fishing – lures BOB CHURCH

We can suffer from gruelling, sun-baked days in August, but my records show this month has produced quite a lot of specimen sized trout for my efforts, particularly on any wet or windy days which may occur. For some reason, browns begin to take more confidently, but mostly in deeper water. So once again where the large lakes and reservoirs are concerned, a boat will give you a great advantage.

As I study my old diaries, I notice specimen fish have been caught from a number of the larger reservoirs, including Grafham, Hanningfield, Pitsford, Blithfield, Draycote and Rutland, and it is significant that most of these were taken on tandem lures 5 inches long. The tandem White Marabou Muddler has been the most successful pattern, followed closely by tandem Appetizers and Goldies. I even caught a 20¾lb pike at Grafham on the White Marabou Muddler. These should always be fished alone on the point on an 18ft, untapered leader of 8lb test nylon.

On many occasions, browns will take a lure that is running along only inches from the bottom, but will not give that self-same lure a second glance if it is fished two or three feet above the bottom. To achieve this it will be necessary to use fast-sinking lead-impregnated fly lines for fishing at anchor or drifting in water of medium depth, or lead-cored line for very deep water and fast drift fishing. August is a month for searching as much of the lake bed as possible, so I advise fishing on the move. One may drift bow first with the drogue streaming out from the stern, but for fast drifting, which seems to be more effective during this month, I advise the use of a drift control rudder, a method which is fully explained in the opening chapters. However, it should be pointed out that this method is banned on some waters, which I feel is a great mistake. On some waters there are official trolling zones which offer the angler an excellent alternative for fishing these big lures.

Now let us discuss the controversial lead-cored line, which will enable us to get down to the bottom in whatever depth we decide to fish and in addition also ensure that our lures hug the lake bed throughout the retrieve.

The lead core line is really an improvised fly line, and I form a shooting head by cutting 10 yards from a 100 yard spool of American or Canadian special trolling line. Despite the critics' claims to the contrary, this shooting head can be cast efficiently on a slow actioned, powerful 10ft rod. After just one back cast, lever the rod forward and throw the line high, straightening everything out by slowing down the backing with the left hand just before the head hits the water.

After casting about 30 yards or more, if possible, square to the drifting boat, let out more backing to ensure your tandem lure reaches the bottom. You may have 50 yards or so out when it comes to the retrieve and, by the way, a fast one usually works best. When the retrieve is commenced the lure begins its movement by travelling in the opposite direction to the boat, it then accelerates in a big, semicircular sweep before finally being retrieved at the stern of the boat. Just as when fishing with slow sinkers for mid water rainbows, these browns take best as the lure curves around that bend.

Towards the end of the month, if high winds are experienced, you can expect to find plenty of rainbows on or near the surface. Although the surface stripped lure or Muddler is still quite killing, the American Popping Bug often works best of all.

It was Nottingham's Tom Saville who first stressed to me how many fish he and his friends were catching at Rutland in August 1979, all on Popping Bugs. I took Tom's tip, and was amazed at the response from the fish, of which 90 per cent were rainbows. The beauty of this type of fishing is that the takes are so spectacular, and as the rainbows are in perfect condition at this time of year the fight is fast, with plenty of aerobatics. These Poppers are best fished on a floating No.9 shooting head. Cast a long line down wind and retrieve in short, sharp jerks; as the water is forced into the concaved head of the bug it lets off a distinct 'pop', and at the same time creates a substantial disturbance on the surface which attracts fish from a considerable distance.

Bank fishing — imitative patterns
BOB CARNILL

Whereas the fishing in July, during a normal season, can be a reflection of the weather and go from excellent to poor as the heat of the month takes effect, quite the reverse can be expected for August. The start of the month finds us slap in the middle of the period that is quite often referred to as the 'doldrums' — that part of the season when the water temperatures are at their highest and the interest shown by the trout is at its lowest. However, as the ever shortening days of August tick by, the longer, cooler nights begin to bring about renewed activity by the trout, and by the middle of the month, with the doldrums having passed, things are once again beginning to look up. From the middle to the end of the month this change becomes even more pronounced as the weather begins to break up. The falling temperatures and the higher oxygen content of the water seems to sharpen the appetite of the trout, giving the angler a taste of the delights to come during that golden month — September.

At the beginning of the month the very early morning and late evening sessions usually provide the best and most consistent sport, and though August is still a very good month for the Sedge Fly, I have found that it is the smaller flies that score most consistently. And for some reason best known to the trout, pale coloured flies tend to kill the best. The colours that I have found to be most useful are as follows: pale ginger, beige, light grey with a tinge of salmon pink mixed in, and a 50/50 mixture of the very pale fur and the light brown fur that are both to be found on the back of a hare's ear. Any of these colours or mixtures incorporated into one's flies has got to be good medicine for August.

For a very early start — that means arriving at the water just before sunrise — I would usually start by fishing a size 10 bloodworm imitation or a size 10 buzzer pupa (beige or light green) on the point, and two size 10 Beige and Ginger (Olive Midge) Adult Buzzers on the dropper. The fly line I tend to use almost exclusively these days is a No.8 weight forward floater — long hours at the waterside mean countless casts to be made, and consequently much energy being spent. But by using the weight forward line false casting can be cut down by at least 50 per cent, the result being that one feels so much fresher by the time the evening rise comes around.

The kind of spot I prefer to fish during August, particularly for an early start, are the areas where plenty of coarse fish fry can be found. These are usually the sheltered bays and creeks with ample marginal weed which can offer the fry some measure of protection from attack; should the margins drop off into relatively deep water then so much the better, for this is the kind of location where one is likely to encounter the better quality fish as they leave the sanctuary of the deeps to feed in and around the shallows at first light. It should therefore go without saying that one should not be in too much of a hurry to get a long line out — do search the margins thoroughly with your flies first of all.

As the day wears on I would still fish the shallower areas, for even when the better fish have gone off their place is usually taken by the fry-marauding shoals of rainbows, and although these fish are not very often colossal they are well worth taking, usually being very plump and like bars of silver. The beauty of these fry-bashing rainbows is that they are very vulnerable to a small fly or nymph — provided that it is presented properly. One of the most deadly methods that I have found is to drift a trio of size 14s round on the ripple to cover the area of greatest activity. In order to achieve this the leader should be lightly greased along its full length, and then the droppers meticulously degreased. The dropper length can sometimes be very important — it is usually the shorter ones that are the most effective, i.e. anything from 1in to 3in. It can be very tempting to cast directly at the fry-chasers, but one should resist the temptation, the flies will prove to be much more attractive if they are allowed to come round naturally on the wind. Do not be tempted either, to retrieve the flies while using the greased-up technique; simply let the wind do the work and wait for the positive drawing-tight of the line and then set the hook immediately. The most effective flies I have found for this technique and situation have been size 14 winged Gold Ribbed Hare's Ears, dressed with the palest of pale hare's lug, the fur teased well out with the dubbing needle. And the most effective nymph is a size 14 Buzzer Pupa, which once again is dressed very pale, either a buffy/beige or a light apple green. I always fish my Poly Rib Buzzer Pupa for this style of fishing because of the fact that the artificial relies mainly on its looks rather than its movement, and the Poly Rib with its wing cases, etc. is designed especially as a close copy artificial.

During the heat of the day one could do far worse than adopt a roving style of fishing — prospecting in and around the weed beds with either a single Sedge Pupa or a Damsel Fly Nymph. Don't be too put off from doing this because of the absence of rising fish, for more often than not the takes will materialise out of the blue — and sometimes from quite large trout.

The dry fly, too, can sometimes prove to be quite effective during the midday heat, the patterns which I tend to favour have a rich reddy/brown colour — usually a small red sedge or a small dry Wickham's. Once again, it is best to keep on the move when fishing the dry fly, dropping the fly into all the likely looking spots and over the far edges of the weed beds.

The evening fishing for the first part of August can, like July, bring some very exciting sport with the sedge. With so many techniques and patterns to choose from, a sedge rise can sometimes lead to a great deal of confusion for the inexperienced. The first thing that the newcomer should realise is that it is very rare for just one species of sedge to be out on the water at any one time. More likely than not, there will be several species involved during a typical sedge rise, and what's more the trout don't seem to give two hoots which ones they take — being opportunists they appear to take whichever and whatever is the nearest. However, this does not mean by any stroke of the imagination that trout rising to sedge are easy meat. The most difficult task for the beginner is to be able to recognise at what stage the sedge is being taken by the trout — which could be any one of the following. It could be to the rising pupa, the hatching pupa, the freshly hatched sedge as it sits on the surface prior to flight, the stage when the freshly hatched fly skitters over the surface prior to take-off, or to the egg-laying adults as they fly low over the water making frequent dips on and off of the water to deposit their eggs. Once the angler is satisfied that he has recognised the type of rise in progress at the time, he can then commence to fish accordingly. However, it should be borne in mind that as the evening progresses, so the rise forms will change in accordance to the varying activities of the sedge.

A typical early evening rise may well start with a hatch of sedge accompanied by the characteristic boils on the surface as the trout intercept the pupae just a few inches under the surface of the water. This kind of activity should be responded to by fishing one, two or even a complete team of three Sedge Pupae. The pupa or pupae should be fished just beneath the surface with a medium to fast paced figure-of-eight retrieve — for it should be remembered that sedge pupae are quite competent swimmers and their prime objective is to reach the surface as quickly as possible.

Alternatively, the pupa trapped in the surface film and in the act of hatching (transforming) can bring about another characteristic rise form, with the trout's neb breaking the surface of the water as the pupa is taken.

For this kind of rise I prefer to fish a hatching sedge imitation — the Invicta or my Fiery Brown Sedge have proved to be excellent patterns for this particular role. The way I fish the hatching sedge is to present the artificial singly, and to grease the leader up to within an inch or so of the fly. I then tweak the line back with a very slow retrieve, and even at this slow pace the fly will throw up a very enticing bulge. This technique has on numerous occasions given me some very exciting and rewarding sport.

Once the sedge fly has emerged from the pupal skin it is quite likely to rest for a short while on the surface of the water prior to making its first attempts at flying. A trout taking the fly in this position is more likely to show a little more of itself in the way of a 'head and shoulder' rise, which is usually clean cut and not in any way splashy (unless it's an inexperienced stockie, that is!). A standard dry sedge pattern — whose numbers are legion — is the best way to tackle this kind of rise. The fly should be cast delicately into the path of an oncoming trout and allowed to remain stationary — if this has been done correctly and the fly has been refused on more than a few occasions, however, then there are two options remaining. The first is to try giving the fly a twitch or two as the trout approaches; if this fails, then a change of size or even pattern may hold the answer.

The next stage in the proceedings is when the sedge makes its first attempts to get airborne. This can be a cumbersome effort, with the fly skittering across the surface of the water and throwing out a considerable disturbance. The response from a trout to a skittering sedge is usually a noisy, splashy, slashing rise — giving the appearance that it is a now-or-never attempt by the trout to secure its prize. One of the most effective flies to simulate the action of the skittering sedge quite perfectly has to be the G & H Deer Hair Sedge. This fly fished singly on a long leader with twitch and draw retrieves can produce some really spectacular results.

And last but not least there is the rise to the egg-laying female as she flies extremely low over the water — so low in fact that on a calm evening her flight can sometimes be seen to make a slight disturbance across the water. This low flying is frequently punctuated by quick belly-flops on and off of the water — an action which can throw any self-respecting trout into a frenzy. The type of rise stimulated by this kind of behaviour can best be described as an 'arching-leaping' rise, as the trout tries to take the sedge whilst in hot pursuit.

The only hope that one has of simulating even vaguely this kind of action on the part of the sedge, is to mount a Walker's Sedge. This fly has a hackle that is much longer than is normal and is quite stiff to boot. The fly, which should have been given a good dousing in Permaflote and allowed to dry, is fished on the point of a long leader and should be retrieved at high speed. Apart from the speed matching the flight of the natural sedge, it also has the effect of making the artificial stand proud of the water as it skates lightly across the surface on its hackle points. And just a word of warning — be prepared for the fly to be engulfed by the trout during the slight pause between draws.

What has been described above could best be termed as a textbook sedge rise, with everything happening in a set or given order. This can in fact sometimes happen, but more often than not there will be an intermingling of different rise forms, particularly as the evening advances, when stages of the life cycles of different sedges are occurring at the same time. Whenever the beginner is confronted with this situation he should not let the diversity of rise forms confuse or throw him. He should simply stand and survey the water for just a few minutes and pick out the rise forms which are most profuse, and then go ahead and tackle them accordingly.

And as a final note while on the subject of the evening rise, just a few words about the probability of a 'switch' by the trout as they turn their attentions from feeding avidly on the sedge in its many forms, to a 'hatch' or a 'fall' of buzzer. This is a very common occurrence throughout the warmer months of summer and should be anticipated by the angler. The 'switch' is most likely to happen as the darkness descends, which will make it difficult for the angler to spot what is happening. However, his best and most positive indication that the switch has taken place will be that his sedge imitations are being ignored — even though there is a good rise still taking place. The safest bet is to mount both Buzzer Pupa and 'wet' adults on the same leader, for there will be precious little time to spare for further chopping and changing in the failing light. I usually put a size 10 dark Buzzer Pupa on the point — either black or dark claret — and on the middle and top droppers a size 10 Ginger and Beige Adult Buzzer. The flies should be fished just sub-surface with a slow to medium paced figure-of-eight retrieve.

From the middle to the end of August all the aforementioned patterns and techniques recommended for the first half of the month will continue to be effective — if not even more so as the weather and the water temperatures gradually become once again more favourable to the sport. However, there is one other important and exciting species of fly that should be in evidence by now (sometimes perhaps even a little earlier), and that is the large, gangling terrestrial, the daddy longlegs.

As with most large flies, be they aquatic or terrestrial, the trout seem to take a little time before they begin to take them confidently, but once this initial shyness has been overcome, all it needs to set the scene for some very exciting sport is for a moderate blow to come off of some old and established grass or meadowland. The daddies, being feeble and cumbersome fliers, are easily and frequently blown onto the water. This, however, appears to give them little or no concern, for their goodly span of long legs allows them to sit quite happily on the surface of the water without becoming trapped in it. Occasionally a daddy riding the waves thus will lift off for a short and laboured flight, only to drop back again onto the surface of the water and resume its resting position with legs outstretched. It is in this position that the trout are most likely to take the daddy, and it is therefore the position that the imitative bank angler should strive to simulate.

Whereas the boat angler, who will more than likely fish his daddy on the dap or the bob, will tie his artificial with trailing legs, the bank angler should make sure that his artificial has six symmetrically outstretched legs which will give the fly a much better support and silhouette when it is cast out to ride the waves.

A little observation and commonsense are the only requirements needed to help one choose a suitable area in which to start fishing. As already mentioned, the daddies will be blown onto the water from adjacent meadows, grasslands or lawns from whence they were borne. Therefore a wander along the windward shore should soon reveal whether or not this is in fact happening, and also which stretch of bank looks to be the most promising. I mention areas and stretches of bank because on uncrowded waters I much prefer to wander along a selected piece of bank fishing a single daddy on a long knotless leader as I go. I don't necessarily need to witness a trout rising to daddies before I make my cast, for experience has proved that quite often a daddy will produce a rise from what appears to be an empty piece of water.

By the end of the month the lake olive should be starting to put in an appearance again in numbers, which will make them the centre of good if not localised 'rises'. This beautiful upwinged dun will be found hatching-off in the shallower, more sheltered bays and creeks of our stillwater fisheries, and is easily recognised by its upright, sail-like wings.

There are two ways of tackling a rise to a hatch of olives — either the dry fly approach, or the wet. For the dry fly approach, one could do much worse than to place ones faith in a size 12 Greenwell's Glory — winged or hackled, both are excellent flies for the job. And for the wet fly approach, a leader carrying imitations of the lake olive nymph and the hatching or drowned adult can be quite deadly. The nymph is best fished on the point, with a size 12 winged wet Greenwell's Glory on the middle dropper, and a size 12 or 14 winged wet Gold Ribbed Hare's Ear on the top dropper. The leader should be rubbed down with soft waterside mud to ensure a fast penetration of the surface film, and the retrieve should be a medium to fast figure-of-eight. However, as with ALL wet fly fishing, it pays dividends to experiment with different rates of retrieve.

Bank fishing — lures SYD BROCK

The doldrums experienced in July often extend into August, so everything depends on just what weather we get. Although many anglers think twice about fishing during this month, I have caught some of my biggest fish towards mid August. Changeable winds are a good sign; rain can relieve a poor period of warm settled weather. I will settle for anything from high winds to continual rain. This has a tendency to cool the water temperature down and bring the fish back on the feed. The lessons learned in July will put you in the right frame of mind for the early part of August. Another sure sign of August is complete bays covered in algae, when hot weather and very little wind are the norm; but this is not too worrying, for using a slow sink line with a lure with orange in it, such as Whisky, Dunkeld, Streaker, Orange Pearly, or even Jersey Herd, you can still get at those feeding fish just under the layer of algae without the line and lure becoming clogged every cast with this green menace. Many fly fishermen will move away from this situation and fish elsewhere, even if fish are showing, but I prefer to try, at least for an hour or so, before moving to clear water.

During August the fish seem to fall into two categories, the ones that take flies at high speeds, and others that seem to want the lure just trickling along very slowly. Let's deal with the former. Using a floating line, 12ft leader, and size 6 or 8 Muddler or White Pearly, the line is retrieved at what I can only describe as breakneck speed to get the fish to take. If the retrieve is slowed down the result will be a boil at the lure with no take felt, almost as though the fish had too good a look at the lure. The same applies to using a slow sink line with either a Black Ghost size 8, Whisky Fly size 8, or even a black lure such as the Ace of Spades. If these flies get no response then use bright, unusual colour variations, such as the Yellow Hammer or Streaker lures in scarlet, yellow, or even blue. This should do the trick, but if there is no response with these variations then slow down the rate of retrieve. There will always be some incident to show that just what you are doing or have done is right, thereby guiding you on to the correct method of fishing.

My other approach is the slow fishing of lures such as Jersey Herd, green back Baby Doll, or Mylar Minnow, all at size 8 or 10. You will notice that all these lures are what I call tied backs; that is to say all have their feathers or wool tied down just before the bend in the hook, so that the lure retains its original shape whatever speed it is propelled through the water. These can be fished on a slow sink line just above the lake bed at slow even retrieves, with an occasional couple of quick pulls in between then back to the slow retrieves again. In this situation the takes are usually felt with not so much a snatch, but a feeling of everything going taut, almost as though you have hooked the lake bed, but the fish are very quick to let go, so your reactions must be extremely fast to drive home the hook.

Along the same lines but with a slow sink line, a short leader of 7ft and moderate retrieves, I would try a Black Muddler or White Pearly. Fish them just off the lake bed rather than across the surface, as I described earlier. This sometimes produces fish coming short at this time of the year, when all that is felt is a bump on the line, and then nothing — then it will happen again. This means you have selected the right lure colour and size but it is being fished at the wrong speed, so speed up a little — this should then bring results. If not, then slow right down with your retrieves and also change to a much smaller lure — the remedy has to be one or the other.

As this month draws to an end, the browns tend to lose a certain amount of cautiousness, as though they have just been released from a pen. My advice now is to double check those hooks and leaders more often.

9 September/October

The weather

The autumn is now with us, although in good summers we may still anticipate spells of warm, dry weather. The warmth of the sun is now decreasing and the water temperature begins to drop quite rapidly. During September and the beginning of October, depressions are likely, bringing windy, squally weather often accompanied by heavy rain, which can make fishing very difficult and unproductive. However, when we experience those occasional days of warm, cloudy weather with a steady breeze, which often occur during the middle of September, we can anticipate some very good fishing indeed. By this time of the year the trout seem to sense the coming of winter, and will for periods often feed avidly. This is the most likely period of the year to contact some of the larger brown trout, and it will be your last chance, as these will be out of season on most waters by the first day of October. Nowadays most of the big reservoirs remain open to the end of October, but you are only allowed to retain rainbow trout, all brown trout must be returned, as their spawning period is now fast approaching. During the latter part of September and throughout October, evening rises are likely to become less and less widespread, and on cold evenings may be absent altogether. The last two or three weekends of the season are usually very busy, with most anglers having a last fling, and unless you book boats well in advance you are likely to be disappointed.

Boat fishing — imitative patterns
JOHN GODDARD

Most fly fishers seem to agree that September and early October can be a most exciting and rewarding period; by now the water temperature will be dropping and, given reasonable conditions, the trout will often feed throughout the day as if realising that the winter and lean times are ahead. September is undoubtedly the best month in which to catch that really big brown trout, as prior to spawning they seem to become more aggressive and move into shallower water where they can be tempted with patterns in mid water or near the surface. This can also be a most frustrating period, as so much depends upon the weather. The boats will once again be in heavy demand and have to be booked weeks ahead, so that you have to take pot luck with the weather. If you are unlucky you may have to cope with cold, squally wet conditions which can be very unrewarding. Conversely, hit the right day and it will be one to savour through the long winter months ahead.

Insect life is now beginning to wane and there is less variety for the trout to feed upon. It is probably due to this reason combined with their increased aggressiveness that our flies once again become more effective. During the early part of September in the mornings or afternoons some good hatches of lake olives are likely to be encountered, particularly on many southern waters, and as I prefer general drift fishing tactics at this time of year in order to cover as much water as possible I would suggest you concentrate on short drifts in shallower water until you find the fish. Fish a fairly short line and mount a wet Greenwell's or Invicta on the top dropper with a Gold Ribbed Hare's Ear on the middle dropper and a Collyer's Green or Brown Nymph on the point. If olives are not present replace the flies on the middle dropper and point with Midge Pupa patterns, as various species of midges are likely to be present on most waters throughout this month. If no offers are forthcoming, change to a team of Sedge Pupa patterns as there will still be plenty of natural sedges on most waters this month and early October. If all else fails, revert to the method which is often so effective in July when drift fishing and mount a big Palmer or G & H Sedge on the top dropper and fish this well greased, bounced along the surface; even during September this will attract trout to your flies from a long way off. In water up to about 6 ft in depth I find a weighted Stick Fly on the point, combined with the bouncing Sedge as an attractor on the top dropper will often account for some very good browns.

From the end of August through the early part of September many trout will start feeding on the corixidae — these are small aquatic beetle-like insects that are present on most stillwaters throughout the year. While trout are not averse to taking them occasionally all season, it is not until this time of year they seem to concentrate on them to any marked degree. This is probably due to the fact that they are only found in shallow water — less than 3 ft — and it is not until July or August that trout make frequent excursions into very shallow water mainly in search of fry. By the end of August most of the fry have matured and left the shallows and it is then I think the trout switch their attentions to the corixa now present in their optimum numbers. By far the best time to take trout feeding upon them is very late in the evening when it is almost dark. At this time it is not unusual to see very large trout, particularly big browns, chasing them in water so shallow that their dorsal fins and even backs are exposed above the surface. Whilst it is better to fish for them from the bank, they can be taken from a boat and it often pays dividends to bear this in mind when the evening rise is either poor or absent. If you are aware of any very shallow areas on the water not frequented by bank anglers then do give it a try, you may be very pleasantly surprised by the result. Allow the boat to drift quietly into this shallow water and then cast a team of unweighted corixa patterns on a well degreased leader as close to the shoreline as possible. The retrieve should be in long steady pulls with frequent pauses.

Towards the end of September and throughout October the patterns and techniques we used in the early part of the season will once again prevail, although late in the season, and unlike the early part, the trout are just as likely to be found in the shallower water as in the deeps. It is also worth noting that the areas we avoided early in the season, such as deep holes, creeks or inlets of running water, will now prove attractive to many fat, well conditioned trout preparatory to spawning. Hatches of midges, particularly the smaller, darker species, will extend right through to the end of October and under the right conditions will often continue throughout the day but seldom on a large scale. When the trout are feeding on these, they will usually be taking the pupae just below the surface, so a team of appropriate artificials cast quickly and accurately will nearly always produce a trout. The ability to spot these feeding fish will only come with experience; in many cases the only indication you will have is a crinkle in the water, or perhaps a slight variation in a wave or ripple that seems out of character. Such powers of observation when developed can often result in a limit as opposed to a blank.

Boat fishing – traditional   JOHN KETLEY

Loch style fishing in early September can be a strange combination of previous months' techniques, depending on the way those months have fished and on the weather prevailing. If August has been hot and windless, the first change to breezier, cooler weather can produce some remarkable hatches of fly and lots of hungry trout in pursuit of them. If, on the other hand, those brassy hot days continue into September the fly and trout may wait for a change in conditions before they become active again.

For the sake of clarity, I will again assume that September gives us the first gentle change in the weather and a return of proper fly hatches. The early spawning trout should start on something of a feeding spree prior to the physical demands made on them by mating. The trout may also go on, or return to, feeding on coarse fish fry, which I dealt with in my July section.

The likelihood of good stiff breezes will give any of you that fancies it a chance to continue to experiment with dapping. In fact September may well be the premier month for dapping, especially as the trout should be seeing far more large land insects like the daddy longlegs being blown onto the water during this month. All in all, September can be the month of opportunity for the drifting boat fisherman and it will pay to be flexible in your choice of fly, line and even technique.

Early September is, in my opinion, as safe a time as any to take a fly fishing holiday, as it seems to offer good fishing in most of the British Isles. (If such a claim can ever be made about any month in the world of angling.)

I am tempted to spend the rest of my available space writing about various venues in Scotland, Ireland, Wales and England where I have enjoyed practising the loch style of fishing with anglers who were taught that way by their fathers and grandfathers, but there is so much else to cover I have resisted the temptation. For most of September, I would venture forth on any English stillwater with a floating line, assuming there was a reasonable ripple. My long cast would feature a really bushy top dropper, on the middle I would have a buzzer imitation, and for the point a fry-imitating pattern. With such a catholic cast I would expect to find which of these types of food the trout were concentrating on that day and amend my fly selection suitably. Should I find rises came to the bushy top dropper I would put a second but different sedge imitation on the point. If the buzzer pattern on the middle seemed to be more favoured by the trout then I would add another buzzer pattern on the point. Should the trout only be interested in my point fly I would put a second such fly on the middle dropper. Now that may sound like I'm backing all the horses in the race, but it is one of the most effective ways I know of isolating the most likely patterns during a month as complex as September.

There will be days when the trout chase fry for an hour in the morning, suddenly switch to taking sedges in the afternoons and end the day with a grand slam at hatching buzzers. When trout are changing from one food source to another it is only too easy to be catching fish and suddenly find they start refusing artificials they were very keen on only moments before. To flog on trying to make them take is usually a waste of time and a new artificial should be tried.

September must be one of the most rewarding months for fishing a loch style bouncing sedge on the top dropper, especially as it is also the month the large brownies seem to emerge hungry from the depths.

Over recent years I have developed a fly to take advantage of the trouts apparent willingness to rise consistently to a bouncing sedge, especially on warm September evenings. The fly is called the Orange John, and details of its dressing will be found in the reference section (see page 168). The Orange John has a seal's fur orange body and the body hackle will allow the angler to hold the fly almost stationary on the water where it wiggles and rolls with the wave action just prior to lift off. The large front hackle helps keep the fly well up in the water on the retrieve, and if you pull a little harder it will break through the surface just like a hatching sedge. The laid back wing adds to the fly's very genuine sedge profile, which I consider important for those well educated large brownies.

One of the more pleasing aspects of the Orange John in use is the way large browns appear from nowhere and gently head and tail over the fly, neatly engulfing it as they slip back down into the depths.

An old trick, not apparently much used nowadays, is to treat a bushy top dropper with floatant, which allows the angler to skate the bob fly for the entire retrieve; this seems to work very well with the Orange John when the fish are feeding on evening sedges. A second bonus from this device is that it appears on occasions, to bring up fish that take the middle and point flies before they reach the surface.

Towards the end of September the weather may start to get too cool for hatches of fly, and the trout can become very difficult. The most satisfactory solution I have found in these circumstances is to put a small Muddler on the point, a flashy fly like the Dunkeld in the middle, and a fluorescent red tailed Zulu on the dropper. Take your boat to the windy shore and drift onto the bank, retrieving relatively slowly.

This method will usually raise fish to the bob fly. They may take immediately in a porpoise over the fly, or they may be hesitant to take. Should this be the case, lift the bob fly onto the surface and let it move in the wind without retrieving further. This will often persuade the fish to rise again and take properly.

The Muddler on the point can be fished over the shallowest water almost on the bank (assuming you are not disturbing bank anglers) in short sharp retrieves with little pauses between. If any reader feels the Muddler is not traditional enough a fly for proper loch style fishing I suppose I must agree, but no other fly seems to have quite the same action in the water.

By the beginning of October the temperature of the top few inches of water will probably have taken a critical drop and the only answer will be a return to the sinking line. If this weather change happens in September and the fish show less and less I would change to the sinking line earlier. The fly life will virtually disappear and the loch fisher is forced to early season tactics. A slow-sinking line or a sink tip will usually get your flies down those few important feet, but once trout feel that nip in the air they seem to become suddenly torpid, so don't retrieve too fast. The most likely flies tend to be large fry imitations, but a size 10 Zulu on the top dropper can often rise fish from 3 ft down if the surface is not too chilled by a cold wind.

Boat fishing – lures BOB CHURCH

Now comes the most interesting time of the year for me. It is a time when the lure fisher needs to be imitative in his approach because great changes in the food chain are now taking place. The masses of fast maturing coarse fish fry have now left the shallow margins and start showing up in their thousands around every weedy area, valve, aearator tower or boat jetty, etc. These small fish are perch, roach, bream or rudd and they can measure anyting from 2 to 5 inches. Naturally, the most successful lures are designed accordingly. With water temperatures now dropping, fly hatches gradually become less frequent, so trout usually start feeding on these small fish in earnest about the second week in September and this continues until the end of October. I can assure you that both rainbow and brown trout often become preoccupied when feeding upon them, and some of the patterns I have taken big catches on are Appetizer, Badger Matuka, Jack Frost, Baby Doll, Squirrel and Silver, Missionary, Muddler Minnow, Pure White Muddler and Jersey Herd. Normally these are used on a No. 6 ordinary long shanked hook, or, if the fry are large, special extra long shanked hooks up to 3½ inches in length. When dressed correctly these lures give the impression of a 5 inch fry.

For the whole of this back end period we revert to anchoring the boat either over well known deep water hot spots or shallow bays with thick weed beds, which will now hold big trout during the day. Let me quote an example. One of my favourite spots for holding bigger fish, both rainbows and browns, is the aerator tower at Grafham. Usually in September water levels are steadily dropping, leaving the depth of water approximately 25 ft. This tower attracts massive shoals of coarse fish fry. Many times my initial efforts at this now well known hot spot have failed to produce, although the odd trout may be observed following the lure. However, if one is patient and prepared to persevere for up to an hour or two, the trout will eventually start feeding, and then those follows will turn into positive takes.

It is a good idea to anchor about 35 to 40 yards on the upwind side of such a tower. First try the lead core head with a long leader, 6 yards of 8 lb nylon. Take note of the size of fry in the water and tie on something similar in size, colour and shape. Appetizers and White Muddlers are my most successful patterns, and frequently when fishing in such an area with a good boat partner we have had great sport with many specimen sized trout to our credit. It is particularly noticeable that our more successful days have occurred when there has been a good wind blowing.

After casting out a long line which catapults my lure so it lands close to the stone work of the tower, I patiently wait. This is important. The reason is that the fry gather thickly around the tower, keeping close to the stonework, but varying their depths. My lead core line lands and quickly sinks to the bottom. Because of my long leader, my buoyant White Middler is still up on or close to the surface. So there is my crude but necessary lead line, well out of the way. One good sharp retrieve sets my Muddler sinking, or should I say slowly swimming, to the bottom. Many times it never arrives, as a good trout takes it on the drop and is hooked against the pull of the lead line lying on the botton. In the main it is rainbows that take in this way.

If nothing happens on the drop the waiting time has not necessarily been wasted for the fish may have been scared by the initial landing on the lead line. It is the first or second long, slow pull of the retrieve that often tempts the trout to take. If this doesn't happen, start stripping faster. Now watch out for a sharp take from a brownie as the lure changes direction as it leaves the bottom and ascends to the surface. If no takes are forthcoming when the beginning of my shooting head reaches my left retrieving hand, I lift my rod sharply. This accelerates my lure towards the surface area in one clean, fast sweep. Sometimes when big, old suspicious brown trout have been following repeatedly (and they do get wary of those jerks, jerk, jerk retrieves) this action induces them to take right at the last moment, when the lure has almost reached the surface. My tip here is don't snatch your lure out too quickly when fishing this way, and be prepared for a last minute snatch take. The method illustrated here will work over any known deep water fry-holding hot spot on your favourite water.

For the shallower water techniques you need a slow sink, sink tip or floating shooting head. Although there are so many ideal looking weed beds which hold plenty of fry, the bigger fish tend to favour certain spots for their feeding. Therefore, if you are lucky enough to find such a spot in early September, it will produce regularly to the end of October. One of my favourites lies 70 yards off the point of Savage's Creek at Grafham, and it is here that I drop anchor. Once such a hot spot is known, it is best to anchor on it and wait for the trout to come on feed. You will know soon enough when this is. The leaping fry and swirls in the weed beds tell it all.

I have found that the trout feed in bursts, then rest up for a couple of hours, presumably to digest such a wholesome meal as a dozen or more fry. My best catches have come by being patient and quietly biding my time. When they do come on the feed it is not uncommon to catch several large trout in a relatively short period. Stomach content checks are useful at this time as it will confirm whether or not the trout are fry feeding; if fry are present you can attempt to match their size and colour with an appropriate lure.

When there are trout in these weedy areas, it can be annoying when many casts are wasted through fouling weed with the lure. So make sure you have a few floating and slow sinking versions of the patterns I have suggested. Those with white chenille bodies, constructed alternatively with strips of white polythene wound on, for floating versions. Appetizer, Missionary, Jack Frost and Baby Doll for example. A Jersey Herd dressed with buoyant materials seems to work best of all. Those with pulsating marabou wings work best as slow sinkers.

Brown trout become less and less cautious as we approach the end of October, and tend to shoal in some form of pre-spawning courtship, usually congregating in selected areas instead of roaming. However, it should be pointed out that some of these trout may now be in poor condition, and should be returned quickly.

In conclusion, it is only fair to advise you that there will be many occasions when imitative or traditional patterns will prove more effective than lures, especially in late April and May, when buzzers are widespread, and again in July when sedge hatches are at their peak. My tip is, study the whole book carefully, and retain a flexible approach, using the right method at the right time; that way you will be taking home a lot of trout.

Bank fishing — imitative patterns
BOB CARNILL

If ever there is a month to be looked forward to with bated breath then it has to be September, for no other month can wreak such havoc with one's emotions. It can be rewarding, it can be frustrating and it can even be heart-breaking — but rarely is it dull. Given anything like the weather conditions we all pray for our final fling, the trout may well oblige by being on the move from before sunrise until very late evening — stoking-up, as it were, in preparation for the harder months ahead of them. It is also the month when the big fish move in close to the bank — particularly the brownies, attracted, it appears, not only by the abundance of food, but also by a natural desire to be in shallow water as the spawning instinct grows ever stronger with their now raidly ripening gonads.

At the beginning of September the need to be at the waterside before sunrise is not as important as it was in the previous weeks, for good fishing can be expected throughout the day, given anything but adverse weather conditions. However, having said that, it is a time of year when I wouldn't dream of coming to the water any later than first light for fear of missing what could be some of the best sport of the season.

For the early morning sessions I would pin my faith on any of the following patterns. Flies for the point: Bloodworm Imitation, Buzzer Pupa, Cove-style Pheasant Tail Nymph and Orange Shrimp. Flies for the droppers: Dark Olive

(Large Green Midge) Adult Buzzer, Beige & Ginger (Olive Midge) Adult Buzzer (both in size 10), Greenwell's Glory (size 12 winged wet, with a D.R.F. phosphor yellow tag under the tail whisks), and Red or Soldier Palmers (size 8 and 10). Choosing a spot for an early start is not quite so exacting as in previous weeks, due to the shoreward migration of large numbers of trout. However, the spot chosen ought not to be too deep, and if possible it should have a hard or stony bottom; such places can be real hot spots, particularly for big browns. Dam walls and draw-off towers can prove to be good holding areas on some waters and should not be overlooked. But even with a greater abundance of spots to choose from, there are always certain places which will habitually fish better than others. In an earlier chapter I stressed the benefits which can be derived by fishing from points and promontories which overlook bays, creeks or coves, and for September this advice still holds good. Any trout which happen to be patrolling a bay will nearly always use the shallower water of the point as a turning place, and an angler positioned on the point will usually fare far better than another angler who happens to be fishing the bay itself.

The daytime fishing, as I have already mentioned, can be very good indeed but that doesn't mean to say that the trout are by any means a pushover. On the contrary, being plump and summer-fed they can afford to be very selective in what they choose from such a varied platter. It is therefore, up to the angler to be adaptable and observant in order to take advantage of the situation.

If there happens to be a rise taking place any time from sunrise to, say, about mid morning, then it is fair to assume that it will be to a hatch of buzzers. Early September can produce some excellent hatches of chironomids, and like early June quite a number of different species may be involved at any one time. There may be some of the larger, light coloured species from August still in evidence, but in the main the majority of the species will be quite small and drab in colour, many a dark, drab olive. It was for this reason that my Dark Olive Adult (Large Green Midge) Buzzer was evolved, and what a killer it has proved to be for this particular month. For the first week or so of September I will quite often mount a Beige & Ginger (Olive Midge) A/B and a Dark Olive A/B on the same leader, with either a Bloodworm Imitation, Buzzer Pupa or an Orange Shrimp on the point — this combination used at the right time can be lethal. However, there are times during a rise to buzzer when the trout will look at nothing but a buzzer pupa — and how discerning they can be at such times. Size, shape, colour, position and presentation, all have to spot-on if one is to stand anything like a chance with these selective feeders. Perhaps the best advice that one could give for dealing with selective trout is to urge the angler not to continue too long with an unproductive method. Do be prepared to chop and change until the correct combination is found, always keeping in mind that a rising trout is a feeding trout, and therefore it is a takeable trout.

From round about mid morning until mid afternoon hatches of lake olives can be expected, especially in and around the shallow waters of sheltered bays. A hatch of olives can be spotted at a glance, as these beautiful up-winged flies drift gracefully across the surface of the water, their wings acting as sails and pushing them forward on even the lightest of breezes, making them appear for all the world like an armada of miniature sailing craft. In calm and settled conditions, trout may well be observed casually picking off the floating duns one by one in a leisurely, unhurried rise with just the tip of the neb breaking the surface of the water. I can think of no nicer way of tackling this situation than to fish a single dry fly attached to a long knotless tapered leader. And what better fly for the job than a Greenwell's Glory — winged or hackled, both are excellent patterns.

It is at about this time of the day also (mid morning to mid afternoon), that there will be a good chance of some daddy longlegs finding their way onto the water, particularly so if it happens to be a warm, humid day with a moderate to strong south-west wind. Because of the fact that the vast majority of the daddies to be seen during August and September are born and bred on grasslands, and only get onto the water by being blown there, it therefore makes sense for the angler to position himself on a windward shore that has suitable grassland bordering the shoreline. The artificial daddy that I tie for bank fishing has six symmetrically spaced legs of double knotted cock pheasant tail fibres, two forward, two out to the sides and two to the rear, imitating exactly the stance of the natural insect. The artificial should be cast out and allowed to ride the waves — only occasionally give it a twitch to impart a suggestion of life into it. It never fails to amaze me how a daddy floating thus can produce a rise from even the most barren looking stretch of water. And just a word of warning, don't be in too much of a hurry to set the hook when you see your daddy taken by the trout. Allow him to turn down before tightening.

The evening fishing for the first half of September can be quite excellent, with good rises to buzzer and sedge — which more often than not occur simultaneously. When this happens it gives the angler the unique opportunity to choose his most favoured style of fishing, as opposed to having to fish purely to the dictates of the trout. I usually choose to fish buzzer imitations at this time, but as an insurance I also have a spare rod ready and waiting with sedge patterns on the leader, just in case. When fishing buzzers in the evening I nearly always choose patterns dressed on size 10 hooks — both for the pupae and for the adults. A typical leader would carry a black or dark claret Poly Rib on the point, a Dark Olive (Large Green Midge) Adult Buzzer on the first dropper and a Beige and Ginger (Olive Midge) Adult Buzzer on the top dropper. An excellent alternative for the Adult Buzzers on the dropper positions are Mallard and Clarets (size 10 and 12). For the leader on the spare rod carrying the sedge imitations I would invariably choose a team of wet patterns. A Sedge Pupa on the point and patterns to represent drowned adults and/or hatching sedge on the droppers, such as a Fiery Brown on the first dropper and an Invicta on the top dropper. However, there are many excellent alternative patterns that are very attractive to the trout at this time of the year — the Soldier or Red Palmer for one, is particularly effective, as can be a large Mallard and Claret dressed on a size 8 hook. There are of course, many more patterns and techniques which one could, and should, be prepared to use during a sedge rise — however, as these have already been covered in detail in the June, July and August chapters, I feel it only fair to ask my reader to refer to these chapters for any further information on the subject.

From the middle to the end of September, all the patterns and techniques recommended for the first half of the month should still continue to produce good results. It will be noticed, however, that the trout population are now beginning to form into shoals which tend to take up residence in certain areas, or territories; this is particularly true of the brownies. If the angler is to take advantage of this situation and secure some first class sport then he must first locate his shoal. On many waters this is not such a difficult task, because many of the regulars will have already done this and will be at their fishing stations for most of the daylight hours. The most difficult task for the uninformed is to be able to get in on the scene. To be but a few yards from the shoal's edge one may just as well be a mile away, for all the response it brings. But if one is fortunate enough to be able to cover such a shoal then large flies, fished slowly, are the order of the day. A good friend of mine takes large numbers of big brownies each season by fishing a trio of size 8s and 10s Cove-style Pheasant Tail Nymphs. The nymphs are fished on a floating line with the leader thoroughly degreased. After making his cast the line is not retrieved, but allowed to drift round on the wind to cover the shoal — the takes are indicated by a positive drawing tight of the line, which can easily be tightened into.

Trout fishing in October is very dependent upon the weather. Some years, if we are lucky enough to have an extended Indian summer, the fishing may well continue from late September and produce some first class sport, even though the trout are by now quite dark in colour, being fully clad in their courting colours. Large flies fished slowly are still good medicine for the brownies (the season for brown trout may be extended on some waters into October — Rutland Water for example), but for the rainbows a small (size 14 or 12) buff coloured fly, such as a Gold Ribbed Hare's Ear (dressed with the special 50/50 mix of hare's lug mentioned in the August chapter) fished extremely slowly can sometimes work wonders. Quite often, however, we are likely to have really nasty north-east winds during this month, which can mean numbed fingers and poor catches. Not a very nice note on which to end the season.

Bank fishing — lures SYD BROCK

The weather now should be cooling down and down with it goes the water temperature and on come the feeding fish. This will only be stopped temporarily by the occasional heavy rainfall, but in general this is the time to catch some big browns, for they seem to become aggressive and determined to feed on something more substantial than ordinary fly life, often hunting down fry in packs and herding the fry into a solid shoal before launching into them in frenzied attacks.

Once this commences, the rainbows join in as well, and all caution seems to go to the wind. It happens on most waters and the only exceptions would be a very newly opened fishery or some of our smaller waters with no shallows. With careful observation they can be detected by the occasional heavy water movement deeper down and also by the fry leaping clear of the water surface in their attempts to escape. This can be observed especially on waters with an island in the middle, for more often than not the fry tend to congregate and move around the margins, likewise around any obstructions in the water such as bushes, tree roots, sunken hedgerows, etc.

I cannot emphasise enough the importance of continual checking of traces or leaders and the occasional check on the fly for damage; now is the time when your patience and careful planning could pay off with a big fish. My approach is to fish the Muddler or Pearly to rising fish on a floating line in the wake method — the results should produce fish humping out of the water in their attempt to take the lure. If this does not happen wait until fish are showing on the surface in bigger numbers. If the odd fish does show to the wake method but will not take, change to a slow sink line, and offer the Black Ghost (size 8) at medium fast, even retrieves — this should get results. The wake method very often excites fish into action, but sometimes when they are close to the lure they change their minds, whereas the Black Ghost fished medium fast will excite and also bear close scrutiny. I would also use the Black Ghost and streaker at all depths, for they are proven lures, at medium fast retrieves.

I will increase my leader breaking strain from 6 lb to 8 lb at this time of the year, especially when fishing deep. Remember that by now the small fry are much bigger so do not be afraid to up the size of your lures to size 6, or even tandems. The Whisky Fly fished on a slow sink line can also be very effective. This period, when the trout start to mop up the fry, can also be a time of complete frustration. When a big fish shows near the surface you must evaluate the situation quickly, for we know rainbows shoal, but very often a big brown will chase other trout from his territory. One effect can be that you are fishing in an area where if you get a take it will be a big fish, but you will not experience the occasional take from the free feeding and moving fish to give you a guide as to method and fly. It will almost seem that you are fishing incorrectly — this is where patience and experience are the major factor.

I would fish the Mylar Minnow (long shank, size 6) under similar conditions, with 8 lb trace, and cover that area at all depths, speeding up my retrieves and then slowing down with the occasional almost stop/start retrieve, twitching the lure with 6 inch pulls, or alternatively long slow retrieves using the White Pearly to its best advantage, so the eyes are really visible. Most of my lures have eyes and are fish or fry imitators, so I would try any of these in this situation before I would pass by where a big fish has shown. On many waters, in addition to the early morning and evening rises, there is also a time when fish take quite freely for a short period during the day. I know, through experience, that at Farmoor it occurs at 11 am, so just enquire from local anglers if this applies to the water you are fishing.

Finally, lure fishing, if it is correctly executed, becomes not a cast and strip method of catching fish, but an art of searching through a mass of water, feeling and probing, more often for a quarry one cannot see; rod, line and hands working in unison to present the lure at the correct speed of retrieve and depth, waiting for a take to guide us to the correct method on this particular day. The takes can be varied, from a gentle tap, a tightening of the line, or a vicious snatch, according to the speed of retrieve.

As the season draws to a close I will be fishing harder and more often, but always there will be a place in my lure collection for the unusual fly — I have proved time and again the benefit of a slightly different pattern. This applies also to my method of fishing, the fast sink line or the slow sink. It is just when we think we have the answer to the secret of a particular day's fishing that we are proved wrong, and while this can be most frustrating it can also be stimulating as it helps to keep alive our interest in the wonderful sport of fly fishing.

10 Fishing in small waters

RICHARD WALKER

The expansion of interest in trout fishing that began in the mid 1960s has led to the construction of great numbers of lakes of modest size by comparison with the large water-supply reservoirs, though these smaller lakes are highly variable, not only in size but in the nature of the water they contain, the system of management by which they are run, and numbers of other factors. Consequently, it is impossible to indulge in generalisations without risk of misleading the reader in respect of individual waters. I shall therefore try to deal with the fishing in such of these smaller lakes as I know well and have fished often with success.

Methods for clear-water lakes

Let us consider first the lake formed by the extraction of sand or gravel to a depth well below that of the water table. The water in such a lake will usually be very clear and there will be a wide variety of trout food, including snails, shrimps and often sticklebacks, as well as sedges, midges and ephemerid flies. Such waters offer scope for many different styles of fly fishing; dry fly, nymph, midge pupa, conventional wet flies and large lures, if allowed, fished variously on floating lines and lines with different sinking rates, can all be successful at times.

Because trout in such waters find a good deal of their food at or near the surface, many anglers prefer to use methods appropriate to surface activity; that is, floating lines and either dry flies or various nymphs and midge pupae fished just under the surface. This is not only because such methods are more enjoyable and interesting than dragging deep-fished lures on sinking lines, but also because on most days they catch more fish.

It is often possible to identify the kind of insect upon which the trout are feeding, to tie on the appropriate artificial, and to cast it to fish that can be seen breaking the surface. Here we come to a very important difference between one lake and another; in some, it is possible to see not only the surface disturbance caused by rising fish, but the fish themselves, often when they are not actually rising. On other waters, not necessarily bigger ones, it is very rarely possible to see the fish; only the rise forms they produce.

The difference is of vital importance to the angler who likes to catch very large trout. He, if he is wise, will concentrate on lakes where the actual fish can be seen reasonably easily, whether rising or not; where the management policy is to stock with a proportion of big fish, and preferably, where some cover exists on the banks. It goes without saying that the water must be reasonably clear.

The procedure necessary for success with big fish on this sort of water is quite different from that which would be used elsewhere. It consists in equipping oneself

127

with every possible aid for seeing into the water, a hat or cap with a very wide brim or peak, of a dark or drab colour underneath; polarised glasses, and a rigid determination not to look at the sky or its bright reflection. The pupil of the eye expands or contracts in respect of the general illumination, so that the more one can exclude extraneous light, the more deeply into the water one can see.

It is also essential to dress drably and move slowly, avoiding footfalls likely to cause vibration detectable by fish, spending a great deal of time peering into the water. A cursory glance is far from enough. You may peer into a given spot for five whole minutes before seeing a fish that has been there all the time. Practice in seeing fish improves ability; try to make a mental list of all you can see; a pale stone, a twig, a strand of weed, a light patch of bottom; while so doing , you will often realise suddenly that you can see a fish, or perhaps several fish, quite clearly.

The easiest areas in which to see fish are where there are dark reflections from objects, usually trees or bushes, on an opposite bank, from which you may deduce that the best lakes in which to see fish are those of modest size where the opposite banks are not too far away. Hand in hand with the mental discipline that is necessary for avoiding looking at bright light, careful movement and proper investigation of each area by sustained looking, is the most important of all; determination to cast only when you see the fish you want to catch.

All the waters of the kind with which I am now dealing have a bag limit; all of them stock with many, many more trout of modest size, than big ones. If you cast at random, without first spotting a big fish, you will nearly always make a limit bag of smaller fish. Not only are the odds against you through the ratio of small to large fish in the water; small fish are much more willing to swim faster and further to take a fly.

It may take hours of stealthy moving about and peering into the water before you see a big fish. In doing it, you will often be tempted to cast to a fish above average size but much smaller than the size you want to catch. Do it, if you like; but if you do, it will reduce your chances of a big one, first by the disturbance it causes and second by the fact that it is one towards your bag limit. Remember that even when you see a big fish and cast to it, a small one may suddenly appear from nowhere, grab your fly and hook itself before the big fellow can take it.

Really big trout don't often take floating insects, and you seldom have the chance to offer such fish a great selection of different patterns, so for this fishing there is no advantage in having many. The following are those I use:

Mayfly Nymph, leaded on a No. 8 round bend long shank hook.

Damsel Nymph, as above.

Leaded Shrimp, on a No. 10 normal shank hook.

Short Orange Partridge, on a No. 6 round bend.

Short Green Partridge, on a No. 6 round bend.

Black Leadhead, on a No. 10 normal shank.

Orange Leadhead, on a No. 8 normal shank.

Muddler Minnow, No. 6, with lead under the deerhair head.

The two Partridge patterns are used when the big fish are cruising within two or three feet of the surface, the orange version early in the season, the green one later, and specially when algae scum breaks from the bottom, in hot weather, and rises to the surface. The Mayfly and Damsel nymphs usually succeed until their continued use by numbers of anglers on a water have reduced their effectiveness, when the Shrimp can be tried. The two Leadheads, or the weighted Muddler, can be used when either the other patterns are refused or where it is known in advance that they have become less successful by over-use.

Equipment and methods

Casting to visible big fish demands accuracy; handling big fish requires adequate tackle. I think my best course is to say what I use myself; a 9 ft carbon fibre 2-piece rod, designated for 7/8 lines, and a 3½ inch diameter single-action reel with an exposed flange. It carries 12 yards of sepia-dyed No. 7 floating fly line, needle-knotted to 100 metres of 27 lb b.s. flat nylon monofil backing, and the portion of thin level line at its business end is cut back to the start of its taper; a 3 yard knotless tapered leader is needle-knotted there, tapering to 0 x ; that is 7 lb b.s., dry. Attach the fly with a Grinner knot.

I am sure that pale lines scare trout; you may think otherwise, so the choice is yours. I would suggest, however, that where you can see the trout and usually your fly as well, there can be no need whatever to see the line, and you may just as well give my opinion the benefit of the doubt and use a dark-coloured fly line. The leader must sink directly it touches the water, so treat it with a sinking agent; a putty-like mixture of Fullers' earth, glycerine and neat washing-up liquid.

Have a landing net of adequate size with no shiny parts and a handle at least 4 ft long. Do not use flip-up nets; they don't always flip up, and the most likely time for them to fail to do so is when you have a 15 lb trout waiting to be netted. It is sensible to have your net handle terminating in a spike, so that you can stick it into the bank, easily reached and not likely to be forgotten if you move to another place.

Not uncommonly, you will see a big fish cruise slowly past, and by the time you have extended line it will have gone out of sight. Stay where you are; these fish nearly always move on a regular track and if you wait, that fish will return. While you are waiting, extend enough line and let it lie on the water. When the fish appears again, point your rod at the spot where you wish your fly to alight, lift off smoothly and quietly, then make your cast. You should be able to see your fly sinking; it may be taken as it sinks, or it may sink past the trout, in which case you draw it up slowly. If you lose sight of your fly, watch the trout; if it opens and closes its mouth, showing a white horizontal line along its jaw, tighten.

There is no way of predicting what will happen after one of these big fish is hooked. It may thrash about in a bewildered way and come to net quite easily. It may dive deep and swim round in circles until it is exhausted. It may go off at very high speed and run a long way; I remember a 12-pounder that took out all but a foot or two of my backing, and another of 13½ lb that ran at least 80 yards before the end of the lake stopped it; I couldn't. Don't be afraid to apply considerable pressure to a hooked fish at all times except when it is going very fast.

Even after a fish is hooked, avoid letting it see you, as far as possible. Slide the net quietly into the water; if you remain unseen, you may have a chance to net the fish long before it has tired. If some well-meaning fellow comes running along the bank to assist you, ask him to desist!

Other small stillwaters

So much for the waters where the trout can be seen and the big ones selected. Now let's think about the other waters, where they cannot. Catching big ones from these is a matter of chance, but accumulated knowledge can help; if you fish a water often, you discover the areas from which the bigger fish are most often taken, and deduce that these areas are favoured by the bigger fish.

I have explained so many times that white or pale lines can scare trout that I risk becoming a bore about it; but it is a fact that at certain angles of sun, fish and line, these lines in the air can alarm trout, and that can also happen when they are seen against a dark background, which is often present on small lakes.

Brian Clarke and John Goddard have also shown that a white line lying on the surface, outside the trout's window, is very obtrusive. I cannot therefore too strongly recommend the use of dark-coloured floating lines on comparatively small waters, and specially where the angler may fish for an hour or more in one spot. David Jacques drew attention, some years ago, to the fact that continuous casting with floating lines drove trout out of the area, but casting with sinking lines had no such effect. I think that the reason is that most floating lines are white!

Small lakes are seldom so deep as to need a sinking fly line; trout feeding near the bottom can usually be reached with a floating line and a weighted fly, using a leader of suitable length. After allowing such a fly to sink, it is necessary to retrieve at a very slow speed indeed to keep the fly at the required depth, and the usual advice is to watch either the end of the floating line, or a greased length of leader, to detect takes. This may well be good advice for many or even most anglers; I find I can detect these takes by feeling them; either as positive pulls, a gentle jerk, or simply as a feeling of increased weight of the line I am retrieving.

I can see no point at all in watching a greased part of the leader; it is easier, if you prefer visual indication, to watch the end of the floating fly line; and if, as many claim, you can't see that because it is dark-coloured, you can paint a couple of inches of its end with pale orange fluorescent paint.

Among the successful fly patterns for deep fishing with floating lines are the Mayfly and Damsel nymphs, the leaded Shrimp and the Leadheads, together with artificial corixae, leaded Black and Peacock Spiders, Longhorns and a variety of other patterns. It is usually impossible to see what deep-feeding trout are eating, ane one can only try likely patterns and hope that one of them will prove successful. In waters known to hold big trout which, however, cannot be seen, it is sensible to give the latter patterns, tied on good-sized hooks, a trial, using comparatively stout leader points of 6 or 7 lb b.s., before resorting to smaller flies fished on finer leaders. Especially on heavily-fished lakes, the first hour or so of each day is much more likely to produce a big fish than later times, after many anglers have tramped the banks and disturbed the water, often with inexpert casting. We have many novices fishing for trout nowadays, and it pays to steer well clear of those who stamp about, dress conspicuously, and flash white lines back and forth in the air.

So far, I have been dealing with lakes that hold big trout; that is, fish from about 7 lb upwards. There are far more waters in which nothing nearly as big is likely to be encountered; where the majority of the fish are from 1 to 1½ lb, a few from 2 to 3½ lb are stocked, with a very occasional 4 or 5-pounder. It is quite foolish to decry such waters, since they frequently offer more interesting areas of fly fishing, involving more attention to entomology and fly design, often at somewhat lower cost.

Above all, such waters usually provide much more surface activity by the trout, as I said earlier, giving the angler the chance to use his knowledge of insects, allied to skilful casting, often to fish that betray their presence by breaking the surface. The way in which they do this often provides evidence of what they are eating.

A gentle sip or kissing effect usually means that a fish has taken an ephemerid spinner, probably a pond olive, lake olive, sepia dun, claret dun, or, on some waters, a spent mayfly.

Fish moving upwind, showing tips of dorsal fins and tails, and barely breaking surface with their mouths, are probably eating midge pupae.

A slashing rise, often accompanied by a furrow in the surface, means the trout are either eating sedge pupae rising to hatch, or taking the winged sedges; it is easy to see which is happening.

Trout cruising around, apparently aimlessly, rising frequently with a modest disturbance of the surface, are eating caenis; when these little insects are very profuse, trout may swim round with their noses above the surface, gobbling up the caenis continuously.

Calm patches in a ripple, suddenly appearing and spreading, indicate nymphs or pupae being taken a foot to three feet below the surface, as they rise to hatch, or sometimes, where corixae are numerous, the trout intercept them as they rise to collect air, producing a similar effect. In calm waters, this activity is much more difficult to spot, but careful watching may reveal small vortices or miniature whirlpools, or a piece of floating weed or leaves may suddenly rotate. It will be appreciated from the above, I hope, that careful and prolonged scrutiny of the water is of great value, and much more likely to bring success than random casting. Good observation not only helps the angler to choose the right fly, but also tells him where to cast it, and often enough, how to move it.

On large lochs, lakes and reservoirs, it is common practice to fish two, three or even four flies, usually all different, at once. This is forbidden on most small lakes but even where it is allowed, I do not recommend it. It increases the incidence of tangles, it makes accurate casting more difficult, it may lead to one fly in a fish and another in weed, snags or even landing-net meshes or, worst of all, two fish hooked at once, which usually means losing the larger, if not both, specially where selective feeding by the trout has compelled the use of small flies and fine nylon.

Equipment and methods

We must now consider what equipment to choose for this kind of water; that is not easy, because the size of the water and the presence or otherwise of bankside cover has to be taken into account. On lakes of modest size with good cover, long casting is not necessary and a rod of 9 ft, carrying a No.6 line, will provide easy casting and delicate presentation, while reducing the risk of breakage of fine leader points, perhaps down to 2½ to 3 lb b.s. Somewhat larger waters with little or no bankside cover, resulting in the fish being driven well out by anglers on the banks, will usually require much longer casting, and then the rod and line I recommended for the big-fish waters is more suitable, remembering that with it, a leader point of less than about 4 lb b.s. is risky.

I can see no advantage in the popular double-taper line for any kind of trout fishing; anglers who dislike handling monofil backing can use forward-taper lines with either the standard 30 foot belly or, if their casting ability is exceptional, the so-called long-belly forward tapers. I have no difficulty in handling a 12-yard fly line backed with monofil, and it saves me half the cost of fly lines, but I appreciate that personal preferences are important; a man will not catch fish so well if he is unhappy with his equipment.

So — we use a single fly, which we will often cast to fish that we have located, rather than indulge in random casting. Furthermore, we will frequently use a fly chosen as the result of observation of what the trout are taking, or most likely to take.

If there is a breeze, it is best to take up a position, if possible, so that casting is done crosswind and obviously it is far better if the casting arm is on the downwind side of the angler. The fly is then drawn across the line of movement of the trout, which, in a breeze, move upwind. When they reach an area where food has become sparse, they turn downwind and swim quickly back from whence they came, usually at a depth of several feet, ignoring for the most part any food items until they reach the downwind end of the area of water in which food is profuse. They then turn again, come up to the surface or near it, and cruise upwind again, feeding as they go. Usually, in a well-stocked water, there will be numbers of trout in a feeding area, all behaving in the same way. Consequently, the fly cast crosswind and drawn back is likely to cross the tracks of several fish and if one refuses it, another may take it. Also, the fish see the fly in side elevation, and any that take it are likely to be hooked firmly in the corner of the mouth. There is never any difficulty in detecting a take when fishing in this way; often the fish hook themselves.

In a stronger breeze, a cast can be made crosswind and the effect of the wind on the floating line used to move the fly in an arc, but winds strong enough for this are not encountered on more than one day in three on small lakes and it is therefore necessary to retrieve. Do not be afraid of moving such patterns as Midge Pupae, Sedge Pupae and ephemerid nymphs quite quickly. I do not mean they should be stripped in really fast, as is often done with large lures, but they can be moved a good deal faster than their natural prototypes, and to do so usually increases their attraction for the trout.

Particularly when fishing the artificial midge pupa, it is important to retrieve fast enough so that the fly is as near to the surface as possible, without actually breaking through and causing a wake. With Sedge Pupae and ephemerid nymphs, a slower retrieve is needed, with pauses to allow the fly to sink a foot or so between pulls.

Anglers are commonly advised to fish midge pupae and sometimes other insect-imitating wet patterns, on leaders greased to within an inch or two of the fly, and to move the fly only in a series of almost imperceptible twitches. It is true that such tactics will catch a few fish at times, but floating leaders often alarm trout, specially in sunshine and when cast over shallow water, and I know I catch far more with a leader carefully treated to ensure that it goes below the surface directly it reaches it.

Another common piece of advice is to use very long leaders, from 15 to 20 ft. I hardly ever use one longer than 10 ft. As I have explained, for big fish I use a one-piece knotless taper 9 ft long; but on waters holding smaller trout, there is a foot or so of 25 lb b.s. nylon needle-knotted to the fly-line, and then knotted in turn, to the thick end of a knotless tapered leader. If for any reason I wish to use a finer point, I add it to the thin end of the knotless taper, which usually tapers to 1x (6 lb b.s.) or 2x (5 lb b.s.).

If the double Grinner knot is used, differences in thickness far greater than would be safe with a Blood knot can be tolerated and it is quite all right to step down from 5 lb to 3 lb for the 18-inch level point.

Dry flies and sunk flies

There are times when a dry fly can be most effective, though I have never found any imitations of small ephemerids as effective on still waters as they are on rivers, and while imitations of midges in their winged stage, fished dry, do catch fish, they usually do so just as well, if not better, when fished sunk. The dry flies that catch most fish for me from still waters are, first and foremost, imitations of sedge flies, followed by copies of terrestrial insects; daddy longlegs, white moths, drone or hover flies, and, where the naturals are common, the hawthorn fly and the heather fly or, as it is called in Scotland, the Bloody Doctor.

It has to be admitted, however, that there are times, by no means rare, when trout will come up and take almost anything that floats. If you make a very simple fly consisting of a pea-sized ball of expanded polyethylene impaled on a suitable hook, cast it out and sit waiting, a trout is quite likely to come up and take it. The frequency with which floating cigarette filter tips are taken is ample evidence that trout will take surface matter of all kinds.

However, when winged sedges are active, or the various terrestrial insects are seen about, it is obviously sensible to fish imitations of them, either allowed to sit floating without being moved, or drawn across the surface, in the case of sedges or white moths, where the real insect is capable of such movement. The Daddy, the Hawthorn Fly, the Bloody Doctor and the Drone Fly are not and should be fished static.

Even when fishing dry flies, the leader should sink — all of it. This means that the fly will be pulled under when retrieved or lifted off, but if it has been proofed in a suitable dip-in waterproofing liquid, a couple of false casts will ensure that it floats again.

The willingness of trout to take flies floating statically at the surface is matched by equal willingness on their part to pick static flies from the bottom, despite much argument to the contrary. It is a rather dull way of fishing, at least until a fish is hooked, and I do not advocate it as a regular practice, but when the casting arm tires, or it is time for refreshment, it is worth tying on a suitable fly, casting it out a little way, preferably where the bottom is clean, and letting it sink. The rod can be rested on one's bag within easy reach, with the reel handle upwards and the check, if adjustable, set lightly.

I find the most suitable flies are tied with stiff cock hackles at both head and tail, with a ribbed body between; colour seems to matter little. If you have no such special patterns, a good-sized Dambuster will do. The object of the 'fore-and-aft' hackles is to lift the hook above the bottom and prevent it from catching débris, but just as trout will take all sorts of floating objects, so they will pick up anything on the bottom that may arouse their interests, and in the absence of special patterns for fishing static on the bottom, any fly is quite likely to catch a fish.

Traditional wet flies

We must now consider the value of traditional wet flies which were at one time the automatic choice for fishing lakes. Such patterns as Peter Ross, Butcher, Mallard and Claret, Blae and Black, Woodcock and Yellow, Teal Blue and Silver and Alexandra found a place in every lake-fisher's fly box. Some of them are still effective, designed as they originally were to imitate various items of trout food. Down the years they have been standardised for mass production to the extent that if they were all dyed black, you could hardly tell one pattern from another; but many still retain the basic recognition points that signal food to the trout. Among the more useful are Invicta, Mallard and Claret, Williams' Favourite and Grouse and Orange; the first and last will often catch well when sedges are about and the middle two when midges, or buzzers, are seen in numbers.

Lures

So far, we have been talking about either trout that are feeding at or near the bottom, or those that are clearly feeding at or near the surface, when it is not very difficult to decide what they are eating. We may also meet conditions when neither bottom fishing with weighted flies nor surface and near-surface patterns seem appropriate; fish are cruising, apparently aimlessly, feeding on nothing in particular or in any special way.

This is when fishing a large lure, where allowed, may catch some fish. Multi-hook patterns are usually forbidden on the smaller lakes, but many allow big single-hook flies up to size 6 or 8. These can be fished on floating lines, but more often a sinking line works better, its grade depending on the depth of the water. For shallow lakes, use a slow sinker; for deep water, a faster sinker. The big fly is cast out, given time to sink, and then retrieved — usually — quite fast. Useful patterns are Sweeny Todd, Whisky Fly, White Lure, Mrs Palmer and Muddler Minnow, though there are literally hundreds more, any one of which may succeed.

It seems likely that these flies arouse either curiosity, aggression or defence of territory; the fact remains that they are often successful, though their use demands little knowledge of trout behaviour or diet, and is therefore far less interesting to the thoughtful angler. The man who seeks the most rewarding sort of trout fishing will fish lures only when no other method produces results, and then only when he can do so without reducing the chances of success of other anglers fishing nearby; while long casting with lures on sinking lines may often catch fish, it may also frighten them, and alarm started in one place may spread a long way. This is hardly the place to discuss angling etiquette, but perhaps, with so many beginners in trout fishing, I should suggest that when one sees other anglers fishing imitative fly patterns on floating lines, one should not commence to fish a large lure on a sinking line anywhere near them; and if they are seen to be catching fish, it will be a hint to the novice that lure fishing is not in any case the preferable method.

Coloured water

There is one more kind of small lake, or perhaps a condition found on some small lakes, with which it remains to deal. This is deeply coloured water, often produced by excessive suspended algae growth but sometimes by mud washed from the banks by rain, or carried in by a feeder stream. A few lakes hold bream or carp as well as trout, and these fish can stir up a great deal of mud.

In conditions of this kind, it may be necessary to fish flies chosen primarily for visibility, which means orange or yellow in greenish water, and black in muddy water; and also to choose a pattern which is large and can be fished slowly, so that it spends longer within sight of a trout. That means fine soft hair for the wing which should be longer than usual for a given size of hook; flexibility increases as the cube of the length, so a wing twice as long is eight times more flexible, important for a slow-fished pattern.

Water is seldom nearly as muddy or alga-stained as it looks; if you dip out a glass jarful from it, you can see that it is actually much clearer; but even so, trout cannot see nearly so far through it as they can through clear water, and it is wise to take that into account in your choice of flies and technique for fishing them.

Concealment

The ability of trout to see brings me to the matter of concealment. No water is so muddy or clouded that fish cannot tell if an angler moves between them and the sky. They always know when some of the light reaching them has been interrupted. If the water is clear, they can not only see the angler against the skyline, but also if he contrasts with backgrounds of other sorts. It is therefore quite amazing to observe how little attention stillwater trout fishers pay to this. In river fishing, trout fishers are very careful indeed to avoid scaring their quarry, but on lakes it is common practice for an angler to stand bolt upright, not even taking advantage of what cover, or outline-concealing background, may be available. In addition, garish clothing seems to be more and more fashionable at the waterside. This happens despite the fact that whereas in a river the trout are all headed upstream, in a lake they may be swimming in any direction and are therefore much more likely to see and be alarmed by a man on the bank.

Since most lakes of the kind we have been discussing are quite heavily fished and are of modest size, it takes only one or two fish-scaring fools to reduce greatly the chances of success of all the other anglers present. Often, the only course left open for you is to fish as far away from such people as possible, even if that means choosing a relatively unlikely spot. At least the fish there — if any — will not be alarmed, though if you catch one, it is more than likely that one of the fish frightening gentry will come pounding along the bank to net it for you, or to enquire which fly you were using.

It is necessary to avoid becoming angry and therefore to adopt a philosophy which regards the fish-frighteners as a part of the sum of handicaps, which include adverse weather, excessive weed, badly-tempered hooks and all the rest!

Think about it

Finally, it is most important to understand that each lake must be considered on its own merits; what succeeds on one will not necessarily succeed on another. In particular, the nature and variety of trout food may differ very considerably. I know one small lake where pond olives hatch about midday on most days, and their female spinners return to the water to lay their eggs in the evening. Imitations of this insect, in all its forms, do very well on this lake, but there are many more lakes where pond olives are never seen.

Some lakes hold sticklebacks and the fry of coarse fish, which trout, specially brown trout, can be seen chasing, usually close to the bank. Judicious fishing of such patterns as the Polystickle can be very successful there, but useless on other waters where there are no small fish. Lakes also vary greatly in respect of surface and bottom feed. In some, huge quantities of snails inhabit the bottom, covered as it usually is in that case with silkweed, and then deep fishing will often be necessary. On other waters, most of the feed is at or near the surface.

It must also be realised that trout behaviour varies greatly with changes of weather, not only from day to day but sometimes from hour to hour. This is convenient for the angler who catches nothing, as there is always something for him to blame. In fact, catching trout is seldom impossible. I remember a day on which catching trout seemed to be so. At the end of it, a dozen of us were assembled in the Fishing Lodge, all without a single fish. I was rash enough to say, 'I don't believe anyone could have caught fish today!' The words had hardly left my mouth when in came the late Cyril Inwood with eight trout, the smallest over 4 lb and the largest over 6.

If you are not catching trout, try always to believe that they can be caught, if you could only find the right fly, or the right method, or the right place to fish. Never think it impossible to catch some. Expect some days to be more productive than others, but be sure that your average catch is a fair measure of your angling ability. If you want to catch more fish, you have to be a better angler; better at casting, better at observation; better at concentration and self-discipline. Success in fishing, despite popular belief, is not a matter of luck. Good luck may help you catch fish you didn't deserve, bad luck may lose you fish you deserved to catch, but over the months and years, the bad and the good luck balance one another, and what is left is what you have earned.

11 Step by step tying instructions

With illustrations by Ted Andrews

List of 40 patterns in alphabetical order

Ace of Spades DAVID COLLYER

Hook	D/E Long shank 6 to 12
Silk	Black
Rib	Oval silver tinsel
Body	Black chenille
Wing	Black hen tied matuka style
Over wing	Dark bronze mallard
Hackle	Guinea fowl

1 Rib tied in, chenille body wound
2 Hen hackle (wing) tied in by the butt

3 Rib taken through the hen hackle and secured
4 Over wing and hackle fibres added

Adult Buzzer (Large Ginger)

BOB CARNILL

Hook	10 (standard shank or Yorkshire Sedge hook)
Silk	Orange or golden olive
Abdomen	Underbody hot orange swan herl, ribbed closely with stripped peacock eye quill, dyed ginger
Wings	Cock hackle points, dyed light blue dun
Thorax cover	Web of hen secondary feather, dyed gingery orange
Thorax	Beige/brown fur
Hackle	Pale ginger or honey hen

1 Silk taken well round the bend and a stripped peacock quill tied in. Length of orange swan herl then tied in
2 Herl wound forward to the point shown and secured. Body neatly ribbed with close turns of the peacock quill
3 Wings tied in as shown

4 Thorax cover tied in, silk dubbed with beige/brown fur
5 Thorax formed. Thorax cover brought over and tied down
6 Hackle tied in and wound. Hackle fibres swept down and secured with two turns of silk to form legs

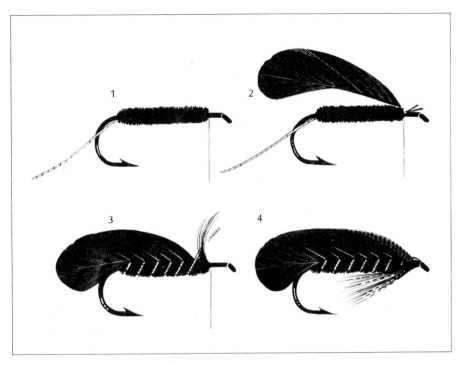

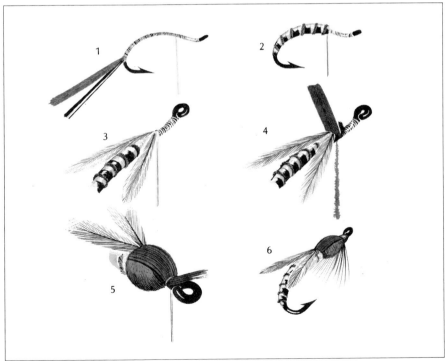

Alder Larva STEWART CANHAM

Hook	8 or 10 Partridge lure hook
Silk	Olive Danville's pre-waxed
Rib	Gold wire
Body	Ginger seal's fur
Wing case and back	Brown raffene
Thorax	Medium olive seal's fur
Underbody	Lead wire
Tail and gills	White marabou
Hackle	Brown partridge

1 Double layer lead wire tied in, the silk run up and down in random turns and varnished
2 Bunch of marabou tied in, forming tail of ½ to ⅜ inch length, forward fibres separated with figure of eight whipping
3 Raffene tied along back of shank, silk run back to the bend. (The marabou fibres are held backwards, still divided.) Gold wire tied in at the bend. Silk dubbed with body fur and wound forward to point shown
4 One bunch of marabou strands gathered, spun into a rope, and stroked so that the fibres are at right angles to the strand

5 Marabou rope laid alongside body and tied off at the shoulder. Other side treated similarly. (Trim waste marabou.)
6 Raffene stretched over the back of the fly and secured at the shoulder. Rib carefully taken up the body, between the marabou fibres (not trapping any), seven or eight turns. Rib secured at the shoulder and trimmed
7 Silk run forward to eye in tight turns. Silk dubbed with thorax fur
8 Thorax formed, back to the shoulder, brown partridge hackle tied in and wound
9 Raffene folded back over the thorax, secured and whip finished, behind the thorax and hackle. Then varnish

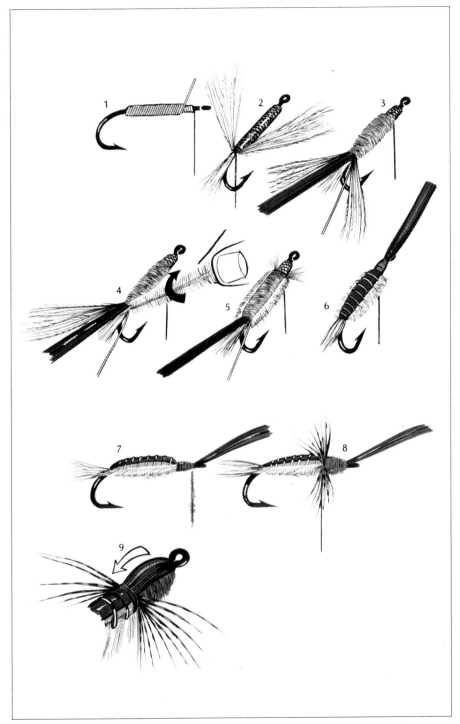

The Allrounder JOHN KETLEY

Hook	Down eye 10
Silk	Black
Tail	4 fibres of honey hackle
Rib	Flat mylar (gold side)
Body hackle	Honey cock
Wing	Rolled teal, strongly barred
Hackle	Honey (dry fly)

1 The tail fibres are tied in, followed by the body hackle and the mylar rib
2 The body hackle is wound to the head, and then ribbed with the mylar, which is tied off and trimmed
3 The wing is added
4 The hackle is tied in

Appetizer BOB CHURCH

Hook	D/E Long shank 6 to 8
Silk	Black
Rib	Silver tinsel
Body	White chenille
Wing	White marabou herl, large spray
Over wing	Natural grey squirrel tail
Throat hackle	Orange, green and silver mallard fibres, mixed
Tail	As for throat hackle

1 Tail fibres tied in, silver tinsel and chenille body tied in
2 Body wound forward and ribbed
3 White marabou wing tied in, throat hackle fibres tied in
4 Natural squirrel overwing tied in

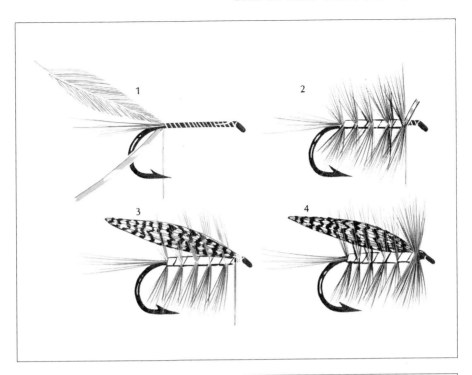

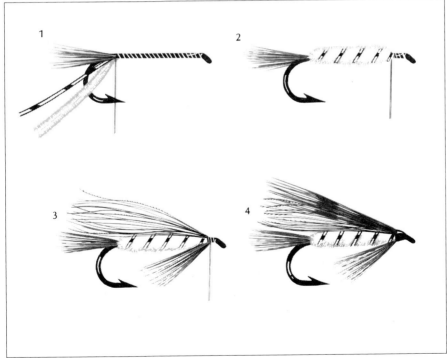

Badger Matuka STEVE STEPHENS

Hook	10, 8 or 6 Long shank
Silk	Black
Rib	Silver wire
Body	White chenille
Thorax	Orange wool or chenille
Wing	Two or three pairs of well marked badger hen hackles
Hackle	Hot orange cock

1 Rib tied in at bend, chenille body wound forward and secured at the shoulder, thorax added
2 Paired badger hackles tied in at the butts

3 Rib taken carefully through the feather fibres up the body and secured at the shoulder (matuka style)
4 Throat hackle added

Black Bear's Hair Lure CLIFF HENRY

Hook	D/E long shank, 8 or 10
Silk	Black
Rib	Oval silver tinsel
Body	Black seal's fur
Wing	Thin strip of black bear skin with hair attached, cut a little longer than the hook shank

1 Cut the bear skin
2 Rib tied in at bend, dubbed seal's fur body wound to eye
3 Wing placed in position, secured with

tight turns behind the eye. Rib taken firmly up the body and between hair fibres
4 Secure and trim waste tinsel

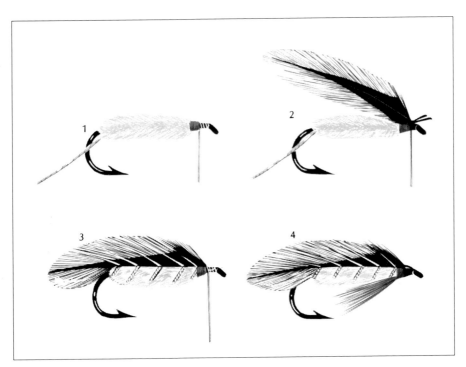

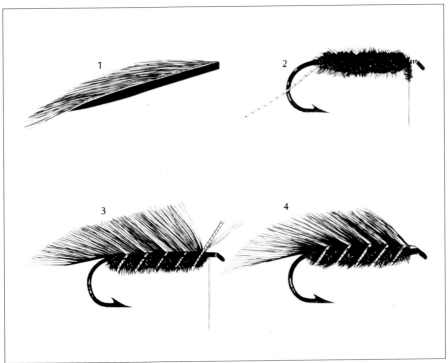

Black Chenille BOB CHURCH

Hook	10, 8 or 6 long shank
Silk	Black
Rib	Silver tinsel
Body	Black chenille
Wing	Four matching black cock hackle feathers
Throat hackle	Black hackle fibres
Tail	Black hackle fibres

1 Tail, rib and chenille tied in
2 Chenille body wound forward and ribbed

3 Wing formed from two pairs of matched hackles, and tied in
4 Throat hackle added

Black Ghost SYD BROCK'S VERSION

Hook	Long shank, 6 or 8
Silk	Black
Rib	1/16" wide strip of white stiff plastic tape
Body	Black stretched pvc or black wool
Wing	Four matched white cock feathers
Throat hackle	Yellow cock hackle fibres
Tail	As for throat hackle

1 Tail, and white and black plastic strips tied in
2 Body wound forward and ribbed.

Throat hackle fibres added
3 Wing tied in

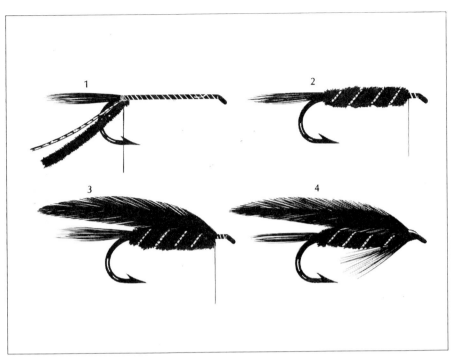

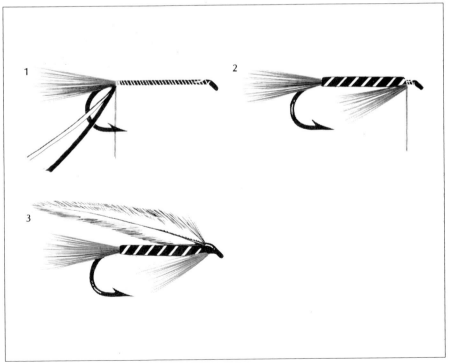

Caenis Nymph BOB CARNILL

Hook	16 to 14
Silk	Brown
Tail	3 fibres from brown partridge hackle
Rib	Stripped peacock quill
Body	Strip of drab brown herl (dyed swan, goose or heron)
Wing case/thorax cover	Quills from narrow side of heron primary
Thorax	Hare's ear
Legs	Partridge fibres

1 Tail, rib and body herl tied in (inset shows detail of tail formation)
2 Body wound forward and ribbed
3 Heron quills tied in as shown, concave faces towards hook shank
4 Silk dubbed with hare's fur

5 Thorax formed and thorax cover brought forward and secured. Partridge legs tied in
6 Shows shape of finished fly, with trimmed quills

Cased Caddis BOB CARNILL

Hook	Long shank 10 or 12
Silk	Black
Rib	Silver wire
Underbody	Lead wire
Body (case)	Hare's ear fur, well mixed
Body (larva)	Swan herl (white)
Hackle	Small black hen

1 Lead underbody wound on and secured with random turns of silk. Silk dubbed with hare's fur
2 Dubbed silk wound forward to position shown. Rib tied in. Swan herl tied in

3 Swan herl wound forward to position shown and ribbed
4 Hen hackle tied in and wound

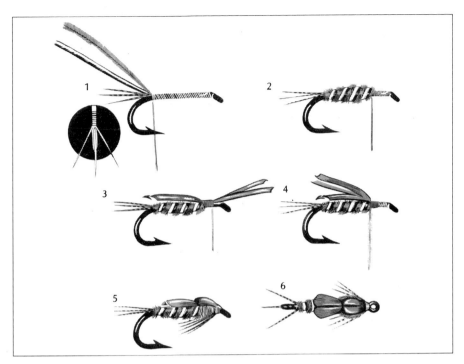

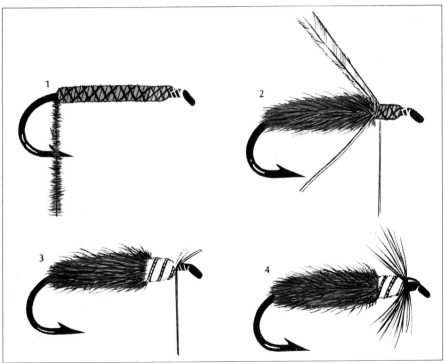

Christmas Tree LES LEWIS

Hook	10, 8 or 6 long shank
Silk	Black
Rib	Silver oval tinsel
Body	Black chenille
Collar	Red fluorescent wool or floss
Wing	Generous spray of black marabou
Tail	Fluorescent green wool or floss

1 Tail, rib and chenille tied in
2 Body wound forward and ribbed

3 Throat hackle added
4 Wing tied in

Fiery Brown Sedge BOB CARNILL

Hook	8 to 12
Silk	Brown gossamer
Rib	No.14 oval gold tinsel
Body	Fiery brown seal's fur
Wing	Dark bronze mallard (two layers, folded)
Hackle	Rich brown hen

1 Rib tied in
2 Silk dubbed and wound forward, neatly ribbed
3 Wing of folded bronze mallard tied in

4 Hackle given four or five turns, tied in and waste trimmed. Hackle fibres sloped slightly rearwards and secured with two or three turns of silk

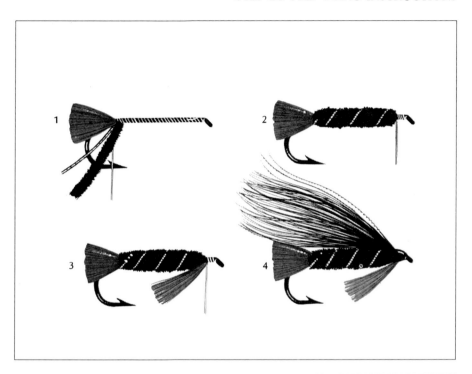

Floating Snail CLIFF HENRY

Hook	D/E wide gape 10 to 14
Silk	Black
Body	A pear shaped section of cork glued around hook shank
Body covering	Partly stripped bronze-green peacock quill

1 Shaped cork body slit along its centre and glued securely to hook shank. Herls stripped to two-thirds of their length, and stripped ends tied in at the hook bend

2 Herls wound forward up the body and tied off against the cork at its widest part. Trim waste herl. Secure silk behind the eye and whip finish
3 Drench the body in varnish
4 Position of the snail as it is fished

G & H Sedge

JOHN GODDARD & CLIFF HENRY

Hook	D/E long shank 8 to 12
Silk	Green
Body	Spinnings of deer hair
Underbody	Dark green seal's fur
Hackle	Two rusty dun cock hackles

1 Tying silk tied on at the bend
2 Separate length of tying silk, about 8 inches, tied in at its mid point at the bend of the hook
3 First spinning of deer's hair placed at the bend
4 Shows spinnings of deer hair all the way along the shank. Silk secured with a half-hitch after the final spinning. Deer hair trimmed approximately to the shape indicated by dotted lines (as close as possible under the shank)
5 Shows rear view of trimmed body — note the triangular section. Pair of silk strands each dubbed with underbody fur

6 Dubbed silks brought down and twisted into a rope, taken underneath the shank, and secured with tight turns behind the eye. Waste dubbed silk trimmed
7 Matching hackles selected, good proportion of butt fibres stripped away, to leave long quills (which form the fly's antennae). Hackles tied in with quills forward over the eye. Wind the hackles and tie off. Trim waste
8 Shows hackles with upper fibres trimmed off, leaving downward facing "legs"

156

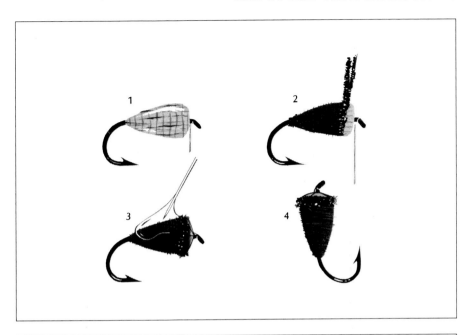

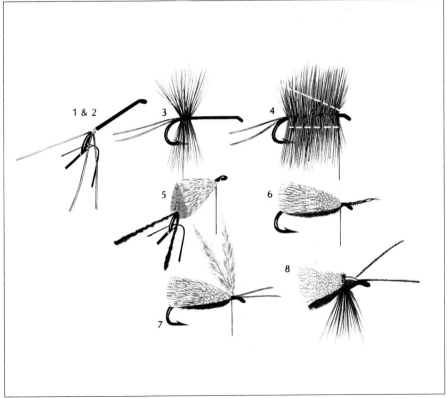

Greenwell's Glory JAMES WRIGHT

Hook	D/E 10 to 14
Silk	Yellow, well waxed with brown wax
Rib	Fine gold wire
Body	Formed from the tying silk
Wing	Paired slips of blackbird wing
Hackle	Coch y bonddu

1 Silk taken to bend and rib tied in
2 Slim tapering body built up from turns of tying silk, and neatly ribbed

3 Matched slips of blackbird wing tied in
4 Hackle tied in and wound

Invicta JAMES OGDEN

Hook	D/E 10 to 14
Silk	Brown
Rib	Oval gold tinsel
Body	Yellow dyed seal's fur
Body hackle	Red game cock
Wing	Hen pheasant centre tail
Throat hackle	Blue jay
Tail	Golden pheasant crest feather

1 Tail tied in. Rib tied in, and silk dubbed with body fur
2 Body formed and hackle tied in at shoulder
3 Hackle palmered to bend and

secured with rib, which is then wound forward to the shoulder
4 Throat hackle tied in
5 Wing tied in

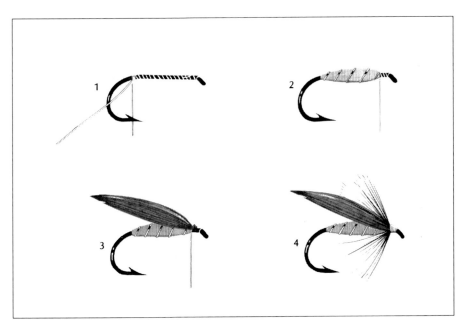

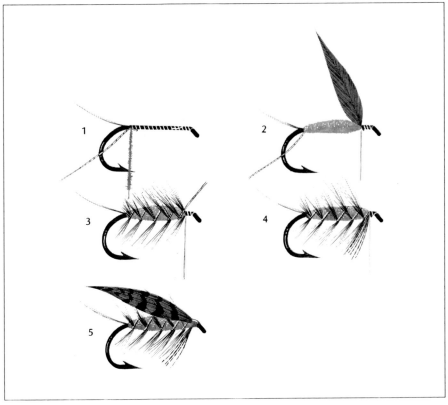

Jack Frost BOB CHURCH

Hook	D/E long shank 6 to 10
Silk	Black or white
Body	White Sirdar baby wool covered by a 1/8″ wide strip of polythene
Tail	Crimson wool
Wing	A generous spray of white marabou
Hackles	Long fibred crimson cock, followed by long fibred white cock

1 Tail tied in, followed by a length of white wool and then the polythene strip
2 Body wound forward, and covered with polythene strip

3 White marabou tied in sloping back over body. Crimson and white cock hackles tied in
4 Shows hackles wound

Leprechaun PETER WOOD

Hook	10, 8 or 6 long shank
Silk	Black
Tail	Green hackle fibres
Body	Fluorescent lime green chenille
Rib	Silver tinsel
Throat hackle	Green hackle fibres
Wing	Four matched green cock hackle feathers

1 Tail, rib and chenille tied in
2 Body wound forward and neatly ribbed

3 Wing tied in
4 Throat hackle added

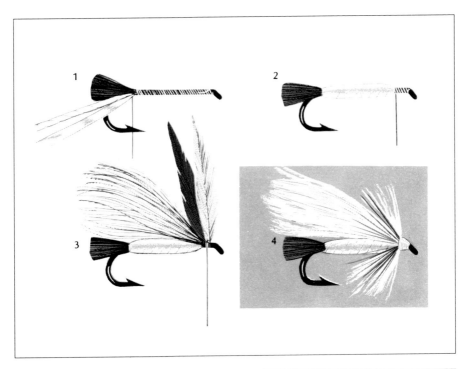

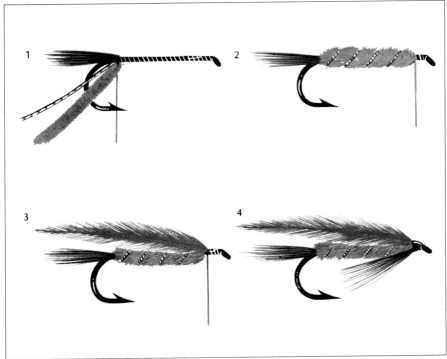

Longhorns RICHARD WALKER

Hook	D/E 10 or 12
Silk	Pale yellow
Body	Amber or pale sea-green, Sepia or chestnut — dyed natural sheeps' wool
Rib	Fine gold thread
Hackle	Short brown partridge
Horns (antennae)	Pheasant tail fibres

1 Rib tied in and silk dubbed
2 Dubbed (amber) body wound forward for two-thirds of the shank length, then ribbed

3 Silk redubbed (sepia), thorax wound forward, horns tied in, twice the length of the hook
4 Hackle tied in and wound

Mickey Finn USA

Hook	Long shank 12 to 6
Silk	Black
Body	Flat silver tinsel
Rib	Oval silver tinsel
Wing	Three parts: yellow, red and yellow bucktail
Throat hackle	Red cock hackle fibres (optional)

1 Rib tied in, followed by length of flat silver tinsel
2 Tinsel wound forward and ribbed

3 Wing tied in in three parts, yellow, red (centre) and yellow bucktail
4 Throat hackle added

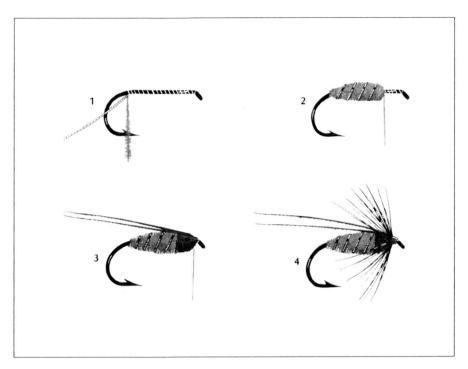

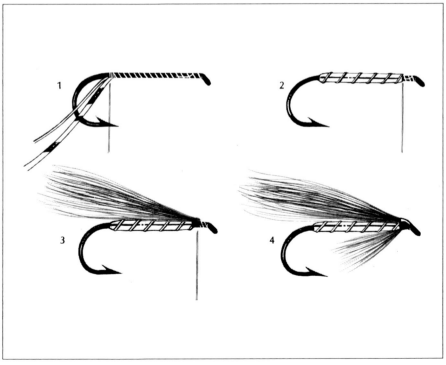

Missionary EARLY NEW ZEALAND PATTERN

Hook	D/E long shank 6 to 10
Silk	Black
Rib	Silver tinsel
Body	White chenille
Wing	Whole silver mallard breast feather
Tail	Bunch of scarlet dyed cock hackle fibres
Throat hackle	As for tail

1 Tail, rib and chenille tied in
2 Body wound forward and ribbed

3 Wing tied in flat to top of hook shank
4 Throat hackle added

Muddler Minnow DON GAPEN

Hook	D/E long shank 12 to 6
Silk	Black
Body	Flat gold tinsel
Inner wing	Bunch of grey squirrel tail
Outer wing	Two large sections of mottled oak turkey wing feather
Head	Natural deer hair
Tail	Small section of turkey wing

1 Tail tied in, and flat gold tinsel body formed
2 Under wing of squirrel tied in, and over wing of turkey added

3 First spinning of deer hair formed
4 Subsequent spinnings of hair applied, then head clipped to shape (leave a few long fibres to trail back)

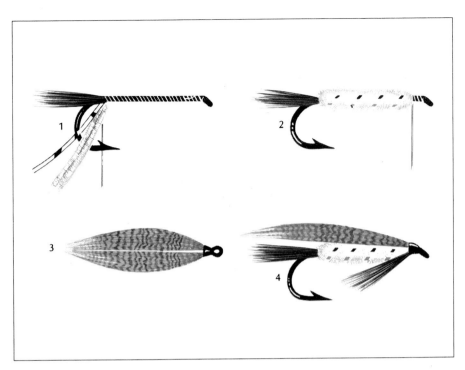

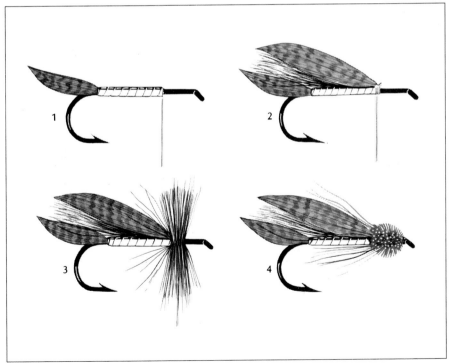

Mylar Minnow SYD BROCK

Hook	D/E long shank, 10 to14
Silk	Black
Underbody	Wool or floss
Body	Mylar piping cut to length (silver or gold)
Back and tail	Peacock herl

1 Tapered underbody formed from wool or floss

2 Mylar piping cut to length, inner core removed. Piping pushed over woollen underbody, and secured at the bend with tight turns of silk. Whip finish the binding at the bend, and leave 8" of silk hanging. Fresh silk reattached behind the eye. Mylar piping bound down behind the eye

3 Generous bunch of peacock herl selected and offered up at the tail, and then secured with original silk reserve

4 Herls gathered and lashed down at the head. Waste herl trimmed, and bold head formed from turns of silk. Whip finish and varnish. Eye detail to be added.

Nailer Fly

Hook	Long shank 10, 8 or 6
Silk	Black
Body	Gold lurex or tinsel
Rib	Gold wire
Throat hackle	Chocolate brown cock
Tail	Red cock hackle or hair fibres
Wing	Underwing of bright red hair (goat or skunk). Overwing of brown hair

1 Tail fibres, rib and tinsel tied in

2 Tinsel body wound forward and neatly ribbed

3 Underwing tied in

4 Overwing tied in, hackle tied in and wound

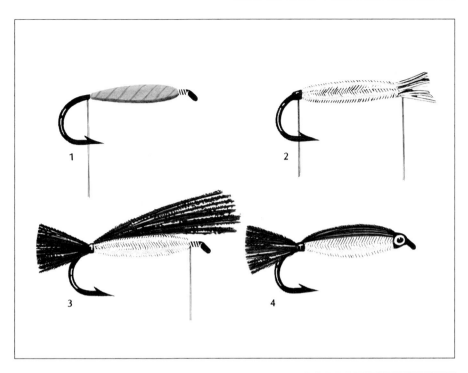

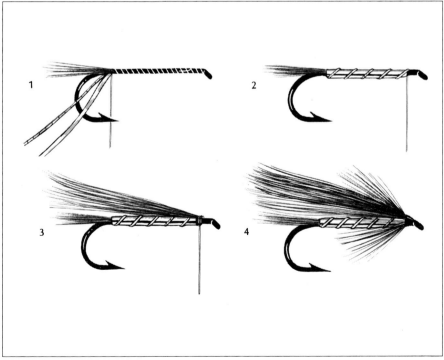

Orange John JOHN KETLEY

Hook	Down eye 10
Silk	Orange or brown
Rib	Goldfingering
Body	Hot orange seal's fur
Body hackle	Light brown
Hackle	Honey
Wing	Flat hen pheasant

1 The ribbing and body hackle are tied in, and the silk is dubbed with seal's fur
2 The body is formed

3 The body hackle is wound on and secured, followed by the rib
4 The wing is added and the hackle is tied in

PVC Nymph JOHN GODDARD

Hook	D/E 12 to 16
Silk	Brown
Underbody	Copper wire
Thorax	As for underbody
Overbody	Three strands of olive or olive-brown condor herl or substitute
Tails	Tips of overbody material or three golden pheasant tippets
Body covering	1/16″ to 1/8″ wide strip of clear PVC
Wing pads	Three strands of dark pheasant tail

1 Underbody and thorax formed with turns of copper wire. PVC strip tied in at bend. Condor herls tied in leaving the tips for a tail
2 Silk returned to the eye, condor herls wound forward over the copper wire and tied off behind the eye
3 Silk then wound back behind the thorax, the PVC strip then wound up over the condor herl and tied off behind the thorax. Waste trimmed off. Silk returned to the eye, where three pheasant tail fibres are tied in
4 Double and redouble pheasant tail fibres to form wing case

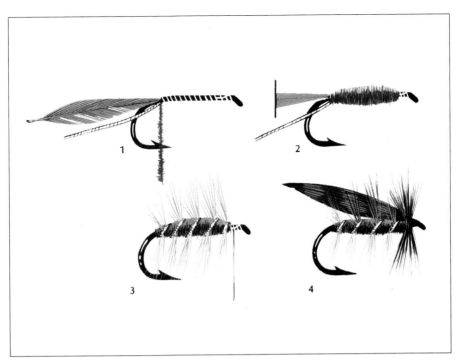

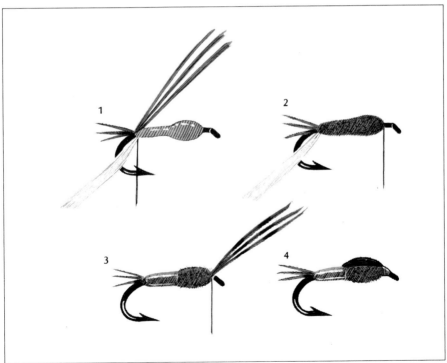

Pearly Nobblers SYD BROCK

Hook	Long shank 10 to 6
Silk	Black
Body	Black chenille
Tail	Bunch of yellow marabou
Head	Black pearl or bead, fixed with 'instant' glue

(This pattern may be tied in a variety of colour combinations.)

1 Marabou tail tied in, followed by a length of chenille
2 Body wound forward and tied off at position shown. Whip finish

3 Bead glued into position behind the eye. (It may be necessary to enlarge the hole to go over the eye of the hook.)
4 Eye detail painted in

Poly Rib C Pupa BOB CARNILL

Hook	14 to 10 (standard shank or Yorkshire Sedge hook)
Silk	Black
Tail	3 or 4 strands of DRF Electron white floss
Rib	Pre-stretched heavy duty polythene strip
Body	¼″ web of dyed black swan goose or heron herl
Thorax cover	¼″ web of body material
Thorax	Mole's fur dyed black
Wing stubs	Quill-like fibres from narrow side of white swan primary
Breather filaments	White nylon baby wool

1 Silk taken to a point well round the bend. Tail tied in. Polythene rib tied in
2 Body herl tied in, body formed and ribbed with seven or eight turns of polythene. Thorax cover tied in
3 Wing stubs tied in, concave faces of fibres towards the hook shanks. Silk dubbed with mole's fur

4 Thorax formed. Thorax cover brought over and tied down
5 Short length of white baby wool tied in horizontally and secured with figure of eight winding. Whip finish
6 Breather filaments trimmed and teased out. Wing stubs trimmed to shape shown

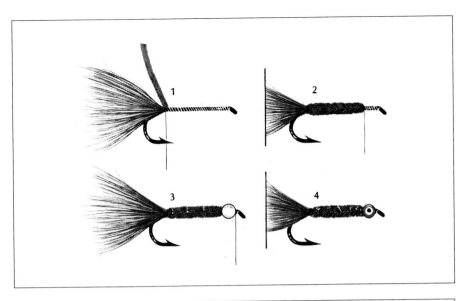

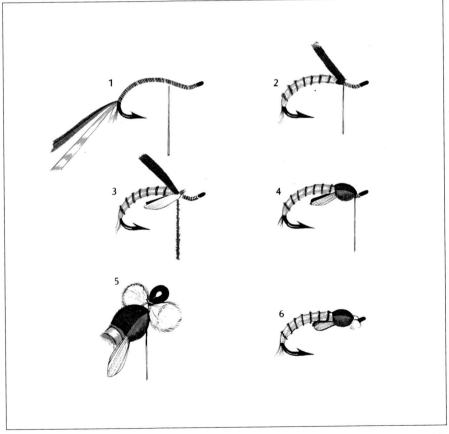

Ruby SYD BROCK

Hook	Long shank 6 to 10
Silk	Black
Body	Scarlet stretched plastic tape
Tail and throat hackle	Scarlet cock fibres
Wing	Four scarlet cock feathers
Cheeks	Golden pheasant tippets

1 Tail tied in; plastic strip tied in
2 Plastic strip wound forward into tapering body, throat hackle added

3 Wing tied in
4 Golden pheasant cheeks tied in, one on either side of the wing

Sedge Pupa JOHN GODDARD

Hook	D/E long shank 10 or 12, wide gape
Silk	Brown
Rib	Narrow silver lurex or oval tinsel
Body	Cream, brown, orange or green seal's fur
Thorax	Dark brown condor herl, or dyed turkey
Wing cases	Two or three pale coloured feather fibres, doubled and redoubled
Hackle	Rusty hen (sparse)

1 Narrow silver lurex tied in
2 Silk dubbed with seal's fur and wound forward to the position shown. Three fibres of condor or turkey herl tied in
3 Herl wound to form a plump thorax.

Three fibres of pale coloured feather tied in at the eye
4 Double and redouble these fibres to form a wing case. Hackle tied in and wound

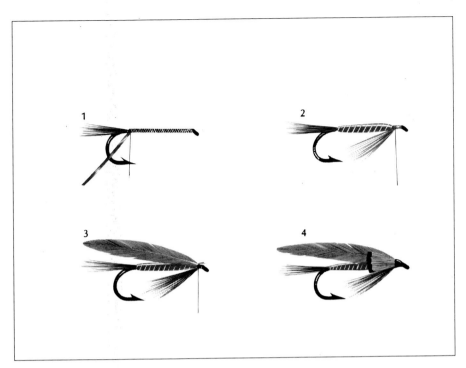

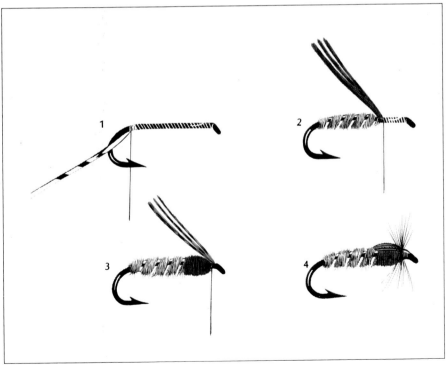

Squirrel and Silver JOHN McLELLAN

Hook	Long shank 10, 8 or 6
Silk	Black
Tail	Tuft of bright red wool
Body	Flat silver tinsel
Throat hackle	Fibres from silver mallard breast feathers
Wing	Natural grey squirrel tail

1 Tail and silver tinsel tied in
2 Tinsel body formed

3 Throat hackle tied in
4 Squirrel wing tied in

Special Baby Doll SYD BROCK

Hook	Long shank 6 to 10
Silk	Black
Body	Stretched black plastic tape; bright red wool
Back and tail	Fluorescent green wool

1 Black plastic strip tied in at the bend, followed by length of fluorescent green wool tied in as shown
2 Black tape wound to form neat tapering body. Tape tied off (and waste trimmed) at the position shown. Short length of bright red wool tied in

3 Red wool wound forward, tied off and trimmed
4 Green wool brought down over the back of the fly and secured at the eye. Waste wool trimmed off, and head built up with turns of silk. Whip finish and varnish. Eye detail added

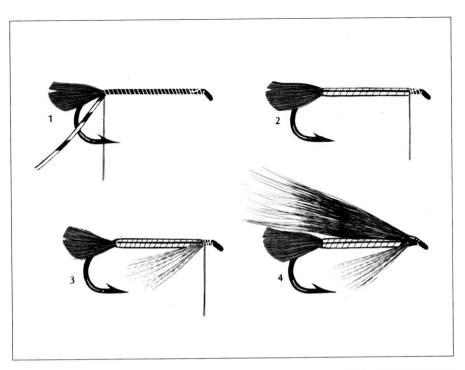

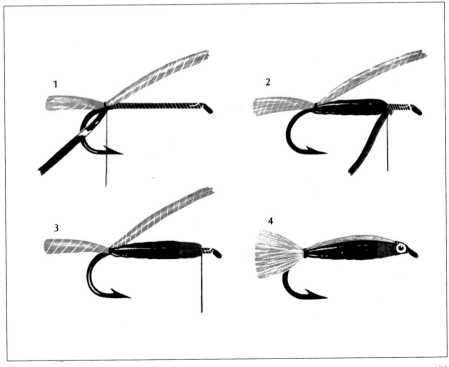

Streaker SYD BROCK

Hook	Long shank 6 to 10
Silk	Black
Tail	Black squirrel
Body	Black plastic strip or black wool
Rib	Silver or white stiff plastic tape
Throat	Orange cock hackle fibres, tied long
Wing	Black squirrel tail
Over-wing	Orange cock fibres, tied long

1 Tail tied in. Body and rib tied in
2 Body formed and ribbed
3 Wing and over-wing added

4 Throat hackle added. Build up a large head with turns of silk and add eye detail

Suspender Midge JOHN GODDARD

Hook	Down eye 10 to 14
Silk	To match body colour
Head	Ball of Plastazote wrapped in small piece of nylon stocking mesh
Tail or Tag	White fluorescent wool
Rib	Fine silver wire or lurex
Body	Seal's fur of required colour
Thorax	Brown dyed turkey herl

1 Plastazote 'head' trimmed to sphere approximately 3/16 inch diameter or large enough to support size of hook used then wrapped in nylon stocking mesh
2 Head whipped to hook shank behind the eye
3 Silk taken well round the bend, tail fibres and silver rib tied in
4 The silk is then dubbed with the seal's fur and wound forward to the point indicated, secured, and ribbed
5 Silk is taken forward and thorax of herl is tied in behind the head
6 Thorax is wound and secured

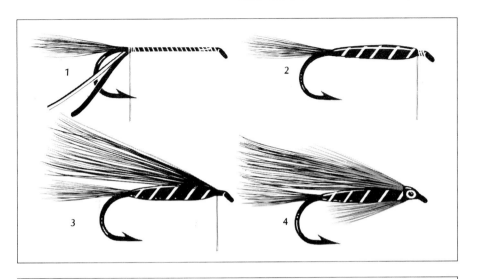

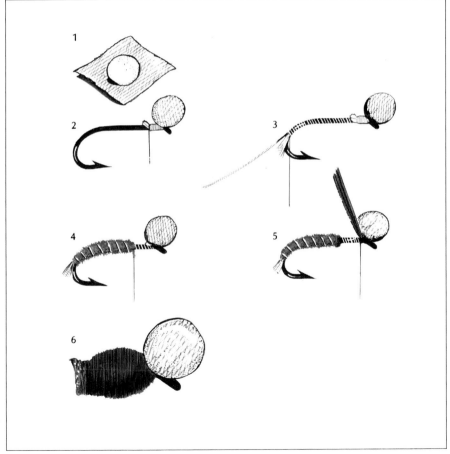

White Marabou Tandem Muddler BOB CHURCH AND MICK NICHOLLS

Hook	Long shank 6 to 10, tied tandem
Silk	Black
Tail & Body	White 'Sirdar' baby wool
Wing	Large plume of white marabou
Head	Natural deer hair

1 Tail and body wound on rear hook, and again on front hook
2 Wing formed on rear hook, by tying in large spray of white marabou. Front wing is formed similarly
3 Head formed, muddler style, by spinning on deer hair in bunches and clipping to shape

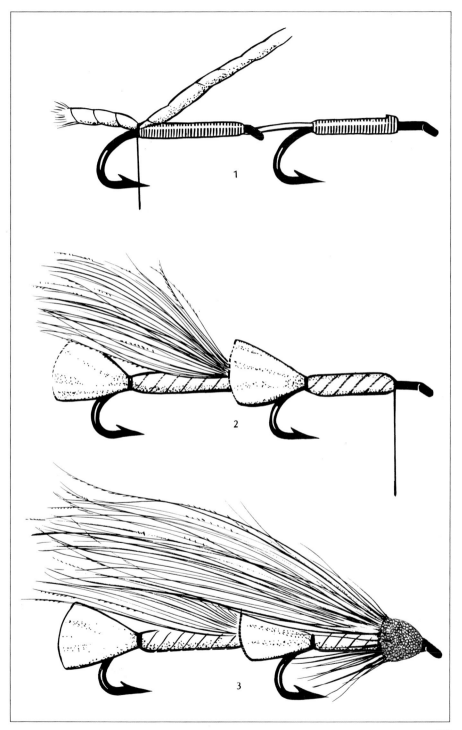

Whisky Fly ALBERT WHILLOCK

Hook	Long shank 6 to 10
Silk	Orange
Body	Flat gold tinsel
Rib	Red floss
Wing	Orange bucktail or orange dyed hackles
Throat hackle	Hot orange

1 Red floss tied in, followed by flat gold tinsel, from which body is formed, in a slightly more forward position
2 Body formed. Butt formed from two or three turns of the floss, which is then ribbed up the shank
3 Secure the body and rib with a coating of varnish
4 Throat hackle added, and wing tied in

Wickham's Fancy T C WICKHAM

Hook	Down eye 12 to 16
Silk	Yellow
Tail	Red game cock fibres
Rib	Fine gold wire
Body	Wide flat gold tinsel or lurex
Body hackle	Red game cock
Throat hackle	Red game cock
Wings	Starling wing quill or grey duck wing quill in larger sizes

1 A few fibres of red game cock tied in for the tail, followed by a length of gold wire and one of flat tinsel
2 Flat tinsel wound forward and tied off at the point shown. Red game cock hackle tied in
3 Palmer the hackle down towards the bend, where it is trapped with the gold wire rib. Rib worked up the shank through the feather fibres and secured. Trim waste wire
4 Wing tied in, red game cock throat hackle tied in and wound in front of wing

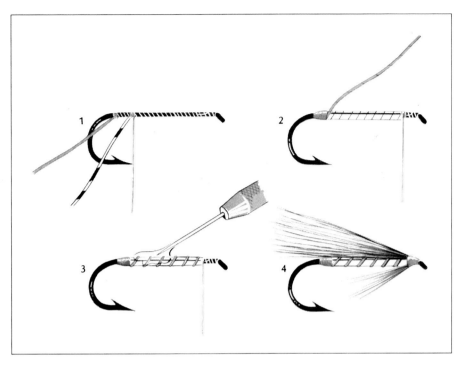

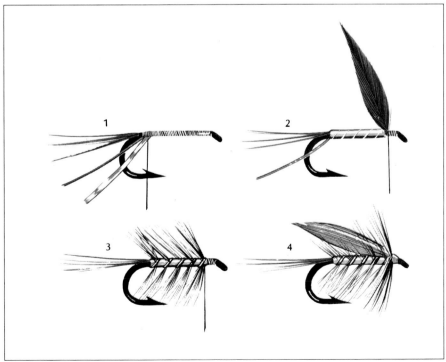

Williams BOB CARNILL

Hook	D/E 12 to 8
Silk	Black
Rib	Oval silver
Underbody	Lead wire
Body	Black seal's fur
Hackle	Black hen

1 Lead underbody wound on and secured with random turns of silk. Rib tied in
2 Silk dubbed with black seal's fur

3 Dubbed silk wound forward and ribbed. Black hen hackle tied in and wound (4 or 5 turns)

Yellow Hammer SYD BROCK

Hook	Long shank 6 to 10
Silk	Black
Tail	Cock fibres dyed yellow
Body	Yellow plastic tape or yellow wool
Rib	Black stretched plastic tape, 1/16" wide
Throat hackle	Cock fibres dyed yellow
Wing	Four yellow cock feathers or yellow marabou
Over-wing	Black marabou

1 Tail tied in. Body and rib tied in
2 Body formed and ribbed
3 Wing and over-wing added

4 Throat hackle added. Build up a large head with turns of silk and add eye detail

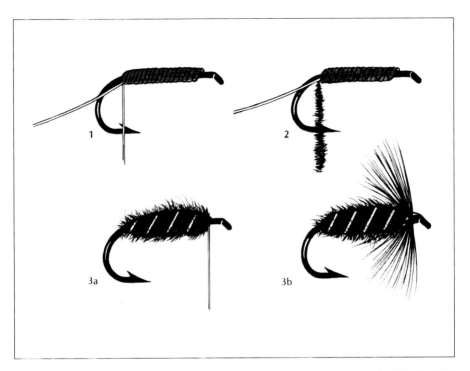

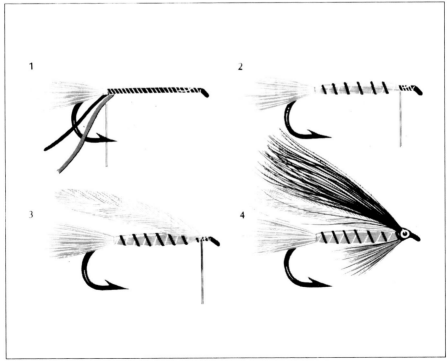

12 Dressings for the remaining patterns

1 BLAE AND BLACK

Hook Down eye 12 to 16
Silk Black
Tail Red dyed hackle fibres or golden pheasant tippets
Rib Flat or oval silver tinsel
Body Black wool or seal's fur
Hackle Black Hen
Wings Medium starling or wild duck (silver grey)

2 GOLD RIBBED HARE'S EAR NYMPH
David Collyer's dressing

Hook Down eye 10 to 14
Silk Black or Brown
Rib Oval gold tinsel
Body Hare's fur dubbed
Wing cases Black dyed turkey
Thorax Hare's body fur
For sinking pattern add lead to shank

3 SHORT ORANGE OR GREEN PARTRIDGE

Hook Down eye long shank widegape 8 to 12
Silk Brown
Body Orange floss silk or phosphor yellow wool. Half length of hook shank.
Hackle Brown partridge

The Adult Buzzers (Bob Carnill)
4 BLACK DUCK FLY ADULT BUZZER

Hook 14 and 12 standard shank or Yorkshire Sedge hook
Silk Black Gossamer, waxed
Abdomen Black herl, dyed swan, goose or heron, no ribbing
Wing Cock hackle points, dyed light iron blue dun
Thorax cover A web of herl, the same as for the abdomen
Thorax dubbed mole fur, dyed black
Hackle Black hen, sparse

5 LARGE GINGER ADULT BUZZER
(Large Red or Ginger Midge)

Hook 10 standard shank or Yorkshire Sedge Hook
Silk Orange or golden olive Gossamer
Abdomen Underbody, hot-orange swan herl ribbed closely with a stripped Peacock eye quill dyed ginger
Wing Cock hackle points, dyed light iron blue dun
Thorax cover Web of hen secondary feather, dyed gingery orange
Thorax Any light beigy brown under-fur will do, but try to avoid using seal's fur due to its coarse texture. I use a beige Crimplene fibre—unfortunately it is not on sale
Hackle Pale ginger or honey hen

6 GREY BOY ADULT BUZZER

Hook 10 & 12 standard shank or Yorkshire Sedge Hook
Silk Grey Gossamer
Abdomen Grey heron or grey goose herl, ribbed closely with a natural, stripped peacock quill
Wing Cock hackle points, dyed light iron blue dun
Thorax cover A web of herl, the same as for the abdomen
Thorax Dubbed mole fur, natural
Hackle Iron blue dun hen

7 GINGER AND BEIGE ADULT BUZZER
(Olive Midge)

The dressing is identical to that described for the Large Ginger Adult Buzzer, the only difference being that the under body for the abdomen is beige instead of hot orange. Either soft under fur, herl or man-made fibre can be used

8 LARGE DARK OLIVE ADULT BUZZER
(Large Green Midge)

Hook 10 standard shank or Yorkshire Sedge Hook
Silk Dark olive Gossamer
Abdomen Dark olive swan or goose herl, ribbed closely with a stripped peacock eye quill, dyed medium olive
Wing Cock hackle points, dyed iron blue dun
Thorax cover A web of herl, the same as for the abdomen
Thorax Dark olive under fur or man-made fibre, dubbed
Hackle Dark olive hen

9 MEDIUM OLIVE
(Golden Dun Midge)

Hook 10 & 12 standard shank or Yorkshire Sedge Hook
Silk Light or medium olive Gossamer
Abdomen Medium olive herl, swan or goose, dyed. No ribbing
Wing Cock hackle points, dyed light iron blue dun
Thorax cover A web of herl, the same as for the abdomen
Thorax Medium olive under fur or man-made fibre, dubbed
Hackle Medium to light olive hen

10 AMBER NYMPH
Dr Bell

Hook Down eye 10 to 13
Silk Black
Wing cases Fibres of any grey brown feather
Body Amber yellow seal's fur
Thorax Dark brown or black (large) or hot orange (small) seal's fur
Legs Honey hen hackle fibres, tied in sloping back under thorax

11 BLACK AND PEACOCK SPIDER
Tom Ivens

Hook Down eye 8 to 12
Silk Black
Under body Black floss silk
Body Three or four strands of bronze peacock herl
Hackle Soft black hen

12 BLOODWORM
John Wilshaw

Hook Yorkshire Sedge Hook 10 to 14
Silk Red
Rib Oval gold tinsel
Body Scarlet seal's fur

13 COLLYER'S GREEN NYMPH
David Collyer

Hook Down eye 10
Silk Olive
Rib Oval gold tinsel
Body & Tail Three or four strands of olive dyed goose or swan herl
Wing case Olive dyed goose or swan herl
Thorax Olive dyed ostrich herl

14 COLLYER'S BROWN NYMPH
David Collyer

Hook Down eye 10 or 12
Silk Brown
Rib Olive gold tinsel
Body & tail Three or four strands of cock pheasant centre tail
Wing case Cock pheasant centre tail
Thorax Chestnut dyed ostrich herl

15 CORIXA

Hook Down eye 10 or 12
Silk Brown
Body White silk floss
Rib Fine silver wire
Wing case Bunch of squirrel tail fibres
Throat hackle Six fibres from a grouse hackle

16 DADDY LONGLEGS
Dick Walker

Hook Up eye 10 or 12
Silk Brown
Body Veniard plastic mayfly body
Wing Light ginger hackle points
Legs Six strands of black horsehair or nylon
Hackle Collar of light red cock hackles — six turns

17 DAMOSEL NYMPH
Cliff Henry

Hook Down eye long shank 8 to 12
Silk Green
Tail Tips of three olive cock hackles
Body Medium olive seal's fur
Rib Flat gold tinsel
Thorax Dark olive brown seal's fur
Wing case Brown mallard shoulder
feather fibres doubled and redoubled
Legs Bunch of six fibres from grouse
hackle

18 FOOTBALLER
Geoffrey Bucknall

Hook Down eye 10 to 18
Silk White
Body Black and white horsehair
Thorax Natural mole's fur
Head Single strand of bronze peacock
herl

19 GRENADIER
Dr Bell

Hook Down eye 12 or 13
Silk Black
Rib Oval gold tinsel
Body Hot orange floss or seal's fur
Hackle Two turns of light furnace cock

20 HATCHING MIDGE PUPA
John Goddard

Hook Straight eye 10 to 14
Silk As body colour
Tag White fluorescent wool tied well
round bend
Rib Silver lurex
Body covering A ⅛″ wide strip of opa-
que PVC wound over body
Body Seal's fur of the desired colour
Thorax Three strands of peacock herl
or chestnut dyed turkey
Head filaments White fluorescent wool
tied into thorax and pointing forward
over eye and teased out.

21 HATCHING SEDGE
Brian Clarke & John Goddard

Hook Down eye 12
Silk Orange
Rib Silver wire
Body Olive seal's fur
Wing Grey mallard wing quill sections
Thorax As body
Antennae Two brown mallard fibres
Legs Green dyed grey partridge hackle
tied in false
The orange version is as above but with
orange seal's fur body and thorax and
brown partridge hackle for legs

22 LAST HOPE
John Goddard

Hook Up eye 17 or 18 fine wire
Silk Pale Yellow
Tail Honey dun cock 6 to 8 fibres
Body Two or three Norwegian goose
fibres pale grey brown
Hackle Dark honey cock very short in
flue

23 MATING SHRIMP
John Goddard

Hook Down eye wide gape 8 to 12
Silk Brown
Back PVC or clear polythene
Rib Oval silver tinsel
Body Strip of lead doubled and
redoubled along shank. Seal's fur, 60%
olive 30% brown 10% fluorescent pink

24 MAYFLY NYMPH
Dick Walker

Hook Down eye long shank 8
Silk Brown
Tail Four or five strands of pheasant
tail fibres
Rib Warm brown nylon thread
Body Pale buff knitting wool
Thorax As above
Wing case and legs Bunch of pheasant
tail fibres doubled and redoubled over
thorax. The fine ends of the fibres are
then divided into two backward sloping
bunches to form legs

25 POND OLIVE SPINNER
John Goddard

Hook Up eye 12 or 14
Silk Orange
Tail Pale badger cock
Body Apricot dyed ostrich herl covered with pale olive dyed PVC
Wing Pale blue dun cock hackle tips tied spent
Hackle Dark honey cock bunched and tied in spent

26 PERSUADER
John Goddard

Hook Down eye long shank 8 or 10
Silk Orange
Rib Round silver tinsel No. 20
Body Five strands of white ostrich herl
Thorax Hot orange seal's fur
Wing pads Three strands of dark brown dyed turkey herl

27 RED AND GREEN LARVA
John Goddard

Hook Down eye long shank 8 to 12
Silk Brown
Tail Two or three curly scarlet ibis feathers
Rib Silver lurex
Body Scarlet seal's fur
Thorax Two or three fibres of pale brown dyed turkey herl
Green pattern as above but tail green dyed heron fibres and body green seal's fur

28 SMALL HATCHING MIDGE
John Goddard

Hook Down eye 14 or 16
Silk Brown Gossamer
Rib Narrow silver lurex
Body Two turns of silver lurex followed by condor herl or seal's fur of desired colour. A few turns of fluorescent silk of same colour may be wound over body
Thorax Two strands of chestnut brown dyed turkey herl
Hackle Small honey dun cock tied sparsely

29 STICK FLY

Hook Down eye long shank 8 to 12
Silk Brown
Body Shank of hook weighted with copper wire if required. Bronze-green peacock herl four strands
Thorax Fluorescent green wool
Hackle One turn of dark honey cock

30 SUPER GRIZZLY
John Goddard

Hook Up eye fine wire 14 or 16
Silk Orange
Tail Bunch of fibres from pale red dun cock
Body Three natural grey heron herls
Hackle One each grizzle and red cock tied in together both short in flue

31 TADPOLLY
John Goddard

Hook Down eye 10 or 12
Silk Black
Tail Three slim black cock or saddle hackles tied in projecting well beyond bend
Underbody Black seal's fur
Body/head Three or four bronze-green peacock herls

32 WALKER'S SEDGE
Dick Walker

Hook Down eye long shank round bend 8 to 10
Silk Brown
Tip Arc Chrome DF wool
Body Three strands of chestnut ostrich herl
Wing Bunch of natrual red cock hackles tied sloping back and clipped square at bend
Hackle Two large stiff natural red cock hackles

33 BLACK AND ORANGE MARABOU
Taff Price

Hook Down eye long shank 8
Silk Black
Tail Orange cock fibres
Rib Oval gold tinsel
Body Flat gold lurex
Wing Bunch of black marabou
Cheeks Jungle cock substitute
Throat hackle Bunch of orange cock fibres

34 CHURCH FRY
Bob Church

Hook Down eye long shank 6 to 10
Silk Black
Tail Bunch of white hackle fibres
Rib Gold or silver oval tinsel
Body Bright orange chenille
Throat Hackle Crimson dyed hackle fibres
Wing Bunch of natural grey squirrel tail hair

35 CONCORDE
Peter Gathercole & Bob Church

Hook Down eye long shank bronze 6 or 8
Silk Black
Wing or Tail Dyed red skunk tail hair over two small well-marked Plymouth rock hackles
Hackle Two plymouth rock hackles dyed red
Nose Copper Candle-lite or red tinsel
Head Black varnish

36 DAM BUSTER
Dick Walker

Hook Down eye long shank 8 to 12
Tag Arc Chrome DF or red wool
Body Peacock herl
Hackle Natural red cock hackles tied fore and aft

37 DUNKELD LURE

Hook Down eye long shank bronze 6 to 14
Silk Black
Tail Golden pheasant crest
Body Flat gold tinsel ribbed with gold wire
Hackle Hot orange cock fibres, tied throat only
Wing Bronze or silver mallard
Cheeks Jungle cock substitute
Head Black varnish

38 GOLDIE
Bob Church

Hook Down eye long shank bronze 6 to 10
Silk Black
Tail Yellow hackle fibres
Body Gold tinsel ribbed with gold wire
Hackle Yellow hackle fibres beard only
Under Wing Yellow goat or skunk hair
Over Wing Black goat or skunk hair
Head Black varnish

39 JERSEY HERD
Tom Ivens

Hook Down eye long shank 6 to 10
Silk Black
Tail and Back Bronze peacock herl
Under Body Any light coloured floss
Body Flat gold tinsel
Hackle Hot orange

40 ORANGE MARABOU MUDDLER

Hook Down eye long shank bronze 6 to 10
Silk Black
Tail Hot orange cock hackle fibres
Body Gold lurex or Candle-lite
Wing Two short, hot orange cock hackles and a generous spray of orange marabou
Head Natural deer hair tightly spun and clipped into ball shape

41 PEARLY (Black, White or Orange)
Syd Brock

Hook Down eye long shank 8 to 10
Tail Cock fibres of chosen colour
Body Wool of same colour tied to
within ¼″ of eye
Wing Marabou of same colour tied up
to eye and varnished
Head Pearl or wooden bead painted in
chosen colour then secured behind eye
with instant glue. Then add eyes using
black and white fast drying paint

42 POLYSTICKLE
Dick Walker

Hook Down eye long shank silver 6 or
8
Silk Black
Body Shank ribbed with black silk for
two thirds of distance to eye, where a
length of crimson floss silk is wound in
up to eye. This is then built into fish
shape body with long strip of polythene
Throat Hackle Hot orange dyed cock
hackle fibres
Back and Tail Brown raffene
Head Black tying silk given several
coats of cellulose varnish

43 SWEENY TODD
Dick Walker

Hook Down eye long shank 6 to 14
Silk Black
Rib Fine silver wire
Body Black floss silk with collar of
neon magenta DF wool at wing root
Throat Hackle Fibres of crimson dyed
cock
Wing Black squirrel

44 VIVA

Hook Down eye long shank 6 to 10
Silk Black
Tag Green fluorescent wool
Body Black chenille ribbed silver tinsel
Hackle Black cock
Wing Four selected black cock hackles

45 WHITE MUDDLER
Bob Church

Hook Down eye long shank bronze 6 to
10
Silk White or black
Tail White swan
Body Silver tinsel
Wing White swan
Head White deer hair clipped cone
shaped

189

Notes on contributors

John Goddard

John Goddard was born in south west London on 27 August 1923. He first became interested in coarse fishing at the tender age of seven, and fished the Thames for many years from his grandmother's house on the great river at Maidenhead. He served in the last war, in the latter half as a paratrooper, and after demobilisation became a dedicated carp fisherman. He first became interested in fly fishing in the early 1950s and this quickly developed into an all-absorbing passion. While he has always enjoyed sea fishing, it was not until the early 60s that he became involved in his other angling love, big game fishing, which he was able to indulge in in the winter months during the trout fishing close season. In recent years he has become increasingly interested in salt water fly fishing abroad, and has now taken many species of salt water fish on the fly.

During his long fly fishing career, his interest has alternated between stillwater and river fishing, and he now enjoys a reputation as one of the leading international authorities on both forms of fly fishing and on angling entomology. His consistent catches of large trout, particularly on rivers, are a matter of record. The author of six books, three of which are now looked upon as classics in their field, he is also a regular contributor to many fly fishing periodicals both at home and abroad, and has been involved in both radio and television programmes concerning angling. In addition, he is a skilled microphotographer and an accomplished fly dresser, with many well known patterns to his credit.

Richard Walker

Contributor on fishing small waters

Photo by courtesy of *Trout & Salmon*

Dick Walker was born in Hitchin, Hertfordshire on 29 May 1918. He was educated at the Friends School, Saffron Walden (1928–34), St Christophers, Letchworth (1934–36), and read engineering at Caius College, Cambridge (1936–39).

During the war he was engaged on the development and testing of airborne radar equipment, and subsequently he has pursued his career in the family business, designing the kinds of lawnmowers used by professional groundsmen. Dick lives in Biggleswade with his wife Pat and small son Robert. He likes cats, and is a good cook.

Dick wrote his first article at the age of 14, a piece about catching carp, for his school magazine. His first earnings from writing was a fee of 15/- in September 1936 for an article in the *Fishing Gazette*. In 1953 he wrote a column for the very first issue of *Angling Times*, and is justly proud of having written an article for every issue of the paper since then, not a break in getting on for thirty years. He has written ten books on fishing, but his first published work was about rabbits.

None of those matters of fact can convey, however, the unique position Dick holds in British angling. He is the country's leading angler, by a considerable margin, and has been for a long time. He is regarded with great affection and awe by a couple of generations of fishermen.

Bob Church

Contributor boat fishing with lures

Living in Northampton Bob Church is geographically situated perfectly for taking advantage of the best stillwater trout fly fishing in Europe. He can drive to Pitsford in 5 minutes, Ravensthorpe in 15 minutes, Draycote and Eyebrook in 25 minutes, Grafham in 35 minutes and, if he hurries, Rutland in 40 minutes. There are many more top class small fisheries and gravel pits within that area too, so all in all he is extremely fortunate.

Bob has written for the national angling press since 1963, including a continuous 8 years with *Angling Times* and an article in every issue of *Trout Fisherman* since it began 4 years ago. In the last 6 years television angling work with Terry Thomas for ATV has been regular, and he has appeared in successful films for Thames and Westward Television. The author of *Reservoir Trout Fishing*, he won the Gladding Masters Trout Trophy and also the prestigious Pro-Am competition at Rutland. Each season he tops 500 fish. His ambitions are to catch a double figure brown trout on fly or lure, and also to win a place in the English Fly Fishing International team now that the professional classification is dropped.

Bob Carnill

Contributor — bank fishing imitative patterns

Bob Carnill, aged 42, has been a dedicated angler for most of his life. A genuine all rounder, even today he still retains an interest in both sea and coarse fishing, despite his almost total involvement in trout fishing. His main interest was in coarse fishing until 1963, but then he had to give in to an overwhelming desire to fish for trout with the fly. He began to tie his own flies during that same year and now, 18 years on, he is becoming increasingly more involved in the two pursuits (fly tying and fly fishing) with each passing year. For the past four years he has instructed a class at the local Further Education College, teaching fly tying and fly fishing. He also contributes quite frequently to *Trout Fisherman* magazine.

His more recent involvement in photography has, in his own words, added a new dimension to the subject of fly tying. He is now gradually compiling a library of slides covering all the different stages of the dressing for his own patterns, as well as their natural counterparts. Once this is completed, he intends to continue with many of the traditional and other famous patterns. The patterns he tends to use almost exclusively nowadays are of his own design — and for very good reason. Over the last 11 seasons (no true records kept before then) they have contributed handsomely to an average of just over 6 trout per outing.

Syd Brock

Contributor — bank fishing lures

Syd Brock was born in Oxford, and it was on the Thames and the many other rivers in the vicinity that his love of fishing began. An avid coarse fisherman for many years, he originally became interested in trout fishing during the coarse fish close season. This very soon changed his outlook, so much so that now his only interest is in game fishing.

His aim is to offer the trout creations of fur and feather they have never seen before, but in a style as lifelike as possible, and his record over the past few years would seem to prove the soundness of his theories.

To date he has taken several superb brown trout between 5 and 8 lb, including one magnificent fish of 10 lb. At the time of its capture this was described as one of the greatest English brown trout taken on a fly. More recently, since the jumbo stocking policy has spread, he has taken many double figure rainbows, with his greatest achievement leading to the capture of an 8 fish limit weighing 72 lb 11 oz.

While Syd is a confirmed lure fisherman, he does on occasion use nymphs and wet flies, while his policy is that a little inventiveness can make all the difference between good sport or none at all.

John Ketley

Contributor — boat fishing — traditional patterns

John Ketley has been fly fishing for twenty years. In 1976, more by accident than intent, he entered and won the South West regions eliminator, which in turn led him to fish in the National, which, to his amazement, he also won. This gave him the opportunity to fish for England in the next International, where he came top rod in the English team. Since then he has fished in the English team for ten Internationals, requalifying every time as is obligatory. During this time he has won the Brown Bowl as the top International Angler and has been top rod in the English team in two other Internationals. For the last three years John has been Captain of the English Team and led them to a resounding victory at the Loch Leven Centenary Match in 1980.

Over the years he has developed his craft from fishing large lures in the early days, through to international rules loch style fishing. He is currently concentrating his time in developing new techniques to expand the pleasures of fly fishing on our major stillwaters by investigating new methods of dapping, dry fly and even nymph fishing. The rest of his fishing time he is, as he puts it, 'just enjoying the most satisfying and frustrating sport in the world'.

Index

Entries in bold type are names or types of artificial patterns. Bold type page numbers refer to detail of fly dressings, while an additional letter 'c' denotes a colour illustration.

Printed in Great Britain by G. Beard & Son Ltd., Brighton, Sussex